Harry Pearson lives in Northumberland in a lovingly restored Victorian post office, which he shares with his partner, the aniseed-ball heiress Catherine Barraclough, their daughter Maisie and two smoke-blue Persian cats, Chekhov and Dai. The household rejects the dubious benefits of the modern broadcast media, preferring to spend their evenings singing Schubert *lieder* while gathered round the spinet.

Pearson's first book, *The Far Corner*, was a runner-up for the 1995 William Hill Sports Book of the Year Award. His second, *Racing Pigs and Giant Marrows*, was shortlisted for the 1997 Thomas Cook/*Daily Telegraph* Travel Book of the Year. His work appears regularly in the *Guardian, When Saturday Comes* and a number of those glossy magazines which smell of after-shave and have women in bras on the cover.

A TALL MAN
IN A LOW LAND

Some Time Among the Belgians

HARRY PEARSON

ABACUS

First published in Great Britain in 1998
by Little, Brown and Company
This paperback edition published in 1999 by Abacus
Reprinted in 2000 (twice), 2002, 2005

PICTURE CREDITS
1, 13, 15, 16: Camera Press;
2, 3, 4, 5, 6, 7, 8, 14: Popperfoto;
9, 10: Robert Harding; 11: Sygma; 12: Topham

A CIP catalogue record for this book
is available from the British Library.

ISBN: 0 349 11206 1

Map by Neil Hyslop

Typeset in Baskerville and Centaur by M Rules
Printed and bound in Great Britain by
Clays Ltd, St Ives plc

Abacus
An imprint of
Time Warner Book Group UK
Brettenham House
Lancaster Place
London WC2E 7EN

www.twbg.co.uk

For Catherine, who got me there.

Introduction

I was at a dinner party in the summer of 1997. When I said I was writing a book about Belgium one of the women at the table laughed. 'I mean,' she said, 'it's funny isn't it, but there just aren't any famous Belgians.'

'Well,' I said, 'there's René Magritte and Georges Simenon; Jan van Eyck, Bruegel, Hans Memling, Rubens and Van Dyck. And there's Victor Horta, Baekeland, who invented plastic; Hergé, Mercator of map-projection fame and Adolphe Sax; Eddy Merckx, Jacky Ickx, James Ensor, Jacques Brel, Jean-Claude van Damme and Peyo, creator of the Smurfs.'

'Oh yes,' the woman said with a dismissive wave, 'but apart from them.'

This was a fairly typical reaction. The other was to say, 'But what will you write about? Belgium is *so* boring.'

On cursory inspection, it must be said, Belgium might appear dull, but that is just a disguise. Belgium has been invaded so often that the inhabitants have tried to make their country look as uninteresting as possible in the hope that, in future, their neighbours will simply ignore them or march right through on the way to somewhere that looks more

1

exciting. Belgian mundanity is a camouflage. But like all camouflage, this one, once recognised, quickly disappears to reveal the solid, eccentric shape beneath.

As you amble around Belgium reality gradually comes into focus. A pair of apparently innocent net curtains hanging in the window of a crumbling ground-floor apartment prove, on closer inspection, to be decorated with woven images of dinosaurs. You come across a window display in a dentist's surgery, four eighteen-inch-high dolls in lab coats each clutching a life-sized pair of false teeth; you pass a sewage farm which is home to a flock of ostriches; a group of men in Ruritanian military uniform march up to your hotel, halt, load and fire a small cannon and then march away again without a word of warning or explanation.

It has always been a tradition in Britain to look to the south for inspiration and colour. You can see that even in the advertising campaign for one of Belgium's most successful exports, Stella Artois. The posters have for years tried to suggest that this lager comes from France. You can imagine the men in their Soho offices pointing to flip-charts marked: 'French sexy, Belgian boring.'

A personal view is that they have got this the wrong way round. It seems to me that the essence of banality is predictability, and who could be more woefully predictable than the French, with their love of fine wine, good weather and chic clothing? Let's be honest – anybody can develop a taste for these things; there's nothing big or clever about it. To carefully nurture a fondness for cacti, canaries and chicory, however, as the Belgians have done, takes rare originality and flair. The only mildly eccentric thing about the French is their pop music, and even here they are undermined by their northern neighbours: Johnny Hallyday, the leading figure of what the French dub, with typical Gallic grooviness, *la musique ye-ye*, is – yes, you guessed it – half Belgian.

It has been a tradition for British writers to head south, too, for the Mediterranean, the Aegean, the Pacific. To go to warm, exotic places. I might have followed them. The Kara Kum Desert seemed relatively unmapped in English prose. But I am a northerner and I burn easily. And besides, I had once met a man in Murton, County Durham who had been to Samarkand, and he said the beer was piss.

Some notes about spellings. Belgium is a country with three officially recognised languages: Flemish (a dialect of Dutch), French and German. This means that towns, cities and geographical features tend to have at least two names. In this book I have generally used the name by which the place is known to the local inhabitants. The exceptions to this are when a city has an accepted anglicised form (for example, Antwerp for Antwerpen, Brussels for Bruxelle/Brussel) or, in the case of the Flemish cities of Brugge and Ieper, when the French names, Bruges and Ypres, are so well-known to British readers that to alter them would be confusing.

A number of books provided me with inspiration, insight and information. In particular Jan-Albert Goris's sprightly *Strangers Should Not Whisper*; *The Coburgs of Belgium*, Theo Aronson's entertaining history of the Belgian monarchy; and Hugo Claus's monumental and brilliant novel *The Sorrow of Belgium*. The General de Gaulle quotation was lifted from Nicholas Fraser's perceptive *Continental Drifts*; the joke about the Belgian pilot from the witty and wise Luigi Barzini's *The Europeans*. Two other works deserve a special mention: Tim Webb's *Good Beer Guide to Belgium and Holland* and *Beers of Wallonia* by John Woods and Keith Rigley. My trips to Belgium wouldn't have been nearly as enjoyable without them, although the country would probably have remained in sharper focus.

With only the rarest exceptions the Belgians I met on my travels were friendly, welcoming and showed a kindness to strangers which went far beyond mere good manners. In particular I would like to thank Liesbeth, Jules and Jacintha, three Limburgers who prove that their home province's reputation for hospitality is well-merited.

Finally, a special mention for my friend Steve Marshall, whose passion for professional bike-racing was what took me to Belgium in the first place and whose, ah, but that's enough of that . . .

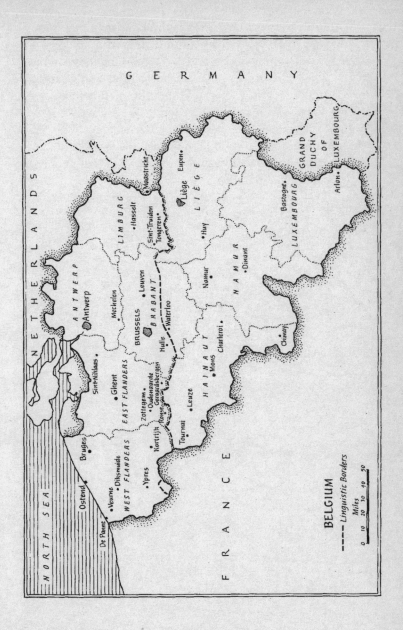

GERMANY

NETHERLANDS

NORTH SEA

FRANCE

GRAND
DUCHY
OF
LUXEMBOURG

Maastricht

LIMBURG

Hasselt •

• Sint-Truiden

Tongeren •

Liège •

LIÈGE

Eupen •

Bastogne •

LUXEMBOURG

Arlon •

ANTWERP

Antwerp •

Mechelen •

Leuven •

BRABANT

BRUSSELS

Waterloo •

Halle •

• Huy

Namur •

NAMUR

Dinant •

EAST FLANDERS

Sint-Niklaas •

Ghent •

Zottegem •

Oudenaarde •

Ronse • Geraardsbergen

Kortrijk •

WEST FLANDERS

Bruges •

Diksmuide •

Ypres •

Veurne •

Ostend •

De Panne •

Tournai •

• Leuze

Mons •

HAINAUT

Charleroi •

Chimay •

BELGIUM

——— Linguistic Borders

Miles

0 10 20 30 40 50

A TALL MAN
IN A LOW LAND

One

My girlfriend Catherine and I crossed the frontier from Holland into Belgium at 10.48 on a grey May morning in 1997. It was raining but that hardly mattered. When you have just arrived in a foreign country everything seems exciting, even bad weather. You marvel at the shape of the chimney-pots, the colour of the number-plates, the odd sloping way the inhabitants write the figure 1. On the other hand some things are puzzling. You can't work out where they hide the fresh milk in the supermarket. It takes you ages to find the right platform on the Métro, and when you do the train leaves without you because you cannot fathom how to open the doors. Being in a foreign country is like a return to the wide-eyed wonderment of childhood, or a sneak preview of senility. At the moment Catherine and I were definitely leaning towards the former.

We stopped at a motorway service station on the E313 somewhere in the flat, sandy-soiled Kempenland near Beringen. The buildings were asphalt-roofed block-houses surrounded by pine trees. I half-expected someone to approach me and whisper, 'The peacock has left his nest and joined the bear in the turnip field,' it looked so much like a border post in Eastern Europe.

Inside, half-way to the restaurant, the toilet attendant, an old lady with the crimped white hair of a poodle, was chatting with a bulky Flemish family who were decked out in velour tracksuits of such vivid unpleasantness they looked like the symptoms of a migraine. Why is it that 90 per cent of all people you see in motorway service stations have leisure-suits on? I suspect that even in Afghanistan there is a special Taliban-approved polyester leisure purdah, so that Kabuli women can go down to the local equivalent and hang around outside the 'travelshop' feigning interest in the machine that tests your blood pressure.

Catherine handed the white-haired lady five francs and disappeared into the lavatories. I loitered, listening to the conversation. Flemish is a language full of metallic consonants, hard vowels and odd, hiccuping squeaks. It is not a romantic tongue. Recited in Flemish the Song of Solomon probably sounds like a sales catalogue for machine-tool parts. Nevertheless, there is something about Flemish – the intonation, the tone of the speaker's voice – which is oddly reminiscent of English, so that if you half-tune in it is quite possible to imagine you can understand what is being said. In this case the father of the family was clearly complaining, 'Four hundred francs for two cups of coffee, a Coke and an apricot Danish? I said to her behind the counter, "Does the cake come wrapped in a hundred-franc note, pet?" And she just sort of laughed, like.'

We drove on. Just beyond Hasselt we came off the motorway and wiggled along country roads, through cherry orchards, neat, low villages and past big, courtyarded farms like the ones the British infantry had defended at Waterloo.

At our hotel in Limburg the owner asked if we were on holiday. 'Tourism is quite a new idea here, I think,' she said. I nodded in agreement. I had had some dealings with the Belgian Tourist Board. The idea of tourism seemed quite new to them, too.

When you phoned the Belgian Tourist Board you got an answering-machine. First it informed you that you were being charged for the call at a rate of 30p per minute, then it ran through a series of computerised questions to which you were supposed to answer 'yes' or 'no'. Like a lot of ideas connected with computers, this was great in theory but in practice led to frustration. After a couple of encounters with the Belgian Tourist Board answering-machine my considered opinion was that they would be better off replacing the whole costly system with a simple taped message saying: 'Thank you for telephoning the Belgian Tourist Board. This call has cost you £3.75. Now sod off.'

Admittedly my view was somewhat jaundiced. The first time I phoned them there was a lot of noise going on outside my house and it kept confusing the machine. Our conversation went like this. The robotic voice would ask, 'Would you like to receive more information on Flemish hotels?' I would open my mouth to reply in the negative, but before I could speak the machine would pipe up, 'I'm sorry, I do not understand your answer. Do you wish to receive more information on Flemish hotels?'

'. . . N—'

'I'm sorry, I do not understand your answer . . .'

After half a dozen failed attempts to reject Flemish hotels, I waited my turn to speak, and when it came, instead of saying yes or no, I yelled, 'Of course you don't understand my answer! It's not a bloody answer at all! It's my next-door neighbour's collie barking because there's a pheasant perched on top of his fucking wood-shed and all the while you're fleecing me at 30p a minute you thieving Belgian bastard!'

The machine took this as an affirmative answer and sent me the brochure on Flemish hotels along with a pamphlet on a James Ensor retrospective in Ostend which finished the following day.

In the end I was glad of that brochure. The 'Holiday Flanders Hotels Guide 1996' is a minor classic. I have read it from cover to cover frequently, and found something fresh to delight me each time. 'Suitable for sailors, tourists and associations,' an establishment in Antwerp proclaims. 'Our multi-lingual receptionists are at your service all day long,' declares the Egmont in Mechelen. 'Green setting. Large collection of old-timers (the 30s). Always welcome, all year round,' explains the Mollenhof in Mol enigmatically. The Keravic at Lichtaart, meanwhile, is closed 'from 24/12 through 8/1 and all construction holidays'. De Croone in sophisticated Ninove has 'excellent comfort and an advanced infrastructure,' while T'Witte Huis in the more stolid environs of Sint-Niklaas is a 'hotel with standing in calm area'. The Viane in Turnhout, on the other hand, advises that 'since April 1995 we have been working together closely with a local beauty parlour. Bicycle rental available', while the owner of an establishment at Zolder, seeking a catchy name, had cast his eye about the local Grand Prix circuit for inspiration and unhappily settled on The Pits. After I had read the latter I went out and gave my neighbour's dog a biscuit. He deserved it.

The following day was brighter. We headed south, crossing the language border between Flemish- and French-speaking Belgium near Heers. At Waremme we stopped and bought a picnic at a delicatessen. It was presided over by a stubby, steel-haired woman with a jaw like a gin-trap and the customer-care skills of a prison bloodhound. We were heading for an area known as the Boot of Hainaut; she might have been its mascot.

Somewhere south of Dinant we got lost and ended up in

France. Anyone who has ever wondered why the Franco-phone Belgians (the Walloons) don't want to be part of France should pay a visit to the town of Givet, thirty or so miles to the north of Charleville-Mézières. Givet is a place of cratered streets. There are clusters of ochre-coloured council flats that look like sawn-off tower-blocks, dead-eyed youths loitering outside the entrances and endless scrapyards. Rimbaud and Verlaine visited Givet, presumably attracted by its suicidal gloominess.

It wasn't the sort of place where we would normally have chosen to linger, but Givet's one-way system quickly took us in its vice-like grip and we did several tours of the centre. The town's brightest spot was one of the dilapidated squares on the western bank of the Meuse. Here, on a sooty brick wall, was a massive poster advertising Suchard chocolate. It featured a young black woman, naked save for a few thin slivers of gold foil. Next to it was an advert for Outspan oranges with the slogan, 'Small ones are the juiciest'. I expect it drew people from miles around.

There were, of course, run-down and forlorn towns north of the border in Belgium, too. But there were strong differences between them and Givet. There are just over three million Walloons, but they have their own Federal parliament, with the possibilities of being heard which that implies. As part of Belgium they are significant, powerful even. As part of France they would be, like Givet, distant and unnoticed, perhaps worse.

The French have a deep-rooted contempt for the Belgians, whom they regard as stupid, unattractive and lacking all finesse. A typical French joke about the Belgians goes: 'How do you make a Belgian spill his chips? Ask him the time!' (Substitute Irish for Belgian and Guinness for chips and you will detect a parallel here, I think). The French hold the Walloons in particularly low regard. 'We speak the language only in a bastardised form,' a restaurateur from Dinant I encountered in the rather unlikely surroundings of North-ampton explained to me. 'And you know what the French are like about their language,' he added, rolling his eyes ceil-ing-wards. 'In Paris they can have you shot for saying *le weekend.*'

While it is true that the Wallonian dialect, which includes Flemish words and pronunciations and outbursts of Ger-manic grammar, is as different from ordinary French as, say, the Geordie dialect is from standard English, it is increasingly rare to encounter anyone in Belgium who actually speaks Walloon (though there is a Wallonian language enclave in Wisconsin, strangely enough). More often than not they talk in French with a strong accent and the occasional indigenous phrase. 'For example,' the restaurateur in Northampton said, 'we say *septante* for seventy and *nonante* for ninety. Now, if you say that to a Frenchman he will just laugh at you.' Possibly so, but in my view it is the bitter mirth of someone who realises he has wasted part of his life saying sixty-ten and four-twenties-and-ten for no logical reason whatsoever.

We eventually fought our way out of Givet by heading south. A few miles outside the town we crested a small hill and found ourselves gazing on the squat cylindrical bulk of a nuclear power station. The French are a notoriously thrifty people. After all, who but they would save grape pips to stick on the outside of cheese? In one area, however, they are gen-erosity personified – the sharing of radiation with their neighbours. Heart-warming. And I'm sure the Irish feel exactly the same about Sellafield.

When we finally arrived at our destination in the Botte de Hainaut, the hotelier and his wife were waiting for us. Monsieur Bonfond, a pear-shaped man in a weekend sweater, greeted us with elaborate formality. 'Welcome, welcome. It is the great pleasure of Minette' – he gave a brief, doe-eyed glance to his wife, who was a good deal younger than him and had the slender, pallid beauty of one of the female revellers in Bosch's *Garden of Earthly Delights* (though she was wearing considerably more clothing, obviously); Minette smiled weakly in response – 'of Minette and myself to welcome you here, dear Sir and Madame, to our amenities and beautiful countryside.' He spoke in a flutey voice, accompanying his words with small and precise movements of his fingers as if he were massaging the shoulders of a particularly delicate pigeon.

'Please come through to the sitting-room, where it is more comfortable. A log fire is lit in there daily and you will find it . . .' – he made a gesture which involved narrowing his shoulders, sinking his head down between them and then rubbing the palms of his hands together – '. . . most cosy,' he said in a little-boy tone.

M. Bonfond ushered us through a side door and into the sitting-room, which was heated to a temperature that would have wilted a cactus. We sat down in dark velvet armchairs around a low table patterned in tessellated veneer. The fringed and tasselled upholstery, the marquetry and the appliqué pictures in the pokerwork frames on the walls were a reminder that minimalism plays as small a part in Belgian interior design as dirty-realism does in the novels of Barbara Cartland.

Minette went and stood beside the fire. Though the blast-furnace heat of it would have caused a salamander to shed his skin, it made not the slightest impression on her pale cheeks.

M. Bonfond came and joined us at the table. 'Your journey was not too fatiguing, I trust?' he asked.

We explained that we had got lost and wandered into France by mistake. The hotelier's eyebrows knitted together and he expressed himself aghast on our behalf: 'But so easily done, so easily done!' he tutted, fingers working away busily on a hard knot of tension just above the pigeon's left wing.

'And now, I am afraid, the formalities,' M. Bonfond said. He took a folder from the coffee-table and began sifting through forms. The wad of paperwork he ended up with looked like the sort of thing you might expect to be confronted with if you were attempting to commit a wealthy and perfectly sane maiden aunt to a mental hospital and simultaneously seize power of attorney over her estate away from her only child.

'But, you must excuse us, Sir and Madame,' M. Bonfond trilled suddenly. 'Of what can we be thinking! We are forgetting ourselves. You must of course be thirsty from your travelling. A drink perhaps?' We said that would be good, a beer and a mineral water. M. Bonfond smiled. 'A beer and a mineral water?' he confirmed. 'Excellent.' He turned to his wife. 'A beer and a mineral water for our guests, Minette.' Minette smiled her faint smile and disappeared.

'You are not familiar with our lovely region?' M. Bonfond asked rhetorically. We agreed. When Minette returned with our drinks and we began to fill in the forms M. Bonfond thoroughly rectified this situation. 'We have here in the vicinity many things of particular interest,' he said. We have, for example, our many fascinating and ancient caves, some accessible only by water. The land above ground, meanwhile, is known for its picturesque gorges and wild meadows. There is also a steam railway. You understand my meaning?' He continued without waiting for an answer. 'It is not a normal railway, you appreciate, but one which is powered by *steam*. Sometimes you may hear from your bedroom the whistle.' He made a little toot-toot noise. 'But,' he said quickly, heading off any possible worries we might have about this before they could develop, 'never at night. The steam train runs only between the hours of 10 and 1800. At night all is quiet. We hear only nature!

'The steam train proceeds from Mariembourg to Treignes,' he went on. 'I would make the following proposal for your consideration: we have at this place' – he indicated a point on the map he had begun unfolding and then refolding into a neat and relevant square a few minutes before – 'a restaurant of great charm and good quality, yet with reasonable prices. The walk to this restaurant is through woodlands and small valleys of simple attractiveness and' – he held up a finger to prepare us for the joyful coincidence he was about to lay before us – 'the steam train stops only one hundred metres from the restaurant's doors!'

There was a pause while we absorbed the import of this information. In case we had missed it, M. Bonfond proceeded to explain the significance further. 'You may,' he said, 'if it pleases you, take the steam train to the restaurant, have lunch and walk back. Or, you may walk there, have lunch and catch the steam train back. Or, possibly, if the weather is fair, walk there, have lunch and walk back.' He smiled at us beneficently. 'It is entirely your choice,' he said. We thanked him. 'And, of course,' he added, 'when you come back from your walking you will always find the log fire lit. For myself it is the thing to which I most look forward. To walk here in the forests and return to a room which is . . .' – he dropped into his little squirrel position and itsy-bitsy voice again – '. . . all cosy.'

At this point Minette, who had returned to her position by the hearth after bringing us our drinks, approached her husband and said something to him in a whisper so soft it would have been drowned out entirely by the noise of a passing butterfly. 'Aaah!' M. Bonfond said with delight, 'my wife has reminded me of something more. You know where you are here?' We shook our heads. The hotelier smiled triumphantly. 'The heart of Europe!' he laughed. 'Yes, the very geographical centre of the European Union is right here!'

'What,' Catherine said, 'in this room?' I think it is the true mark of linguistic mastery when you can be sarcastic in more than one tongue. If only they had introduced a modicum of smart-arsed irony to O-level French I'm sure I would have done better than a grade D.

'Oh, no, no, no, Madame!' M. Bonfond cackled politely if condescendingly, 'you take me too much at my word! No, the site is at a distance of some twelve kilometres from here. The point is marked by an obelisk and you may buy souvenirs in the nearby village, if you wish. It occurs that market day in the village of which I speak is on a Monday. I might therefore suggest that you visit the Centre of Europe on this day, thereby combining sight-seeing with shopping opportunities.'

Listening to M. Bonfond talk I started to think that Catherine had actually been spot-on. His hotel may not have been at the geographical heart of the EU, but M. Bonfond was surely at its psychological epicentre. He was just the man to lay down a thirty-page directive defining the exact nature of turnips. Fortunately – or unfortunately, depending on your point of view – M. Bonfond had other ways to occupy his time. 'Now, if you are ready, Sir and Madame, I will guide you to your room, outlining our facilities here as we proceed. Do not worry about your luggage. Minette will bring it.'

A few days later, ignoring all M. Bonfond's proposals, we drove northwards. We past Nismes' Tunisian restaurant and crossed a narrow little hump-backed bridge over the Viroin river. Nismes had once been famous for its clog-makers, and it may be the subconscious impact of this knowledge more than anything I actually saw that has left me with the impression of a robust, chunky sort of a place. We stopped outside a bakery and I nipped in and bought a baguette and three cherry turnovers. I'd actually been hoping for some of those pastry cylinders filled with Gruyère cheese and white sauce, but I'd lost my nerve when I got inside. I'd tried to buy some once before, in Couvin, and things had gone awry. I asked the middle-aged woman behind the counter for *roulottes aux fromages*. Even though she was obviously a kindly sort of person who would normally have offered nothing but gentle encouragement to a patent idiot such as myself she could barely suppress her mirth. When I got back and looked in a French–English dictionary it transpired that I had requested a brace of cheese caravans. That's pretty much the way it is with me and the French language.

Like many British people I cannot speak French or any other foreign tongue except at the most basic level. The continental view is that the British failure to learn foreign languages stems from a combination of arrogance and laziness. A personal view is that it is the result of nothing quite so glamorous. As far as I can tell, the British eschew foreign languages not because we are idle or scornful but because we are embarrassed. The British fear humiliation above all else, and what could be more guaranteed to make us look ridiculous than the failure to pronounce words correctly? After all, the correct pronunciation of words is integral to British life. The Americans may get away with saying *bay-zil* and stressing completely the wrong syllables in 'oregano', but let a British citizen stumble on Magdalen College, Beauchamp Place or the Forest of Belvoir and he will be reminded of it from now until his dying day. I know this for a fact, because I once asked a London bus conductor for a ticket to Vauxhall, pronouncing it 'Vorks-hall' instead of 'Voxall', and even now, a decade or so later, I still sporadically find Catherine sitting on her own giggling quietly about what I have come to think of as The Incident.

The only area of the French language in which I am normally remotely competent is food. I can read a menu without any bother. This is the result of spending three years at catering college. At English catering colleges you learn classical gastronomic French. This is because while the British are prepared to resist French claims to any other kind of intellectual or cultural hegemony, even we are prepared to admit that the French are the masters of cooking. The French probably take this as a grudging compliment. It is nothing of the sort. It merely confirms the depth of the contempt in which the British hold food.

At my college they had a kitchen organised into the old system of *parties*. A chef called an *envoyeur* would call out the orders and the sections responsible for preparing the dish would yell affirmatively to let him know they had heard it. When you took in an order from the restaurant and handed it to the *envoyeur* he would bellow in a London accent, '*Der pooly so-tay avic sauce dee-arb-la*' and the meat section would roar 'Oi' in response. At least I took it to be 'Oi' at first. After a while I realised it was a Cockney version of '*Oui*'.

Classical menu French is based on the tenets of Edwardian chefs such as Auguste Escoffier. It is a deeply encoded, archaic and in many ways redundant tongue, the caterer's version of Latin, but if you are starving and in a foreign land it is bloody useful. While I may struggle to ask for a rail ticket or engage a Francophone in even the most diminutive form of small talk, I know the French word for every cut of meat, internal organ, species of fish and crustacean, vegetable and fruit. I also know what all the garnishes and sauces are. I know, for instance, that any dish with *du Barry* in its name will contain cauliflower (Madame du Barry's powdered wig supposedly looked like rosettes of that pallid brassica); that *Parmentier* indicates the involvement of potato (Parmentier was the government minister who introduced the potato into France); and that *Normande* signifies butter and cream (key food products of that dairy province). When others hear the word 'Florentine' they think of the Medicis or the Ponte Vecchio; I think of spinach and béchamel.

When I say I know all these things, I do not mean that they are at the forefront of my mind. Far from it. As the incident in the Couvin bakery proved, my knowledge is buried deep in my mental archives, along with cricketers' bowling averages, historic dates and the fact that RWD Molenbeek of the Belgian football league once fielded a player named Lambic Wawa. Or, indeed, that the RWD of RWD Molenbeek stands for Racing White Daring. Nevertheless, given enough time I can rummage around in there and invariably find the necessary information. This is fine in a restaurant, where I can ransack the cerebral cupboard-under-the-stairs at leisure, chucking aside the knowledge that there is an amateur football club in Antwerp named Old God Sport, that Belgium's leading 'serious' novelist Hugo Claus has a child by Sylvia Kristel from the *Emmanuelle* films (what would the British equivalent of this be, I wonder? Salman Rushdie and Suzanne Mitzi? A. S. Byatt and a Chippendale?), until I come across the fact that *perdrix* are old partridges (young partridges are *perdreux*, obviously), or that *Polonaise* implies the involvement of breadcrumbs, parsley and hard-boiled eggs. It is in any situation where a more immediate answer is required – such as a shop – that I run into problems. My solution to this has always been simple. If I can't ask for the thing I want I settle for the thing I know. Since most of the things I know are food, I rarely go hungry. Though the number of times I have gone into a little grocery store to buy toilet paper and come out with an apple and frangipane tart are beyond counting. And it is no substitute, believe me.

To circumvent the inconvenience that can result from my somewhat random selection criteria, before I go shopping on my own these days Catherine – who has lived in France and Brussels – teaches me the sentences I need to know to get the things we actually need. Only after I have repeated these to the shopkeeper am I allowed to start extemporising. This works very well. Most of the time.

Later that first week we left the tender care of the Bonfonds and moved into a cottage in a nearby village. On our second day there I went to the shop fully primed. My mission was a simple one. I was to pick up the bread and milk ordered by Catherine the previous day. Then I was to ask the shopkeeper if he had any eggs. If he did, I was to buy six. Then I was to buy a quarter of a kilo of butter. Catherine had me rehearse the weight quite a few times. This was because of an incident that occurred once in the Garrigues, when I was sent to buy a similar quantity of langoustines and made a bit of a hash of the pronunciation. A quarter of a kilo of langoustines makes a tasty starter for two. Four kilos of langoustines is slightly too much even for a main course, or indeed several main courses, light lunches and buffet breakfasts. God, how we were sick of the crusty pink black-eyed bastards by the end of that week. Unfortunately, as I had spent close to £50 on them, we didn't have much money left for an alternative.

Having memorised my vital purchases I went off to the shop. At first everything proceeded brilliantly. *Bonjour, monsieur. Ça va? Je vais bien, merci. Vous avez le pain et le lait pour Madame Barra-clew? Ah, bon, merci.* Then came my supplementary question: *Est-ce que vous avez des oeufs, monsieur?* The shopkeeper, who had the jutting ears and rotund torso of a body-double for Babar the Elephant, fixed me with a quizzical look. '*Mais oui, monsieur,*' he said, a little suspiciously, and with a slow movement of his hand he drew my attention to the fact that the entire counter of his shop was covered in neatly stacked egg cartons. '*Des oeufs,*' he added for emphasis. I didn't get the butter.

Beyond Nismes the countryside began to flatten out and lose its vaguely Alpine feel. Towns and villages, jumbled and compact in the valleys around Couvin, started to stretch themselves out along the roads until they interlocked with the elongated arm of the next settlement. In any other nation this might have led to a rather dull drive, but not in Belgium.

You see all kinds of strange and wonderful things from a car window as you pass by the gardens of Flanders and Wallonia: sheet-metal models of windmills, vinyl giraffes propping up clothes-lines, laden coal bogies mounted on steel rails – oh, and Belgians, of course. The same urge that drives the local DIY enthusiast to transform a pretty stone-built Ardennais farmhouse into a convincing replica of a Las Vegas bordello, complete with mock-alabaster Doric columns, Grecian-style portico with relief of capering maidens and bile-green roof-tiles, also afflicts many Belgian gardeners. Ornamentation begins at the gate, with the mail-box. To many Belgians this is merely a utilitarian item, a simple rectangular receptacle with a post-horn embossed above the slot; to others it is a field of dreams on which their imagination can caper barefoot and free; a place where the fervid desire for adornment which powered the flamboyant explosion of Brabant Gothic architecture in the sixteenth century can be unleashed, frothing, once more. There are mail-boxes made from miniature Tyrolean chalets and Roman temples, or straw beehives, or shaped like wine barrels bestraddled by Bacchus; there are little Chinese pagodas, metallic pink pigs, rendered pyramids and, in a nod towards post-modernism, concrete inverted commas to indicate the irony of it all.

Once beyond the mail-box into the garden proper, we enter a fantasy land wherein seven brightly-painted dwarves are attended by a blue-dressed glowing-cheeked Snow White; a cavorting Bambi watches, a smile upon his face, as a plaster Renaissance lovely who has gone to the marble fountain to collect water discovers that her dress has slipped from her shoulders revealing her nipples to passing motorists; pixie-heighted ballerinas pirouette amid the privets and naked nymphs cavort unselfconsciously across lobelia beds; a painted resin dalmatian stares hungrily at a pot chicken, while from nearby, atop its personal plinth, an imperial Napoleonic eagle surveys the scene with gimlet eye and wonders at the nerve of the sparrow who has just crapped on his head.

For me, the zenith of horticultural tableaux was reached in the tiny front garden of a modern brick bungalow as we approached the outskirts of Philippeville. Here, a life-sized white plaster twelve-point red-deer stag leapt from a rockery mound, head thrown back, front hooves treading air, muscled flanks straining with noble endeavour. Meanwhile, the beast's proud owner, a bulbous and bearded Walloon, stood on his veranda surveying the scene, bare-chested and wearing grey camo-patterned combat pants. Man, the Hunter.

In Philippeville we parked the car and caught the train into Charleroi. Charleroi was the centre of the Pays Noir, the Belgian Black Country. The Sambre valley in which it lay had been a rich coalfield and the hub of the Wallonian steel industry. Artists who visited the area at the turn of the century, such as the Parisian, Maximilien Luce, painted scenes of smoke and raging flame, confined inside a loose picket of brick chimneys, beneath sky the colours of a well-established bruise. Nowadays the coal has gone, the steel business, once the heart of all industrial production, is in need of a pace-maker and the sky above the Sambre is a less violent shade of blue. Unemployment is chronic even by the standards of Belgium, which has the third highest rate of joblessness in Western Europe.

Charleroi has a reputation for being run-down, but there was more to the atmosphere there than economic hardship. I had been to poorer places in Belgium. Mouscron, which lay across the border from the French rust-belt town of Roubaix, a grim satellite of Eurostar Lille, for instance. In 1995 my friend Steve and I had changed trains in Mouscron. As we had had forty-five minutes to wait for the connection to Tournai, we'd decided to go and get a beer. We wandered aimlessly around empty, terraced streets for ten minutes in a light drizzle until we came upon a car-boot fair in the lay-by of a dual carriageway. People were selling single pre-owned training shoes. The sole bar we could find was presided over by a character of indeterminate sex who looked like Mick McManus after a makeover from a short-sighted Avon lady with a bad case of the shakes. The only other customers were a man and his young son absent-mindedly playing a game which involved flipping beer mats. The bar smelled of yesterday's cabbage and was so grubby you suspected there might be a sign on the inside of the front door advising departing patrons to 'NOW WASH YOUR HANDS!' We decided to go back to the station and put the waiting-room to the use for which it was provided. Mouscron was depressing, sad, haunting even, but it wasn't disturbing. Charleroi was, though, and how.

At first things didn't look so bad. The area in front of the railway station had recently been done up. It was an open sweep of concrete, shiny terrazzo flooring and tarmac, with fountains and ultra-modern street lights that looked like they had been bought in bulk from the Heal's catalogue. Once across this gesture to the space age, however, and up through a few narrow streets of hostess bars, sex shops and second-hand tool emporia, you began to ascend into the wilds of Charleroi proper.

Catherine and I strode up the hill towards the town hall. Ahead of us, groups of strapping young men with slicked-back hair lurched about or lounged on public seating. Their trousers were hitched up to their chests; their T-shirts were tighter than George Best after a night in a gin factory. Moving or stationary, their limbs stayed akimbo as if they had a coconut under each arm and a pineapple tucked in the crotch of their Y-fronts. When girls came into view the macho-men yelped and wolf-whistled. Quite often the girls yelped back. Two youths walking towards us ogled a passing woman, and when she had gone one cupped his hands in front of his chest as if to explain to his mate the concept behind the phrase 'big breasts'. This would have seemed slightly over the top anywhere, but in Belgium, where people normally behaved quietly and impeccably in public, it was nothing short of a debauch. It was as if Oliver Reed had staggered on stage naked during a piece of Noh theatre.

Up in Charleroi's main square, the Place Charles II, things were no better. In the now baking heat, the coconut boys sat astride chairs outside the pavement cafés as if mounted on horses, black trilbies tipped back on their heads, mirrored shades glittering, white shirt-collars spread over dark jackets. They shouted, pointed, gestured. Motorbikes and mopeds circled, roaring and whining. In the centre of the square (which is round, incidentally, a state of affairs with which the English language is unable fully to grapple) was an elaborate fountain. As a piece of civic ornamentation it was pleasant enough, but I felt that it rather missed the point. What the Place Charles II was really crying out for was not spouting water. It was flashing blades and a smattering of automatic gunfire.

Disoriented, Catherine and I stumbled off down a side street looking for something to drink – or somewhere to hide – but instead found ourselves outside a shop called Panty World. Two traffic policemen strolled into view. They wore baggy uniforms in a shade of mid-blue that seemed far too bright to command respect, though since they also had hefty revolvers riding on their hips perhaps the psychological effect of their garb wasn't a major consideration. 'Ask them where the Musée du Glass is,' I hissed at Catherine. 'What, there's a whole museum devoted to ice-cream?' Catherine replied. 'You know what I mean,' I snapped crossly. I had no particular interest in glass, it just seemed like a museum might offer some kind of sanctuary.

The Musée du Verre turned out to be just a few hundred yards away. We walked around a corner and into a tree-lined street. Many of the tall, slim houses had the ornate doors and curved, pale wooden window frames of Art Nouveau. They were run-down now; elegant, slightly racy structures gone to seed. There were gaps in the tiling on the balcony friezes and clear panels among the stained glass, yet they were also a reminder that life in Charleroi, for the middle class at least, had once been rather refined.

There were further glimpses of Charleroi's past in the Glass Museum. Glass production had once been a staple industry of the Pays Noir, but then changes in the market had decimated it just as they had coal and steel. The main danger to the glass in the museum came not from changing fashion or increased overheads, however, but the heating system, which seemed liable to melt it like, well, *glace*. Someone had clearly set the thermostat to cope with a Siberian winter rather than a sunny day in June. If anyone had brought in a barometer the needle would have swung round to forecast a volcanic eruption. We struggled up and down looking at the exhibits and uttering the odd croak of delight. There were delicate Venetian ampoules, vivid blue flasks, slender-necked *fin de siècle* vases painted with intertwined wild irises. It had cost £1.20 to get in, which, including the free sauna, represented staggeringly good value.

Spiritually fortified we went in search of more corporal sustenance. Unfortunately all the restaurants we came across looked like the kind of places that would end up costing an arm and a leg. Literally. In the end we settled on alfresco dining at a mobile *friterie* down by the bus station.

Frites are one of Belgium's great contributions to British life. It was a Belgian who first brought deep-fried strips of potato to our attention; he sold them from a handcart in Dundee in the 1850s. Sadly he chose to pair them with carling peas. As you might imagine, this combination never really caught on, and it was left to an Italian to ditch the peas in favour of fish and start a gastronomic tradition. Belgium's other major impact on our culture was the introduction, by Flemish weavers, of hops into southern England. Chips and bitter beer: without them Britain would be a poorer place – though I dare say the medical services wouldn't be quite so busy.

The woman behind the counter of the *friterie* had purple nail-varnish, nicotine-coloured hair, dangling golden earrings and skin that appeared to have spent considerable time in her own deep-fat fryer – the face that launched a thousand chips. Anywhere else she'd have appeared fearsome. In Charleroi she looked like an earth mother.

Catherine ordered fried chicken croquettes and chips. When she asked me what I wanted I said, 'I think, half a baguette, split, with chips in it and samurai sauce.' Samurai sauce was a speciality of the mobile *friteries*. The recipe was a closely guarded secret, though frequent tastings led me to conclude that it certainly involved mayonnaise, red chilli paste, possibly with a dash of lighter fuel.

Catherine outlined my request to the woman behind the counter. She seemed perplexed, and ran through the instructions again slowly in a voice with such a gurgling rasp to it that it loosened the plaque from your teeth.

'*Un sandwich des frites!*' I said to the woman helpfully, and with what I hoped was a hint of reckless *joie de vivre*. The woman laughed (or at least I assumed she did. It may just have been somebody unblocking a nearby drain). '*Un sandwich des frites,*' she repeated to the vaguely disreputable-looking men who always seem to loiter in pairs around the side doors of such establishments in Belgium. The men chuckled gruffly, grinned and raised their heads in a gesture of acknowledgement to me. A Belgian had introduced the chip to Britain and now I had introduced the chip-butty to Belgium. Somehow I always knew I was destined to make a serious cultural impact on the world.

The Musée des Beaux-Arts in Charleroi is on the third floor of the 1930s town hall. We walked in through the main front doors and found ourselves in the middle of a wedding party waiting to go up to the register office on the floor above. The boys with the large fruit in their pants were much in evidence, now with their girlfriends who wore short, pastel strappy dresses that showed off their tans and the serpents tattooed on their shoulder-blades. At the top of the stairs surveying the scene were the key players in the coming drama. The groom had the slicked hair, dark suit and spread collar; the bride a white full-length gown with lace train. She was wearing a mantilla and a nervous expression. The pair of them were incredibly young-looking. In fact, I think if a truant officer had turned up at that moment the nuptials would have had to be abandoned.

Charleroi's art gallery is dedicated purely to artists born in Hainaut province, or who had come to paint in the Sambre valley. It is a narrow remit, but since Hainaut had produced Magritte (whose family lived for a time in nearby Châtelet, and whose mother drowned herself in the Sambre), Delvaux and Pierre Paulus, and lured in the likes of Constantin Meunier and Maximilien Luce, it was justified by more than mere parochialism. The bulk of the collection is work depicting the heyday of the Pays Noir. Paintings by Paulus, Meunier, Luce, Marius Carion, Alex-Louis Martin and Arsène Detry filled wall after wall. They showed the winding gear, the slag-heaps, the chutes, the coal barges and the railway marshalling yards in all their grim reality. The only thing that detracted from the work as a social document was the sentimentalism that seemed to overwhelm the artists when it came to the workers. In the paintings the women were universally rosy-cheeked and radiating pluckiness, while the men were Jean-Paul Belmondos – tough, craggy and indomitable. There may well have been men and women who looked like this in the Pays Noir, but my feeling is that they were probably in a minority. Studying photos of turn-of-the-century mine and steelworkers in Yorkshire and County Durham you find a few who are stoically handsome, but far more who are small, bandy-legged, pinched, cross-eyed and generally demented-looking. And, given their diets, work-load and living conditions, that's hardly surprising.

Something about this Hollywoodisation of the pit and steel-men and their families irritated me intensely. I knew the Pays Noir painters had been motivated by good intentions. Upstairs, above the gallery, there was a small museum devoted to another Charleroi man, the poet and politician Jules Destrée. Destrée was a key figure in the socially concerned Walloon nationalist movement that began to emerge in the 1880s. He is best known for his declaration, made in a letter to King Albert I in 1912, that 'there are no Belgians'. To an outsider this might seem like a clarion-call for a break-up of the kingdom. It was not, for it is one of the central paradoxes of Belgium that it is possible for its citizens to deny totally the existence of their nationality while still believing passionately in their country. Destrée went on to plead with his King for more autonomy for both Flemings and Walloons, and a Belgium 'united precisely because of their mutual independence'. This suggests that if the poetry and the politics had ever fallen through Jules Destrée would have made a good marriage-guidance counsellor.

Destrée was a close friend of Pierre Paulus. His concern for the Wallonian poor infected the work of the painter from Châtelet and the artists who came to surround him. They wanted to show the Belgian public the appalling conditions the workers were living in, and at the same time persuade them that these were people who merited better. Somewhere behind the glowing cheeks and sturdy brows was the concept of the deserving poor, and the notion that goodness has some kind of physical manifest. The artists of the Sambre valley were working in a visual medium, of course, so perhaps they had no choice but to show the virtue of their subjects in this way. In the end, though, the paintings put me in mind of something the American comedian Denis Leary once said: how come everyone wants to save the beautiful dolphin, but nobody gives a fuck about the fat old tuna?

We descended the stairs from the gallery and emerged into the late afternoon sunlight of the Place Charles II. Flocks of greedy pigeons were gobbling up the remains of the nuptial rice and the extras from the wedding party had now merged with the muscle-bound youths in the nearby cafés. It looked like a scene from a Martin Scorsese movie – though not, unfortunately, *The Age of Innocence*. Catherine and I headed for the station as fast as we could. Nightfall was only a few hours away, and neither of us relished the thought of Charleroi after dark.

Later in the week we bumped into Minette Bonfond at the market in Nismes. She was carrying a snuffily French bulldog named Gargoyle who was plainly too tubby to actually walk. We told her of our experiences in Charleroi. She smiled wanly. 'Ah, yes, Charleroi,' she said in her feathery voice. 'It is not a reassuring place.'

The cottage we had moved into was a few miles from the Bonfond's hotel. It was in a little row midway up a slope, overlooking a school and a church. There were children living in the house next door whose like had ceased to exist in England. They were urchins. They wore ancient white plimsolls, flapping shorts and V-necked jumpers; their hair looked like it had been cut with one of those comb-cum-razor home barbering kits you used to see advertised in the back of the *Sunday Express*, between the donkey-shaped novelty cigarette cases, the hernia appliances ('Ruptured but on top of the world!') and the Swedish army-surplus brassieres.

In keeping with their old-fashioned appearance the urchins exuded the innocence of an earlier time. They were unfailingly polite and monumentally inquisitive. After a few days, when they had got used to our presence, they began pressing their faces up against the front window to see if we were in. If we were they would yell questions to us in that husky tone children adopt when they are trying to keep their voices down and talk loudly simultaneously. And if we weren't in, we would know they had dropped by because of the little smudges their noses had left on the glass.

Catherine and I spent the week meandering about the pleasant local towns of Couvin, Chimay and Walcourt, doing very little except eating extremely well. The area we were in prided itself on its gastronomy, and we were disappointed only once, when we bought a pot of the local delicacy, *escavêche*. *Escavêche* is a type of pickled fish, usually trout or eel, the marinade of which is thickened with flour. I only had one mouthful. It reminded me of something one of the chef-lecturers at my catering college had once done with a carton of jellied eels. 'These,' he'd said to us, 'are a famous Cockney speciality. I will now show you the best way to serve them,' and he'd lifted the lid off the dustbin and dumped the jellied eels into it. I did the same with the *escavêche*.

One afternoon Catherine and I went walking in the surrounding hills to burn off some of the calories. On the way back we saw the urchins in the playground of the little village school. They were with a couple of teachers and two dozen other children. On a table in the middle of the yard was one of those old-fashioned square portable record-players with red dimpled leatherette sides and lid. Hurdy-gurdy and accordion sounds echoed across the fenced yard and the children skipped around in boy–girl pairs. It was like a bonsai version of Bruegel's *Bridal Dance*.

There were four, possibly five urchins living in the house next door, and a couple of others who regularly came to join them on the strip of scrubby grass across the street from the house. The only toys I ever saw them playing with were sticks and stones. They ranged in age from eighteen months to seven years. This was a bonus for me because it meant my French was just about good enough to have a conversation with all but the eldest of them. They were particularly fascinated by our nine-month-old daughter, Maisie.

'Where is the baby?' the urchins would say when I went out to the car. 'She is in the bedroom,' I would reply. Though quite often I was lying. There was no malice in this. It was just that I could never remember the French words for living-room (*la salle de vie*?).

'Is the baby sleeping?'

'No, she is having breakfast.'

'What does the baby have for breakfast?'

'Some milk.'

'And some bread, too?'

'It is possible.'

On our last morning in the Viroin valley I went into the back garden to take some photographs. We had sat out on the terrace but never ventured far up the garden, which sloped steeply and had recently been treated with one of those evil weedkillers that shrivels everything it touches. The hill was covered with twisted, blackened plants. It looked like a snake farm that had been attacked with a flamethrower. I scrambled up to the top and sat down. The view was terrific: the church, a whispy mist along the river, the thickly wooded hills opposite brightened with pockets of vivid yellow rape. I took some photos and began my descent. Then I noticed the roof of the urchins' house. It was fashioned from corrugated iron, and there were holes in it as big as footballs. One of them had been patched with what appeared to be an old tea-tray.

When we had packed up the car and were about to leave, the urchins appeared. One of them, a little girl with a serious face and a slight cast in her right eye, came forward. She had a wrapped sweet in her hand. She looked at Maisie. 'She is like a little doll,' she said, then she looked down at the sweet in her hand. Half of her clearly wanted to give it to our daughter, while the other half wanted to keep it for herself. You could almost feel the battle that was raging inside her. Eventually, after she had stood silently in front of us for what seemed like a long time, we said goodbye to her and the other urchins, got into the car and drove away.

Two

Catherine and I had rented the house in East Flanders unseen. When we walked in through the front door we knew straight away it had been a mistake. The interiors of Belgian houses are often dark, as if some rogue troglodyte gene were still loose in the land, but this one was positively Stygian. The walls were covered in brown velvet. The curtains were the colour of Franciscan robes. All the wood had been stained a sombre shade of mahogany. If the carpet pattern had a name, it was probably 'Swamp Thing'.

The room was decorated with religious icons and medieval weaponry. Arrangements of pale dried flowers decomposed in bell-jars or lay limply across the tops of armoires and chests-of-drawers, the occasional seed-head falling to the floor with a hollow, skeletal rattle. On the roof-beams spiders waged war for the last square inch of *lebensraum*. Switching on the lights made little difference. The brown walls sucked in brightness and burped back dust. It was the only living-room I have ever been in that would have been cheered up by the presence of a few bats.

If the lounge was *The Addams Family*, the kitchen was strictly

The Young Ones. There was rat poison next to the tea-towels. In the fridge an opened jar of béarnaise sauce was so far past its sell-by date the bacteria in it had evolved to the stage where it was capable of hot-wiring a Ford Escort. The grease on the cutlery was sufficient to lubricate a combine harvester. Extended families of dark beetles eyed us reproachfully from the saucepans whenever we mentioned cooking.

'Well, I wonder what we'll find through this door,' Catherine said, with all the unconvincing jollity of a scout-master who's just realised the youth hostel he and his troop have checked into is actually a crack den.

What was through the door was a classic piece of Belgian DIY. The owner had converted the garage into a dining-room. The Belgians love doing this sort of thing. They pride them-selves on it. When a friend of mine was working in Brussels, a Flemish colleague mentioned that his brother was putting a new roof on his house for him. 'I didn't know your brother was a builder,' my friend had said. 'All Belgians,' the man replied proudly, 'are builders.' This is quite accurate. Although based on the evidence presented to me I should say the insertion of the word 'gerry' would render the description even more apposite.

After a few visits to Belgian homes you have only to eye the light-fittings snaking from the walls on grey cable, or glimpse the winking sparks that fizz around the dimmer-switches to know that at some point the owner will say, 'You like the house? I did all the work myself, you know.' And you will have to try to look surprised and impressed while simultaneously endeavouring to find something rubber to hold on to.

This is not a problem confined to Belgium, of course, it's just that the have-a-go spirit which makes the Belgians such good linguists magnifies it. What happens nine times out of ten with major pieces of DIY the world over is that the person doing them gets bored or distracted or runs out of energy before they are finished. The garage conversion was no exception. As a consequence it was the first dining-room I have ever eaten in which had an up-and-over door. The bathroom above it was mercifully free from incident – if you could ignore the unsealed plug sockets and condensation. The bedrooms looked like sets from a '70s porn movie.

We went out for a walk to try to cheer ourselves up. We had a footpath map, but it wasn't really necessary. Belgium is one of the most densely populated countries in the world. There are ten million Flemings, Walloons and German-speakers crammed into an area roughly the size of Wales. That works out at about three hundred people per square kilometre. The Ardennes forest and the farmland of southern Hainaut is so under-populated, however, that a town like Chimay, with 3,000 inhabitants, is considered a metropolis, and villagers gaze on mighty Arlon (pop. 23,000) and wonder how the townspeople stand such a dizzying pace of life. These areas take up around a sixth of the country. Somewhere has to make up the average, and that somewhere is the hinterland of Brussels. The part of East Flanders we were in is so overcrowded nobody could get lost there – not even Lord Lucan. You can't wander more than a few hundred yards amid the tussocky, cow-strewn meadows and bristle-headed, pollarded willows without coming across houses, or more often halfcompleted houses.

'Every Belgian has a brick in his stomach' is a popular proverb in Belgium. Apart from being a reasonable explanation for the state of many Belgian waistlines, the expression also sheds light on why so many building sites, deserted during the week, become hives of activity at weekends. Belgian DIY doesn't stop at putting in a corner bar, or banging a stone-faced arch through between the sitting- and dining-rooms, you see, it also encompasses constructing entire homes from drawing-board stage to the screwing-on of the ornamental door-knocker. Not only is every Belgian a builder, they are a nation of architects too. The effects are unmistakable, and not all live up to the standards you might expect from a country that has produced Rombout Keldermans and Victor Horta.

Some of the self-designed houses reveal the personal obsessions of their owner. One had no front windows at all, presenting to the street a solid wall broken only by a thin strip of opaque glass bricks. Dark, yet private, the home of a shy albino nudist, perhaps? Others had clearly been influenced by foreign holidays. There were hints of Spanish fishing village here, a touch of Alpine chalet there and a little glob of Habsburg baronial every once in a while. In theory this might have seemed like a grand idea, but there were a couple of problems no one had fully resolved. First there were the materials. The brick and the pantile have served the Flemish well over the years, and the great cities of Flanders, Bruges, Ghent, Kortrijk and Ypres are testament to their durability, versatility and attractiveness. The Flemish are, therefore, justifiably fond of the brick and the pantile. Faced with a choice between stone, wood, lathe-and-plaster or brick-and-pantile, the Fleming opts for the latter every time. In Flanders 90 per cent of all structures are built out of bricks and pantiles. Post-boxes, garden sheds, rabbit hutches, nothing is too small to be blessed with the magic of baked clay. Indeed, the absence of a Flandrian automobile industry is almost certainly down to the difficulty of resolving the horse-power-to-brick-weight ratio. Wonderful as the brick and pantile may be, however, they have their limits. Some things are not meant to be built out of bricks and pantiles. Log cabins, for instance.

Secondly, there is location. There are wines which do not travel, and buildings, by and large, are more difficult to transport than wine. Just outside the village of Brakel was a three-storey tower-like house the entire front of which was made of curved glass. It was the sort of building which, facing an azure sea and coated with white stucco, would have had you cursing the good fortune of whoever lived there. Made from burnished ochre brick and plonked in the middle of a damp-looking leek field, however, the effect was quite the reverse.

My father was a structural engineer in the steel industry. To a structural engineer architecture ranks slightly below phrenology in the league table of hard science. If the word 'architect' is ever mentioned by my father it is invariably part of an anecdote which runs along the lines of, 'And then, of course, the bloody architect swans in and says, "If you alter it you'll dissipate the aesthetic impact." So Kenny says, "And if we don't bloody alter it the bugger'll collapse and make an aesthetic impact on some poor sod's head, and it'll be you up in court for criminal negligence." And the silly pillock just turned on his heels an' flounced out again.'

I was therefore brought up to believe the airy-fairy jottings of the architect were suitable material only for the covers of progressive rock albums. If you said 'Norman Foster' in our house you were sent to bed without your supper. Having seen the self-designed houses in Flanders, however, I am now willing to set aside years of indoctrination and risk paternal wrath of biblical proportions to acknowledge the absolute and utter necessity of Sir Richard Rogers.

For all its faults this mania for epic DIY has some major compensations. There are no executive housing estates in Belgium; no avenues and closes of identical starter homes in which individuality is expressed as subtly as in Chinese Opera and the colour of a door, or the festoon blinds hanging in the *en suite* bathroom are a landmark of Himalayan significance. Belgian buildings may not be to everyone's taste, but at least they keep you interested.

We plodded dutifully around, trying vainly to enjoy ourselves. It was a hot day and many people were out tending their gardens. There is some law of human nature which dictates that those people who are least inhibited about their bodies are always the ones who have most to be inhibited about. All along the route old men with the leathery folded skin of sun-tanned rhinos pruned roses in micro-briefs, while their bikini-clad wives spilled out over herbaceous borders like collapsing and over-done soufflés.

On we marched, un-uplifted save by the occasional glimpse of miniature goats capering in miniature farmsteads, until we spotted a dozen men playing pétanque outside a café in Sint-Maria Oudenhove. The Flemish don't have any time for their French-speaking Walloon compatriots, but perversely they are rather fond of France. The pétanque players were clearly Francophiles. Not content with playing boules they were also dressed in berets, neckerchiefs and mid-blue smocks. We stood and watched for a while. It was fascinating stuff, not least because several of the players carried a length of cord with a magnet on the end so they could retrieve the metallic boules without the athletic effort of bending over. Better still, the two teams had sponsors' names plastered over their backs, and one carried the logo (dancing pink elephants) of a local beer named Delirium Tremens. This, I'm sure you'd agree, is an unusual moniker for an alcoholic drink, and one that suggests possible new marketing strategies for British companies looking to expand their operations in Belgium. An enterprising English butter manufacturer might do well with a product named Stroke or Slightly Salted Triple By-pass Surgery, for example, while the slogan 'A Mars a day helps foster tooth-decay' would surely send sales of the chocolate bar soaring. As far as I know, there is as yet no Belgian ale named Cirrhosis, so get cracking, British brewers!

Buoyed up at last we wandered off, waving merrily at the

scantily-clad horticulturalists and pygmy nannies and their tiny kids as we went (I'm referring to goats again here – as far as I'm aware there are no midget child-care facilities in East Flanders, though I wouldn't rule it out). In the narrow strips of garden behind a row of terraced houses on the edge of Sint-Goriks we saw a group of black rabbits gambolling in a wire-mesh enclosure in the middle of a plot which also contained a neatly maintained vegetable bed, a stretch of lawn which was home to a heavily pregnant sheep, a small family of brightly coloured gnomes, a pigeon coop and a fat fortyish man in a vest and the kind of high-thighed shiny shorts seldom seen these days except on Moroccan middle-distance runners. We pointed out the rabbits to our daughter and the man, hearing us speak English, lumbered up his garden path to have a chat. He had dark, oily hair, a cigarette wedged in the corner of his mouth and the narrowed eyes of someone who spends a lot of time with smoke in his face.

'On holiday?' the man asked. We said we were. The man told us he drove a lorry for a builder's merchant. He said the money was no good and he was away too much, and now his wife was sick. 'In the hospital two weeks, out and then back again. They take from down here,' the man rubbed the underside of his belly, 'I don't know in English.'

I decided to change the subject, because if I'd really wanted to hear strangers talking about surgical operations I'd have simply got on a bus in County Durham and saved some cash. I told the man we had been admiring his livestock. 'The sheep,' the man said gravely, 'in a month a lamb, I hope. Last time a dog came, attacked her and the lamb it *purrrf*.' We commiserated with him on the miscarried lamb. 'A bad thing,' he said, bringing his hand up to his mouth as if holding an invisible sandwich. 'Lamb is good to me.'

'Do you race the pigeons?' I asked. The man laughed. 'No,

no. Him,' he replied, pointing to a red-brick pigeon loft across the way. 'He races them. Me, I eat them.'

'And the rabbits too?' I asked rhetorically. It was becoming clear that there was nothing in his garden the man didn't eat. Even one or two of the gnomes had limbs missing. The man looked at the rabbits with a scowl. 'Ja,' he said, 'but the rabbits, it is a problem. I must put them in a box because . . .' He thought for a moment. 'Ah, sorry. It is a long time since I speak English. Maybe fifteen years. The rabbits they . . .' He tapped the side of his head in frustration. 'Wait, wait,' he said, 'I will get it one moment.' We stood looking at each other, the man's brow creased with effort, his fag crushed between pursed lips. Suddenly his face brightened. 'Ja, I have it!' he said exultantly. 'The rabbits . . . they feed only for fucking.' I was very pleased we'd been patient with him.

We wandered back to the house greatly cheered. Once inside, however, our dismal mood quickly returned. As the sun set we put our daughter to sleep amid the satin, wicker and macramé of the upstairs rooms and sat down to eat. The dining-room was not just a microcosm of Belgian home-improvement, but also a reminder that Belgium, particularly the Flemish-speaking part, is a profoundly Catholic country. Scattered about the walls were various graphic depictions of Christ in his final torment. As we sat at the table they seemed to fill every line of vision: the scratches from the crown of thorns, the spear and nail wounds oozing vivid gore. Perhaps I am being rather English about this, but while I readily acknowledge that the crucifixion is a pivotal moment in the history of Western civilisation and a cornerstone of the faith of many hundreds of millions across the globe, I don't think it is the sort of thing you really want to look at while eating your tea.

'Perhaps,' Catherine said, 'it would look a bit better if we opened all the doors and windows.' We did so. Right on cue, storm clouds rolled in over the clumps of shadowy poplar trees. Thunder clapped, lightning flashed, rain hissed and scampered across the roof and from somewhere deep in the impenetrable Flandrian night came the piercing shriek of a soul in anguish. Or possibly a peacock.

We picked at our food, drank heavily, locked all the doors, checked that all the doors were locked, went together to the bathroom, checked all the doors were still locked when we came back down again and then went up to bed.

I woke some time around 3 a.m., my bladder swollen to the size of a medicine ball. To get to the lavatory meant going down the stairs, through the velvet catacomb, the squalid kitchen and the garage/dining-room where drooping grey bouquets glowed in the pallid moonlight like severed limbs and up the stairs at the other side. That I didn't simply piss out of the window showed incredible fortitude. Though the fact that the only window I could prise open was directly above the laden roof-rack of our car was also a contributory factor.

The following morning we made another brief attempt to rally. Who knows, we might well have done so had I not noticed something mysterious poking through a gap between the ceiling tiles in the kitchen while washing up. In a quest for the truth I stood on tip-toes and slid one of the tiles aside slightly, straining my eyes to see in. There was definitely something in there. I shoved the tile some more. As I did so I caught a brief glimpse of a large hank of limp grey fibre before it dropped down on to my face, causing me to yell out in horror and alarm. When you're on edge, in a macabre house, in a small country where a trio of serial killers – including the so-called 'Beast of Mons' and whoever it was who left the remains of ten women buried in the cellar of a Lutheran pastor in Brussels – have been on the loose simultaneously, it's amazing how much like human hair dusty roof insulation can look.

'We can't stay here,' Catherine said after she'd calmed me down by slapping me repeatedly. I knew she was right. Catherine had planned to visit friends in Munich, leaving me alone for a week or so to write. I had already imagined the scene that would have greeted her return: me barricaded in a cupboard, surrounded by chocolate wrappers and empty Trappist ale bottles, head twitching, eyes glowing with terror.

The following day was Sunday. Unable to contact the holiday company we had rented the house from we decided to do the next best thing: phone up our friends and relations and moan. We drove into the nearby town of Geraardsbergen, where Union Jack pennants hung from the lamp-posts and a sign strung above the main road said, 'Welcome British Old-Timers'.

Parking next to a health-food store with a window display devoted to the attractively named Colon-Clean, we walked up Geraardsbergen's steep main street looking vainly for somewhere we might be able to buy a phonecard. The only shops that were open, though, were bakeries. In Belgium Geraardsbergen is famous for three things. The first is the Krakeling-enworp, a festival held on Ash Wednesdays in which local civic and religious dignitaries gather on a nearby hill, the Oudenberg, drink a glass of wine containing a live fish and then throw thousands of sugary biscuits to the watching throng. Really.

The second thing for which the town is famous is a cake called a *mattetarte*. Piles of these cheese curd-filled pastries towered on the counters of shop after shop. Geraardsbergen was plainly readying itself for some kind of world *mattetarte* shortage.

One of the bakeries was run by a grey-bearded man named Olav. I know this because it was called 'Olav's Mattetarte

Shop', outside it was a wooden cut-out of Olav bearing a tray of *mattetarte*, and inside there were postcards of Olav standing proudly in his doorway holding a plate of yet more *mattetarte*. In a bid to do our bit towards demolishing the *mattetarte* mountain we bought a couple and enquired of Olav about the phonecard. 'You can buy from the post office,' Olav said. 'But not today because it is Sunday.' He stroked his long, silky facial hair thoughtfully. 'And maybe not tomorrow either. Because here Monday is a little bit Sunday too.'

Thwarted, Catherine and I walked up the cobbled road to the top of the hill and sat down on a bench near a little domed chapel to eat our *mattetartes* and gaze at the surrounding countryside. By the time we had finished a small crowd of fifty or so people had assembled around us. Thankfully this proved not to be an angry mob of local vigilantes alerted to the fact that a pair of foreigners had been raiding vital *mattetarte* stocks, but a group of cycling fans waiting for the riders in an amateur race. Bike-racing is big in Flanders, and the hill we were sitting on, the Muur of Geraardsbergen, was the third famous thing about the town. It is one of Flemish cycling's great historic sites. I had sat on top of it once before, in 1995, on a day when the crowd was numbered in thousands.

Every nation shapes its sport to test the human characteristics it values most. British football examines courage and commitment more than it probes creative flair. Ours is the land of Drake and Wellington, after all. Let others admire long-haired artists if they must. Road-race cycling is particularly suited to highlighting desired virtues, since the national cycling associations determine the course over which the contest will be run, and the course determines the exact nature of that contest. As a consequence, the outcome of most Italian races hinges on the macho panache of the bunch sprints; the

Spanish on the tight-jawed determination of the mountain stages; and the French on the merciless endurance and self-discipline of the time trials. (If the latter doesn't sound particularly French to you, remember we are talking about France here, not Paris. If it had been left up to the Parisians French sport would have died out long ago. Scabby knees and sweat just aren't chic. Cycling is the preferred sport of rural France – it is the peasant and the farm labourer's game.)

While these three great cycling nations are large enough to hold multi-stage races which at least nod in the direction of other disciplines, Flanders is big enough only for a major one-day race. The Tour de France lasts for twenty-five days; the Ronde van Vlaanderen – the Tour of Flanders – for just over six hours. It is a rugged test of stamina, hitting its most crucial section in the south among the wooded hills around Oudenaarde and Ronse.

The so-called 'walls' (*muur* in Flemish) of the optimistically named 'Flemish Ardennes' are not particularly high, but they are very steep, and the ascents are cobbled with the dreaded *pavés* or 'Belgian slabs' – big blocks of stone that form a surface as uneven and gappy as a village idiot's grin. The riders scale a dozen of them in under forty miles.

The Tour of Flanders takes place on the first Sunday in April, a time when the elements are least friendly to cyclists. In the rain and sleet the uneven cobbles become slippery with mud and motor oil, so that a molar-loosening climb is followed by a nerve-shattering descent. The Flandrians, you see, admire fortitude and coolness and unprotesting bravery. The Flemish, in short, like phlegm.

Road-race cycling became organised as a professional sport in Europe at the turn of the century (in Britain it was banned soon afterwards on the grounds that it frightened carriage horses. The law prohibiting it wasn't repealed until the 1950s, by which time British cyclists were so far behind they still haven't caught up forty years later). Right from the start Belgium was a dominant force. Belgian riders won the Tour de France on all seven occasions the race was held between 1912 and 1922, and in 1920 filled the top five places in this prestigious event, a feat no country has managed since. In the decade leading up to the Second World War Belgians won the race a further four times. Between the end of the war and the present day they have notched up half a dozen more victories. Though this may not seem very significant to the average British sports fan, it is immensely important to their European counterparts. Despite our nation's relative indifference to it, the Tour de France remains the biggest annual sporting event in the world; the third largest of all after the Olympics and the football World Cup finals.

The Tour of Flanders may not be of quite the same epic scale as the Tour de France, but it is big news in Belgium. The morning of the race *Het Volk* newspaper devotes four or more pages to analysis of it. The following day's edition offers five pages of post-mortems and a full-page photo of the day's critical moment.

The Ronde is a top Classic, one of eleven in the World Cup series, ranking alongside such races as Milan–San Remo and Liège–Bastogne–Liège, and only slightly below Paris–Roubaix in the hierarchy of cycling prestige. It has been ridden since 1913 and, much to the delight of the indigenous population, the majority of winners have been Flemish. There was, it must be admitted, a sticky period in the late 1940s when the Italian, Fiorenzi Magni, crossed the finish line first three times in a row, but the locals blunted the pain by nicknaming Magni 'The Lion of Flanders' and claiming him as one of their own.

Much to the disgust of the old, bow-legged, chapped-cheek fans in their faded woollen cycling caps who lurk along the fringes of any bike-race crowd, the top riders of the modern era tend to ignore history. They rarely deign to grace the Ronde with their presence, preferring to conserve their energies for the gruelling, big-money stage races that come later in the season and guarantee the team sponsors more widespread media coverage. As a consequence the Spaniard Miguel Indurain (then standing at four consecutive wins in the Tour de France, soon to rise to a record-equalling five) was not at the start in Sint-Niklaas, a windswept town between Ghent and Antwerp, the heart of the Waasland. Nor were his main rivals: the egomaniac Russian, Yevgeni Berzin; the shaven-headed and lunatic climber, Marco Pantani; and the mouse-like world number one, Tony Rominger, whose one eccentricity was to insist that the publicity girls who traditionally posed alongside winning riders weren't wearing any lipstick when they kissed him. The top Englishman, Chris Boardman, was also sensibly saving himself for Le Tour.

An hour before the start of the race, on a stage in the centre of Sint-Niklaas's town square (the biggest in Belgium – and that's official!), a bulky middle-aged man with sleek black hair and an even sleeker camel-hair sports jacket was introduced to the crowd. This was Eddy Merckx, the greatest cyclist in history – perhaps the only one whose name is widely known in Britain – and a man who might just be the most famous non-fictional Belgian of all time.

In this day and age the star cyclists pick and choose which events they enter. In Merckx's era, from the mid-1960s through to the early 1970s, things were different. Back then top riders entered every race they could, and in Merckx's case won most of them.

Nowadays Eddy Merckx is rotund to the point of globularity. Putting on weight is a problem for the retired pro cyclist. Riding burns up lots of energy, and they eat accordingly; chomping down a 3,500-calorie breakfast is a hard habit to break. Once they slip off the saddle for the final time many bike-racers balloon up as if someone has just pulled the rip-cord on a life-jacket beneath their shirt.

Despite the change in shape Merckx was easily recognis-able. He still has the wide sharkish smile and *those* eyelashes. Merckx's eyelashes are easily the longest and most luxuriant in the history of sport. Even Betty Boop envies Eddy's eye-lashes.

Merckx's mastery of his sport was complete. He was the Bradman of the bicycle. Like the Don, he ruled with a com-bination of iron will and skill, and a dash of the sort of cunning that would have put a grin on the face of Niccolò Machiavelli. In 1996 King Albert II made Eddy a Baron, pre-sumably on the grounds that a country with a bicycling monarchy needs a bicycling aristocracy to go with it. Baron, with its connotations of swagger and the brutal exercising of power, is the perfect prefix for Eddy Merckx.

Jorgen Leth's film *Stars and Water-carriers* covers the 1973 Tour of Italy. During the race José-Manuel Fuente repeatedly attempted to break Merckx's hold on the leader's pink jersey. The film shows the Spaniard attacking one day on a mountain stage, breaking away from the pack and building a substantial lead. Eventually Merckx heads off in solo pursuit, catches Fuente on a steep, pine-fringed incline and cycles past him without so much as a second glance. Fuente tries to respond, but like a man in a nightmare struggling to get to an appoint-ment on time, he is racing as fast as he can only to find himself stuck in some kind of treacle. As Merckx disappears up the hill the narrator announces, in stilted *Tales from Europe* tones: 'This is how Merckx deals with those who challenge him!'

There is a myth in sport about 'the hungry fighter'. Merckx was from a comfortable middle-class background, yet he had a formidable will to win. An American football coach once taunted a less successful rival with the comment, 'The trouble with your guys is they all have their own teeth.' In this dental index of competitiveness Merckx makes Nobby Stiles look like the Osmonds.

Merckx had a number of bitter rivals. Many of them were Dutch or Flemish, and blessed with the sort of names – Zoetemelk, Godefroot, Van Springel – you wouldn't want to shout with a mouthful of carpet tacks. Merckx gobbled them all up with such relish he was nicknamed 'The Cannibal'.

Cycling is a good game for nicknames. Not for this sport the dull practice of adding an 'o' or an 'ie' on to a surname. Romain Maes, Flemish winner of the 1936 Tour de France, was 'The Yellow Devil'; Marco Pantani is 'Il Elephantino', in honour of his pendulous ears; Luis Bahamontes of Spain was 'The Eagle of Toledo'. If David Ginola was a cyclist he'd be 'The Swooning Swan of St Tropez'. One of Merckx's greatest foes was Roger de Vlaeminck. De Vlaeminck had wild, sunken eyes and the knot-jointed legs of a rangy marsh bird. He was known as 'The Beast from Eeklo'.

Merckx is from the Brussels suburbs, a no-man's-land between the warring Belgian factions of Flemings and Walloons. De Vlaeminck is fiercely Flemish. He speaks Italian, a bit of English, a smattering of Spanish, but if anyone addressed a question to him in French during his riding days he looked through them as if they did not exist. De Vlaeminck regarded French as the language of the enemy. Speaking to him in it was an affront. People say De Vlaeminck's reputation for hostility was undeserved, but in my opinion it is wise never to upset anyone known as 'The Beast'.

De Vlaeminck and his elder brother Eric raced for the same team. They set out to defeat Merckx. They went after him in race after race. They became obsessed. Eventually Roger de Vlaeminck saw sense; he eased off on Merckx, joined an Italian-based squad and started winning races. Eric didn't. He ended up seeing a psychiatrist.

Like De Vlaeminck, Freddy Maertens from De Panne was Flemish to the core. He had the body shape of the archetypal Flandrian cyclist: short, columnar legs and a bow-fronted torso. Maertens was tough, but he was simple. His experiences at the hands of Merckx are recorded in his autobiography, *Fall from Grace*. Had Maertens been a stand-up comedian rather than a cyclist, his catchphrase would have been, 'Once again Eddy Merckx had stabbed me in the back.'

When Donald Bradman started dominating cricket in the 1930s Douglas Jardine came up with bodyline. The only way to defeat a cyclist of Merckx's superhuman powers was to slip a lump of kryptonite into his *bidon*. Kryptonite not being available, his competitors did the next best thing: they waited for him to get old or injured. In the meantime they fed off the crumbs that fell from his table. Unlike Eddy these days, they didn't have to worry about their weight.

In *Stars and Water-carriers* an Italian rider takes over the film-maker's mike during a dull stage. He rides up to Merckx. 'Eddy,' he asks, 'isn't it possible for you to ease up and let someone else win every once in a while?' Merckx, smiling, replies in immaculate Italian, 'I hear your complaint, but I am indifferent to it,' and pedals away laughing. No wonder the crowd at Sint-Niklaas greeted him with polite but hardly adulatory applause – Merckx is a man who commands admiration, but perhaps not affection. He was too good for that.

Despite the absence of the top stars, the field of close to two hundred riders assembled at Sint-Niklaas was still a strong one: a mix of young hopefuls not yet ready for the hardship of the major tours, ageing stars and men who have come, often painfully, to the realisation that they do not have the long-term strength, the all-round ability or the incredible recuperative powers needed to make an impact in the stage-races. There is no disgrace in this. Some of the greatest riders in cycling's history fall into this category. Among them were Flemish idols Rik van Steenbergen (Rik I, as he is known in Belgium); Rik van Looy (Rik II, or simply 'The Emperor'); Jules van Hevel, winner of the Ronde in 1920 and a man who missed out on becoming World Champion eight years later only because he collided with a cow near the finish; and Roger de Vlaeminck himself. Another was the honorary Flandrian Sean Kelly. Kelly is an Irishman so quiet he is alleged to have responded to questions from a radio interviewer by nodding his head. He spent most of his cycling career lodging with a Flemish family in Vilvoorde, and was tough as teak, mute and inscrutable. In Ireland Kelly was considered an oddball; in Flanders he fitted in perfectly.

Before the start competitors circled listlessly round Sint-Niklaas's Grotemarkt, their huge, shaven legs warm inside Lycra pop-socks. Accompanying them were groups of teenage boys riding replica bicycles and clad in replica cycling kits. These were the Cycling Saddoes, a group of adolescents who appear at the start of all the major races and inveigle their way into the clusters of professionals in the vain hope that they will be mistaken for somebody famous. Some of them even have numbers on their bikes, and if you sarcastically wave at them they wave back in the distracted way of men concentrating on greater things.

That Sunday the Saddoes were rubbing shoulders with 'Il Diablo', world number three, Claudio Chiappuci; two-time winner of Paris–Roubaix, the silver-templed French smoothie, Gilbert Duclos-Lasalle; the flying Uzbek sprinter, Djamolidine Abduzhaparov, whose thighs are so thick it's a surprise he can actually squeeze a bike in between them; and Franco Ballerini, who in the following week would dislocate a shoulder in a crash during Ghent–Wevelgem, pop it back in himself and finish the race, then four days later ride to victory across the bone-jarring *pavés* of Paris–Roubaix. There was the

American former World Champion, Lance Armstrong, with his Steve McQueen haircut and trendy Oakley eye-jackets; pink-clad Latin glamour boy, Maurizio Fondriest; and the local lads: the two Johans, Capiot and Museeuw; Wilfried Nelissen; Edwig van Hooydonck (crushed after a promising start to his career by being dubbed 'The New Merckx') and the bronzed and hot-tempered Eric Vanderaerden (a 'New Merckx' several years before Van Hooydonck), who displayed the worst sporting bubble-perm seen since the retirement of Charlie George.

As ten o'clock approached the riders cycled up to register for the race. TV cameras homed in on them and a team of pundits – including Eddy Planckaert, once a Flemish cycling hero but now, with his unruly hair, stubble and beer-gut, looking more like the kind of man who'd corner you in a Muswell Hill pub and start going on about his days as the bass-player in Brinsley Schwartz – sprang out to interview the top contenders. The array of languages – Flemish, French, German, Italian – the TV presenters have at their disposal is impressive. Or at least it is until the Dane, Rolf Sorensen, pedals on to the podium:

PUNDIT: Rolf, we will talk in English, yes?
SORENSEN: Okay.
PUNDIT: Well, Rolf, you are here today.
   (*Long pause*)
SORENSEN: Er . . . It would appear so, yes.

The start of a major cycle race is symbolic, a spectacle. Nothing is decided here. The riders make a stately progress around the town, giving off a poisonous cloud of embrocation fumes that has asthma sufferers reaching for their inhalers, then disappear out into the countryside. After they have gone the crowd thins out until all that's left are a deflated hot-air balloon, unstable slag-heaps of advertising material that threaten an avalanche on passing poodles, and knots of old men, still muttering about the modern generation of riders and their lack of respect for tradition. Sint-Niklaas quickly goes back to what it is for the other 364 days of the year, a quiet, well-scrubbed place set among sub-sea-level fields and famous for having a big town hall, a museum devoted to the history of barbering and scores of bronze statues of naked women, many running as if in response to an anonymous tip-off as to the whereabouts of their missing undergarments.

In a bar in Geraardsbergen four and a half hours later people sat eating their lunches, knives, forks and jaws working on automatic pilot, eyes fixed on a giant TV screen in the corner of the room. The cameras followed the Italian rider Andrea Tafi as he crossed the cobbled mound of the Kwaremont hill fifteen or so miles to the west. Tafi had been leading the race for over one hundred kilometres by this stage. He was over a kilometre clear of the rest of the field, but as he forced his bicycle up the next steep incline you could see him begin to wobble. In the bar in Geraardsbergen the watching Flandrians paused over their dustbins of mussels and Himalayan ice creams and smiled maliciously. Tafi may have been two minutes in front, but the drunken swaying of his cycle and the lolling of his head showed that he was already a goner. And the local favourite, Johan Museeuw, was heading the chasing pack.

Dark-haired and jug-eared, Museeuw is the latest in a long line of great Flemish cyclists, all of them with names that look like anagrams – Briek Schotte is a personal favourite. The line has been running somewhat thin in recent years, to such an extent, in fact, that many were calling Museeuw 'The Last of the Flandrians'. When this was put to Museeuw he patriotically denied it, adding cryptically: 'You don't have to be Flemish to be a Flandrian.' (As I write this, things are brightening somewhat. Frank Vandenbroucke has just won Paris–Nice, the first Belgian victory in a major stage-race for over two decades. With dull inevitability Vandenbroucke has since been dubbed 'The New Eddy Merckx' . . .)

On top of the Muur of Geraardsbergen there was a large and happy crowd. Loudspeakers gave a commentary on the race and people with hand-held TV sets yelled out their opinions. Tafi's lead was gradually eroded. With every incline the pursuers clawed back more time. The Italian struggled on, but he was a hooked fish and they were reeling him in inch by inch.

At each announcement of the narrowing time-gap the crowd on the sunny hillside nodded and muttered approvingly. At each mention of Museeuw they cheered. Soon Tafi was swallowed up by the main field. Simultaneously another Italian, Fabio Baldato, broke for the front. Museeuw was on his back wheel. Taken by surprise the main bunch initially failed to respond, and the break took a couple of hundred metres off them before they could organise a pursuit. In front of me a group of lads raised their chalice-like glasses of chocolatey Trappist beer in the air and began to sing. It was a jaunty tune, a marching – or, more likely – a drinking song. All bar two words of it were unintelligible to me. It went: 'Rumpty pumty pum / RUMpty pumty pum / RUMpty pumty PUUUUM / Johan Museeuw!'

Soon the singing was drowned out by the whumping of rotor-blades. The race was approaching. Three helicopters circled above the hill, their noise obliterating the commentary. Cut off from news of the race the crowd waited silently, craning forward to peer down the winding cobbled road that led to the summit. A skein of motorbikes flew up into view, deposited photographers and sped off again. A car appeared. The hill at Geraardsbergen is thankfully too steep and narrow to allow the passage of the full publicity convoy that normally precedes a race, blaring out jingles, hurling sweets and knocking small children unconscious with well-aimed packs of promotional sun-visors. Instead there was just the track marshals, a couple of police motorcycles and then, after a pause, Baldato and Museeuw.

They came up towards the crest of the Muur side by side, legs pumping, heads down, bodies hunched. As they reached the sharp final bend before the peak, Museeuw sprang past. Baldato gritted his teeth and tried to respond. That this was the decisive moment of the race was written on the Italian's face. Baldato was working as hard as he could, but his legs had turned to custard. Museeuw hammered away from him, over the crest. The crowd applauded wildly, the lads began to sing again. Then something strange happened. At the appearance on the slope of a lone, gaunt-faced rider in a red and black shirt, the mood of jollity evaporated. People began to jeer and hiss. There was real venom in it. The rider was the Moldovan, Andrei Tchmil; a top man, winner of the previous year's Paris–Roubaix. The Flemish hated Tchmil.

Tchmil's sin was rooted in the labrynthine world of cycling diplomacy that Eddy Merckx had exploited so well. The Russian rode in the Belgium-based Lotto team. One of his team-mates was Wilfried Nelissen, a popular Fleming. Tchmil was Lotto's best rider – a *rouleur* or all-rounder, extremely capable in all the various disciplines of cycling but a specialist in none. Nelissen is an out-and-out sprinter. Some weeks before, in another race, it had been decided by the Lotto team that as the course suited the sprinters they would all ride in support of Nelissen, pacing him, protecting him from the cross-winds and leading him into a favourable position for the final kick. When the moment for that kick came, however, Tchmil led Nelissen out, then, instead of peeling off to the side to let his sprinter through as planned, he simply belted away to victory himself. The miserable Nelissen finished well down the field. To the rest of the world it may have looked like a simple case of the best man winning. The popular verdict in Flanders, though, was that Andrei Tchmil had, to borrow Maertens' phrase, stabbed their man in the back (despite their much vaunted toughness and self-reliance, the Flandrians also have a reputation for paranoia and moaning. As a Yorkshireman myself it is a combination I find surprisingly familiar). The 'act of betrayal' had raised feelings high. At the foot of the Muur of Geraardsbergen a spectator had jumped over the barrier and attempted to push Tchmil off his bicycle. Other, more restrained fanatics contented themselves with simply spitting at him or holding up banners reading 'Judas'. At the finish near Ninove a heckling crowd reduced Tchmil's wife to tears. In Flanders, cycle-racing aroused the kind of passion normally associated with religion, or football.

After this illuminating if unedifying episode, the crowd settled back into its previous festive spirit. Riders were arriving all the time. Sean Yates, the only Englishman in the race, went past looking furious, heading a bunch containing the Italians' idol, Mercatone Uno rider Mario Cippolini. Some people play up to a national stereotype so wholeheartedly it's a delight. Cippolini is one such character. Arguably the best sprinter in the business, 'The Lion King' (as he styles himself) has designer stubble, a dark tan and a mane of Renaissance curls permanently adorned by a pair of sunglasses. On the stage at Sint-Niklaas they'd asked him who he'd thought would win, and he'd replied 'Museeuw' with a cheesy grin that had 'that should charm the locals' splashed over it like the ink on a forged banknote. Off his bicycle Cippolini drove a Ferrari and lived a playboy life. 'I like to do everything very fast,' he told reporters, 'except making love.'

After the main field there was a long delay before the backmarkers appeared. These were the riders who were really suffering. Grey-faced, besmirched with dirt, their legs bloody from clashes and collisions, they laboured up the hill past the vast memorial to the Great War dead and roadside calvaries as if on some tortuous pilgrimage. The crowd applauded them as warmly as it had done the front-runners. Like penitents, there was something noble in their self-flagellation.

By the time I walked back down to Geraardsbergen, Museeuw had already crossed the finish-line a minute or so ahead of Baldato. In the square there were klaxons sounding. The veterans in the woollen cycling caps grinned madly and the lads outside the bars sang: 'Rumpty pumty pum / RUMpty pumty pum / RUMpty pumty PUUUUM / Johan Museeuw!' Inside, beer was being swilled, backs patted and shoulders slapped. The Flandrians were delirious. Despite the unseasonably warm conditions their man had taken on the best that Europe and America could offer and beaten them hollow. The best Frenchman finished 55th, the Dutch were nowhere. The Flemish had out-phlegmed the rest of the world.

Nothing so exciting greeted the arrival of the amateurs. There was a smattering of applause as each appeared, the odd cry of support from a brother or girlfriend, and then they were gone. The crowd wandered back down the hill again in search of waffles and chocolate sauce and the last million *mattetarte* in the shop.

On the way home we stopped at a café in a village near Zottegem, and sat in the garden trying to fathom why one of the local householders had elected to fill his entire garden with large model bi-planes made from yellow, blue and red plastic and mounted on six-foot-high poles.

'What part of England are you from?' a man on a nearby table asked. When we told him Newcastle, he smiled. 'Philippe Albert!' he said, naming the Liège-born Belgian international and Bob Carolgees lookalike who played centre-half for United. The ice thus broken, the man came over and sat down with us. He was in his early forties, with cropped reddish-blonde hair and a menacing scar which ran down one side of his face. He looked like Vincent van Gogh during a bad patch, albeit with a full complement of ears. He was drinking a 75cl bottle of N'Ice d'Achouffe, a special festive beer from the Ardennes with gnomes on the label. It is so strong you could flambé a Christmas pudding in it. The man wasn't sharing it with anyone.

Despite his fierce appearance the Albert-man turned out to be amiability personified. We talked about football. Middlesbrough had just played Chelsea in the FA Cup Final and lost 2–0. When I told him I was a Middlesbrough fan the Albert-man asked if I had watched the game. I shook my head. 'I think maybe it is as well for you,' he said sadly.

'So,' the man said when we had discussed various Belgians who had played in England and expressed mutual incredulity at the fact that the Belgian league had been won in successive years by Excelsior Mouscron and Lierse, 'what are you doing here in Flanders?'

'We're on holiday,' we said.

'On holiday here?' the man chuckled. 'But why? It is flat and crowded and . . .' He stuck a hand out from under the parasol into the light drizzle which had begun to fall a few minutes before, '. . . it rains all the time.'

At that moment it felt like a tough one to answer.

On Monday morning I obtained a phonecard with surprisingly little effort. Then we began looking for a telephone-box. We drove around for half an hour through what seemed like one big suburb. A couple of times I yelled, 'There's one!', but when we screeched to a halt and reversed, they both turned out to be bread-vending machines. In the end we gave in and went back to Geraardsbergen.

We parked near the station, phoned the travel company

and arranged to go into their Brussels office. There was an hour before the next train, so we walked into town, past a shop called Health and Beauty the whole front area of which was filled with shelves laden with chocolate, and a poodle parlour with an arresting English name above the door. There was some kind of subconscious link in the Belgian mind between dogs and the British. Many canine beauty salons had English appellations. As a dog-lover I found this rather flattering, though I couldn't help thinking the owner of Dogs' Toilet might have chosen her words a little more carefully. Still, at least she hadn't been as ill-advised as the proprietor of Doggy Style in Couvin.

We walked along past the creaking heaps of *mattetarte* in the bakeries' windows. In Geraardsbergen, as in many Belgian towns, there are speakers mounted in the shopping streets broadcasting jaunty tunes. The PA in Geraardsbergen that morning was playing what appeared to be a James Last version of the Clash's 'Should I Stay Or Should I Go'. It was definitely different in style from anything I'd heard from the shopping-street PAs before, but it had the same artistic merit. The music broadcast over such things is almost always crap and usually badly dated too. If back in the 1980s you vowed to shoot yourself if ever again you heard Ryan Paris singing 'La Dolce Vita' my advice is: don't go to Belgium without your revolver.

I went into a bank to cash a traveller's cheque. Since it was Monday morning the bank was full. There was only a pair of positions open and I found myself queuing at the one that was the special preserve of people doing very complicated things with money while having a chat with their friend behind the counter about the events of the weekend. At first I wondered why Belgium hadn't gone over to the single queue system which avoids this sort of thing. After a while, though, I began to see that the Belgians rather enjoyed standing in lines. Getting it over with as quickly as possible wasn't the object. For them it was the journey, not the destination.

Twenty minutes elapsed before I found myself facing the teller. 'I'd like to cash a traveller's cheque,' I said. The teller, whose thick round glasses gave him the startled appearance of an owl that has just landed on a hedgehog, shook his head dolefully. 'We do not have the facilities,' he said. 'There is another bank down the street which may be able to help you.'

I found this slightly aggravating, but reminded myself that in foreign countries things are done differently, and that it is these differences which create the world's colourful tapestry, thereby enriching us all. Bio-diversity, I muttered to myself, as I wandered off down the street; the great blue whale, the natterjack toad, the Belgian banking system – all must be preserved.

In the next bank I queued for fifteen minutes. 'I'd like to cash a traveller's cheque,' I said to the young woman behind the glass partition. A sorrowful smile spread across her round, butter-coloured face. 'I'm afraid we do not have the facilities,' she said. I was overcome by an urge to yell, 'What facilities do you actually need to cash a bloody traveller's cheque? All that is necessary, as far as I can tell, is a newspaper with the tourist rates in it and some fucking money. I've worked in little shops in England that take traveller's cheques, for Christ's sake!' But what would have been the point, besides saving me from hypertension and a stomach ulcer?

In the next bank I came to there was, miraculously, no queue. 'I would like, if at all possible, to cash a traveller's cheque,' I said to the sturdy young woman at the desk. 'It's American Express,' I added hopefully, as her face began the drop into negativity. She held out a hand for the cheque and, after I gave it to her, studied it for a second, holding it up to the light as if searching for a watermark. 'One moment,' she said.

I watched her saunter across to the back of the room, where a man with a pencil moustache and a pale green blazer sat behind a desk. She spoke with him briefly and handed over my traveller's cheque. The man held it up for inspection, ruminatively smoothed his moustache between thumb and forefinger, then shook his head, picked up the phone and punched in an extension number. He said a few words and put the receiver down again. A few moments later a man with hair like a Brillo pad emerged from a side door and marched purposefully across to the young woman and the man in the blazer. He took the traveller's cheque in his hand and held it up to the light. Then he glanced across at me, said something to the young woman and returned the cheque to her. She nodded and came slowly back towards her counter. The suspense as her measured tread carried her across the grey-blue carpet tiles was immense. When she arrived back she arranged herself very deliberately in her chair, lined up several dozen pens in a neat row, shuffled some papers around and then looked up at me. 'Yes,' she said, 'we can do this for you.' We got our train with thirty seconds to spare.

When we outlined the problems with the house to the very elegant Bruxelloise lady from the travel company she took a lot less time to agree that it had all been terribly unfortunate. She offered us our money back without hesitation. We agreed that it might be for the best. 'For you certainly,' the elegant lady said to me. 'A journalist like you, you have only to show your press card and immediately you get 30 per cent, 50 per cent off everything.' I made some noises about not compromising my integrity by getting involved in that sort of thing.

'Oh, but every journalist does it,' the elegant lady said with one of those slight, knowing smiles that seemed designed to irritate.

'Well, I'm afraid I don't,' I said firmly, and immediately wished I hadn't. Why is it that the sort of sentence which, coming from the lips of James Stewart or Gary Cooper, would resonate with dignity, honesty and decency, makes me sound like a pompous and priggish ninny?

That night, when we got back to the house, we packed for an early start. 'Where do you want to go?' I asked Catherine. 'Somewhere normal and safe and boring,' she said.

We were on our way at six. As we drove away cockerels in a nearby chicken coop emerged rubbing their eyes with their wings and clucking grumpily at us. The roads were empty. On the outskirts of Geraardsbergen a woman in a cotton dressing-gown and battered mules, her hair in curlers, stood blinking fuzzily on the roadside outside her house as if she had taken a wrong turn on the way to the bathroom. She was the only person we saw until we crossed the provincial and linguistic border into Hainaut.

Soon after, as we crested the last of a series of low, steep hills, we saw the five grey spires of mighty Tournai Cathedral standing sentry over the city a dozen or more miles ahead. You could see how a medieval peasant might have gazed on this very same scene and drawn comfort from the obvious power and merciful omniscience of the one true God. I felt something similar. Only in my case the comfort came from the knowledge that somewhere waiting for us in the shadow of that cathedral was the merciful omniscience of the one true Holiday Inn.

Three

Tournai was a good place to recuperate. In the morning Catherine and I pottered along the banks of the Escaut, watching tubby cargo barges chugging by, expressing mild admiration for the fortified thirteenth-century Pont des Trous and chuckling at a sign for a local estate agent with the apt surname of Git.

At lunchtime we found a fantastic restaurant. From the outside it looked ordinary, a little run-down even, but once you went through the door you were in another world. There was Duke Ellington playing on the tape deck, and a smell of rich sauces reducing and cognac and cigars. A group of businessmen were sitting having dessert. Their puddings looked like they had been fashioned by Fabergé.

We suddenly felt very awkward and scruffy. I had Maisie in a carrier on my back and Catherine was holding a polythene bag with baby food, plates and bottles in it. We stood in the reception area thinking of retreat.

The owner of the restaurant, a woman in her late forties, with the look of a Gallic Katharine Hepburn, advanced towards us. 'I am very sorry,' she said. I began to mumble something about it being all right, we fully understood, then heard the woman finish her sentence. 'You must forgive me. I have no baby chair. Will she sit on your knee? I cannot think why I do not have a baby chair. It is a terrible oversight. I must get one immediately. Today you must make do, if you can, but next time you come there will be a chair for the baby, I promise you.'

After we had eaten our lunch, the owner came to chat with us. We said how much we had enjoyed our meal. 'It was not difficult because of the chair?' she asked. 'I should have brought one from home when my own kids grew up, but . . .'

I said it was nice to be able to come in at all; in England some restaurants didn't welcome children. 'Really?' the woman said, aghast. 'But this is terrible. When they are that age they need these things. They must have new tastes, new experiences, they must have' – she paused dramatically – 'life.'

Later, Catherine and I walked across a broad, open square where young girls in navy-blue pinafore dresses waited with their music cases outside the grand, porticoed entrance to the Conservatoire, and up through a small public gardens. It was five o'clock when we arrived at the Musée des Beaux-Arts. The gallery was designed in the 1920s by Victor Horta, father of Art Nouveau. Art Nouveau could justifiably be said to be a Belgian invention, because the phrase was coined by Brussels journalist Octave Maus in 1881. Not only that. There was something about Art Nouveau, the way it piled ornamentation on top of opulence, that expressed part of the national character. The Belgians cannot get enough of rich things – mayonnaise, pralines, Gothic architecture; to them *more* is more. Patronised by a new, merchant class made wealthy by their country's rapid industrialisation and King Leopold II's acquisition of the Congo, Art Nouveau flourished in Belgium. There were examples of Art Nouveau buildings in most of the nation's major cities. In Tournai there are half a dozen houses and shops designed by the architects Strauven and De Porre.

The old man at the ticket desk at the Musée des Beaux-Arts, who looked like he'd been designed by someone with rather less aesthetic sense, was very reluctant to let us in. 'It is only twenty minutes until we close,' he snarled, tapping at the face of his wristwatch with a yellowing, talon-like fingernail. 'Twenty minutes, do you see?' He pursed his lips and peered at us. He had one of those elaborate thatched hair-dos; the sort where you start off trying to work out if they're concealing a bald patch by mentally unravelling the interwoven strands and eventually get so confused and bored you give up. I was sure there was bare pate under this one, however, and if the man ever raised enough cash for a hair transplant his nostrils would have seemed an obvious and rich source of live follicles.

'On the door it says you close at half-past five,' Catherine said. The man glanced at the door and then down at his watch and hissed at the betrayal. He paused, temporarily vanquished, then rallied. 'Yes,' he said, 'but we must lock up everything and turn off all the lights before then, you understand.' He saw that we were as yet unimpressed. 'It is regulations,' he snapped.

'Well,' Catherine said to him, 'I don't . . .' The man jabbed his watch agitatedly, *taptaptaptap*, if he was trying to send us a subconscious message in Morse code: Fuck off English people.

'Seventeen minutes now . . . Seventeen minutes until we must switch off all the lights and lock up.' It was 100 francs each to get in. £1.80 was a lot of money for seventeen minutes looking round an art gallery, but for a guaranteed means of irritating this nasty old tosser it was cheap at twice the price.

We walked around the museum, the man with the elaborate hair and long fingernails following ten yards behind us as if in purdah, switching off the lights as we went to deter any thought we might have of returning to look at something. In truth there wasn't much that was worth a second look. The art could hardly match the setting, which was beautiful: natural light filtering down into a series of small marbled galleries.

There was one eye-catching canvas, a massive Victorian oil painting called *The Plague of Tournai in 1090* by someone named Galliat. The scene depicted was one of gruesome devastation, with people weeping and wailing and mad dogs tearing at the flesh of unburied bodies. I couldn't help noticing in the centre of it all that several young women had reacted to the crisis by tearing open their bodices and bearing their perfectly formed breasts. At first I thought this was simply gratuitous. Later, though, I wondered if Monsieur Galliat hadn't based his work on historical records. After all, people did all sorts of weird stuff to prevent the plague – wore masks, burned incense; Arnold of the Abbey of Oudenburg near Bruges even insisted his parishioners drank beer instead of water, and became patron-saint of Belgian brewers as a result – perhaps this was just another of them.

I imagined a meeting of Tournai Town Council. 'What will we do about this dreadful plague?' the mayor asks.

'Why don't we get all the nubile women of the city to expose their bosoms?' cries a councillor.

'And will that stop the plague?' asks the mayor.

'Who cares!' replies the councillor.

'Thank you so much for your trouble,' Catherine said to the talons-man as he unlocked the door to let us out. 'My pleasure, madame,' he replied. If nature truly abhors a vacuum, the total lack of sincerity in these two remarks must have sucked in genuine feelings from hundreds of miles away.

That evening I went for a walk. The first time I'd been to Tournai was with my friend Steve. We'd come to see an amateur bike race that looped round and round the city centre.

As we walked along beside the river we spotted a gents' urinal. 'Obviously for the tourists,' Steve said. 'What do you mean?' I asked him. 'Well,' Steve said, 'no true French-speaking male is going to bother going into a public toilet when he's got the street, is he?'

'Steady on,' I said, 'I think that's a bit of national stereotyping.' No sooner had the words died on my lips than the portly middle-aged man walking along in front of us suddenly stopped, unzipped and relieved himself on a handily placed pile of sand. 'I'm saying nothing,' Steve said oxymoronically.

The cycle race proved highly entertaining, if only because of the efforts of the track marshals. Armed with what appeared to be primitive table-tennis bats and given licence to direct city-centre traffic all Saturday afternoon, they reacted with an officious fanaticism that suggested Tournai might prove a fertile recruiting ground for the Traffic Warden Service. A particularly savage duel was played out between the officials in the car that preceded the riders and the local bus-drivers, some of whom seemed to have formed the impression that ferrying the public to and from the shops might be more important than a local bike race. In one notable mêlée the official car actually pursued a bus for a quarter of a mile or so before finally forcing it into the kerb with a mixture of frantically waving bats and those clutched-fingers 'arsehole' gestures of which Francophones are so fond. I think a Pole won.

Now I retraced our steps that day, past the public toilet and along the river-bank. It was dark now and the street lights reflecting on the water gave everything a pallid, shifting glow.

In a bar near the fish quay I ordered a beer made by a brewery close to Ronse. It came in a bottle with a witch on it and had a tannic edge so hard it felt like it was scraping the enamel off your teeth and using it to sand-blast your taste-buds. The only way I could get through the bottle was by stuffing my mouth full of peanuts before I took a swig. The salt seemed to act as a neutralising agent.

It was around nine o'clock and I was the only customer in the place. Anywhere else you might have thought the bar was on the verge of closing up, but in Belgium bars have a habit of staying open unfeasibly late. In sleepy little towns it is not uncommon to find cafés still serving at 3 a.m. Anyone planning to pursue the age-old British custom of nipping out for the last hour can get a decent kip in first.

The chef and the waitress were sitting at one of the tables eating shrimp croquettes and listening to the radio. From what I could make out, the first findings of the investigation into the Dutroux killings had just been made public. When the woman brought me another little bowl of peanuts I asked her what the magistrates had discovered. She shrugged. 'Nothing, of course,' she said. 'Absolutely nothing.' Only she didn't say 'nothing', she said something that sounded far more contemptuous: *rien*. She delivered it with an extra flourish on the rolling, phlegmy 'R'. It was nothing with spit on it.

Yet for all the waitress's anger there was also a cynic's bitter enjoyment in her tone of being proved right again about the baseness of human affairs. All the Belgians I had met and talked to about the Dutroux killings and their aftermath had expected this outcome, and all of them knew that when it came they were not going to believe a word of it.

Corruption, or a belief in its existence, was ingrained. A couple in a Flemish village surrounded by cabbage and maize fields said, 'To protect our countryside, the government has introduced laws to prevent people building houses on green sights, but, naturally, if you know someone . . .' and the man held a hand up in front of his face and rubbed the thumb across the tips of his fingers, the international gesture for money.

'Belgium,' a middle-aged hotelier said to me later on in

our trip, 'is the most corrupt country in Europe.' I wasn't surprised. I had got used to hearing such things. Belgians suffer from low self-esteem. Even Flemings who trumpet the glory of Flanders become oddly unnerved when you join in the praise and try to dissuade you from it as if heading off a malicious punchline.

In Ghent I had sat in perhaps the only wholefood *patisserie* in Flanders. It was the first time in Belgium I had eaten a cake that felt as if it was doing me more good physically than spiritually. As I ground my way through a slab of what may have been carob-coated carpet-tile I overheard a Flemish music student from the nearby college talking to a Brazilian classmate. They were using English, the global Swahili. The Fleming asked the Brazilian what he thought of Ghent. The Brazilian said, 'I like it very much,' and took a bite of whole-some walnut cake. When he had finished chewing it ten or so minutes later, he added, 'You know, I have lived in Holland and in Paris, also, but I prefer it in Belgium. The cities are pretty, the countryside is open. Things are sympathetic here.'

Ear cocked, I waited for the Fleming's demurring response. It came in a split-second. 'Really?' he said. 'But maybe you have not seen all of Holland. The islands to the north are very beautiful and, naturally, there is Amsterdam . . .'

I therefore knew from experience and observation that protest against the hotelier's statement was fruitless, but still, I felt politeness required some kind of token denial. 'No, no,' the hotelier continued, waving aside my half-hearted mur-muring of 'Oh surely not', 'it is true. Here the white economy and black economy are so well-established people have two bank accounts, one for declared and one for undeclared earnings. In other countries the tax authorities calculate what you owe on what you say you earn. Here the tax authorities base their assessment on your lifestyle.'

I laughed and asked how such a system could possibly

work; after all, people spend their money differently. Such a system would penalise the spendthrift and reward the hoarder. 'It can only work in Belgium,' the hotelier said, 'because here everyone is obsessed with how they look to other people. If it is a choice between putting food on the table and a new set of curtains, a Belgian will choose the curtains.'

In a country which organises its day so thoroughly around mealtimes it is a surprise not to see the opening hours of public buildings listed as 'From quarter to coffee and macaroon to half-past *coupe belle Hélène*', I found this rather hard to believe, but the hotelier had got his momentum up and there was no stopping him.

'Once a month here in our town,' he said, 'the council collect large domestic refuse. People put all the bigger things they no longer want – furniture, building waste and the like – out on the pavement beside their houses and a lorry comes and picks it up. On the morning of this day, no matter if it is freezing cold, pouring with rain, or there is a tornado blowing, everyone in the town will be out and about, so they can inspect what the neighbours are disposing of. "Mmm," they say, "Mrs Cnudde is throwing out that chair and it only looks a few years old. Mr Cnudde must be doing better than we thought." I am sure,' the hotelier said, 'people put things out that are still new just to impress the people next door.'

At the time I wasn't sure if I believed this, but a few weeks later Catherine and I came on just the scene he had described, in a village south of Ghent. We had become momentarily lost in a suburb so posh and leafy that the only way you could tell there were houses set back from the road were the chain-link fences and the barking of monstrous dogs, but then had suddenly emerged into a more familiar street of tiny brick bungalows. The refuse lorry was coming slowly down the road towards us. There was so much stuff on the pavements outside the little houses ('Look, an avocado-coloured bathroom suite!') that it was amazing it had ever fitted into them in the first place. And people *were* standing out alongside their heap and casting anxious glances around at the piles of their neighbours. Once or twice people who plainly felt they weren't matching up nipped back indoors to get something else – a lampshade, bed-head or entire fitted kitchen. In Belgium it was rubbish. In Britain it would have been a swanky car-boot sale.

The hotelier forked a large slice of chocolate mousse cake into his mouth, then took a swig from a cup of coffee that had a raft of whipped cream floating on top of it of a size Thor Heyerdahl might have sailed the Atlantic on. When he had swallowed it he sighed, 'Belgium, Belgium!' and shook his head sadly.

The provocation for the hotelier's outburst was another radio report on the Dutroux killings. I asked him what he thought. 'That, as always, there will be talking and talking and then . . .' He shrugged and then began his assessment of his country's many failings.

To an outsider it was sometimes hard to see the connection between the grisly paedophile activity of Marc Dutroux and his associates and political graft. But in a country where corruption is rife, nothing – from the bungling of the police to the insensitivity of the judiciary – appears motiveless. Everything can be explained, by money.

The situation was not new. Nor was the effect of the black economy difficult to find. In a beautiful five-storey townhouse in Antwerp the owner complained to us about the stone floor. 'The builder,' she said, 'was supposed to clean, polish and then seal it. So he comes, cleans, polishes and goes away again. He comes back again only eight weeks after. By then the floor is dirty because it is our kitchen and we must walk and cook in here. But instead of cleaning and polishing he just puts the seal down on top. Now if we want to get rid of this,' she indicated a smear of red on the dark stone with the chiselled toe of her Chelsea boot, 'We must remove the seal again.'

The owner of the house wore a pale grey hacking jacket with dark velvet collar and cigarette-legged trousers in the same colour. Her house was both luxurious – the stair carpet was so thick the term shag-pile barely did it justice; this was fifty-years-of-love-and-commitment-pile if ever I saw it – and stylish. A reminder that Belgium was the nation of Hankar and Van de Velde as well as the last remaining natural habitat of the black-and-tan leatherette tuffet and matching drinks coasters.

'Can't you make the builder do it for you?' I asked.

The woman pulled a face. 'How?' she said.

'Well, you must have a contract with him or something. If he didn't do the job properly you can take him to court.'

The woman shook her head with a kind of wise sadness that makes it in many ways *the* characteristic Belgian gesture. 'No, we can't do that. We paid half the money' – she made a movement with her hands which indicated that if there had been a counter her money would have gone under it – 'so now . . .'

That was the problem with the black economy: you got involved in it and it messed you up. If you paid a builder on the black and he did the job badly, or didn't do it at all, what recourse did you have, short of going round to his house and putting a shotgun to his head? Sometimes I wondered if it was this that left so much of Belgium looking half-completed rather than just DIY overload.

It doesn't end there, of course. Once a system of corruption is in place it develops a momentum of its own. Just as Prohibition in the US created a climate in which organised crime could flourish, so the black economy created an atmosphere in Belgium which benefited the unscrupulous, the lazy, the incompetent and the blatantly evil.

For years the situation was simply allowed to drift. Certainly Belgium had problems, as people acknowledged. There were strikes, conflict between linguistic groups. There was a costly and unwieldy system of government, in which the national parliament oversaw three regional parliaments (Flanders, Wallonia and Brussels) and the eleven provincial assemblies. The result was an extraordinary number of politicians. In Belgium, for example, there are over ninety Cabinet ministers. If Andy Warhol had been Belgian his most famous pronouncement would have been slightly different; he'd have said, 'In the future everyone will be Foreign Minister for fifteen minutes.'

There were murders, too. A former Deputy Prime Minister, André Cools, was gunned down near Liège in 1991, allegedly by hitmen brought in from Tunisia by colleagues in the Walloon Socialist Party who were worried about what his probe into political corruption might be about to uncover. In Brabant in the early 1980s twenty-eight people were shot in random attacks in supermarket car-parks. There were rumours of a right-wing conspiracy, but nobody could be sure since the killers never announced their aims, or even if they had any. The murders stopped as suddenly as they had begun. No one was ever caught.

Despite these inconveniences and interruptions, life for the average Belgian is pretty good. The education system is excellent, the crime rate generally low, food is superb, there are smart things in the shops. Why rock the boat? Then children started to disappear. You see blurred black-and-white photocopied images of the missing in the windows of houses all across the country. They seem as ubiquitous there as memorials to the dead of the Great War are in Britain.

The Belgians love children. Not just mothers, like the

woman in the Tournai restaurant, but all generations. We had stopped in Mons on the way up to Flanders. It was a strange place in many ways. The Grande Place was lined with handsome buildings and gave the impression of prosperity, but just off it was a street in which the first shop you came to was a tattoo parlour (glancing in through the window I saw a mother sitting beside her teenage daughter. So important, I feel, for parents to share those rites-of-passage moments: first steps, first words, first communion, first tattoo . . .). We were sitting on a bench eating ice creams when a very glamorous girl of about eighteen came rushing up to us. Her dress was orange, but there was hardly enough of it to cover a satsuma. 'Your daughter,' she said, 'she is so beautiful! May I kiss her?' She did so and scampered off, leaving a little smudge of dark mauve lipstick on Maisie's forehead.

But despite all the affection, the missing children didn't come back. Paralysed by a mixture of incompetence, disorganisation, arrogance and – most Belgians continue to believe – something more sinister, the Belgian authorities seemed incapable of doing anything to stop it. For the first time people became agitated with the system. The White March in Brussels in October 1996 was seen by many as a turning-point, the moment when the Belgians finally looked beyond the comfort of their own lives and decided to change things. Not everyone agrees, however.

A local councillor I spoke to later in the month the Dutroux commission delivered its interim report said, 'The trouble is you have millions marching but only about 10 per cent know what they are marching for. In our local school the teachers and pupils went on strike for a day in honour, they said, of the dead children. At three o'clock in the afternoon I went through the square and there were the teachers sitting outside a café drinking beer.' She smiled. 'In honour of the dead children.'

You might think from this that the councillor was some kind of embittered, hard-nosed political bruiser. In fact she was in her thirties and a member of Anders Gaan Leven (Live Differently), the Flemish Green Party. In Belgium political cynicism is so widespread even idealists are infected by it.

'The trouble here,' the hotelier said after he had demolished his cake, 'is that everyone blames everyone else. Since the Dutroux business I hear people all the time saying, "Arrest these politicians, round up these businessmen. They are rotten, they are corrupt." But the same people who say that are boasting two minutes later about how they fiddled some VAT, or dodged paying all their tax. It is like they won a game. When you point out that this is hypocritical, they say: "Yes, but I am only a little person, they are taking more than me. They must get the higher-up people first. *Then* I will clean up my life." It has become a national trait to blame the people in power for everything that is wrong, but sometimes the fault lies with all of us.'

It reminded me of a line from *The Legend of Tyl Ulenspiegel* (set in the mid-seventeenth century, this book is thought by many to be the one which most encapsulates the spirit of Flanders. It was written in the 1860s, in French, by a German, Charles de Coster). Claes, the father of Tyl, observes of his nation's rulers, 'On high the thieving hornets, below the busy bees.' Not much has changed.

When I reported this to the Green Party councillor she nodded. 'Belgium was occupied for centuries,' she said, 'so people came to see government as something imposed on them. Belgians always laugh at the Dutch because the Dutch do what the government tells them. People here say, "What a bunch of arse-kissers the Dutch are. Look, they even obey the speed limit!" But the Dutch have been independent for a long time. The Dutch people do what the government tells them because they, the people, *are* the government. What

Belgians have not come to terms with is that in a democracy you get the politicians you deserve.' She laughed drily. 'And just look at our politicians.'

And then there was the police. When it came to public relations the Belgian police were perhaps the only organisation on Earth who would have benefited from lessons by Gerald Ratner.

I found myself in Brussels on the afternoon of the White March. Steve was trying to go back to Luxembourg City. We went to the Gare Centrale to find a huge crowd of people waiting outside. The massive wooden doors of the station were locked. A pair of police officers stood guard in front of them. As we watched, a stream of people approached the policemen to ask what was going on. Were the trains running? If not, when would they start? When might the station be open again? The policemen offered not a word in reply, they simply stared straight ahead. On a day when 250,000 people were protesting about judicial handling of a series of brutal child murders you might have thought the constabulary would have taken the opportunity to begin repairing their damaged image. Instead they reacted with the surly petulance of rebuked adolescents.

Perhaps the incident that illustrated this best came a year or so later in Charleroi. When the police had belatedly got round to thoroughly searching Dutroux's many houses they found a huge quantity of children's clothing. Announcements were made that the clothes would be put on display; anybody with a missing child could come to see if they recognised any of the items. The parents of children who had disappeared came to look at the garments. The police had cleared out an old stable and dumped the clothing in piles on the floor. The parents were expected to rummage through it as if at some grisly jumble sale. It was an act so insensitive as to be actually contemptuous. (In April 1998 the situation plunged into black farce when Dutroux escaped, briefly, from custody simply by pushing his guard over and running away.) That the police were corrupt was never proven; that they were unintelligent was beyond doubt. Only people of boneheaded stupidity could be so arrogant with so little cause.

The woman from the Green Party had echoed the words of Adlai Stevenson, 'Your public servants serve you right.' I took her point. In a democracy you'd have to say that that is correct. However, it was hard to see how ordinary Belgians, kind and courteous people with hardly an exception, could have deserved a police force like this one.

The following day we left Tournai and drove north along the river. Just before we crossed the linguistic border and the Escaut became the Schelde, we came across a small shanty settlement of pigeon lofts. Old men stood outside, scanning the air as if for a sign. It was a common sight. Belgium is the home of pigeon-racing. The sport's world governing body is based in Brussels. Pigeon-racing had begun in the coalfields around Liège in the late eighteenth century and spread rapidly. By 1820 it was a well-established part of Belgian life. Between the wars it was estimated that there were as many homing pigeons in Belgium as Belgians. Then the Germans invaded. The Nazis became convinced that the pigeons were being used to send messages across the Channel and so thousands upon thousands of the birds were burned alive in their coops or simply machine-gunned. The sport survived because Belgians take pigeon-racing very seriously. Top events are shown on TV and there is illegal use of drugs – and not only by those forced to watch it. Not that doping pigeons is a new thing; Georges Simenon remembered how, before a big race, queues would form outside a certain chemist's shop in Liège whose owner was famous for his pigeon laxatives. If he'd been a real entrepreneur he'd have sold umbrellas too.

The Walloons invented pigeon-racing; the Flemish invented the less celebrated finch sport. There is a whole cabinet devoted to finch sport in the excellent Folk Museum in Ghent. Basically (for there are certainly subtleties I have missed) a linnet, or other songbird, is placed in a little basket by its owner. He and other like-minded souls then sit beside their birds for a specified length of time and make a chalk mark on a length of wood each time the finch chirrups. The finch which chirrups most in the time allotted is the winner. Old photos of the event in the Folk Museum show it taking place on city pavements. This, I imagine, is a thing of the past. Nowadays finch sport takes place in an area which is easier to police, since the excitement generated among finch sport spectators must have created many a riot.

We drove on past villages and farms with barn doors painted bright shades of blue or dusty brick-red. We were heading back to Limburg but weren't in much of a hurry. By now we'd got used to the scale of Belgium. When we'd first arrived we'd look at places on the map we were planning a trip to and say, 'It's three whole squares away. Better get an early start if we want to see anything.' And we'd arrive at our destination in time to watch the newsagents lifting their shutters.

We got to Oudenaarde at a more civilised hour. According to a magnificent brochure picked up from the tourist office, 'history has left its traces of gratitude, still visible in its examples of beautiful monumental architecture' in Oudenaarde, making it 'the 2nd Town of Monuments in East Flanders' as well as 'an important economic metropole with a keen eye on textile'.

With a keen eye on lunch Catherine and I sat down in a café opposite the ornate late-Gothic town hall. The waitress was young, black and very jolly. She said, 'If you need me to explain anything from the menu, just ask.' There was an

American tinge to her English, the effect, I suspected, of MTV. The Belgians are mad on MTV. In practically every house or hotel we stayed in, when the owner showed you how to operate the TV set, they said proudly, 'Look, you've got MTV!' and pushed 18 on the remote control. MTV would come on. And it was always Jon Bon Jovi singing 'Midnight In Chelsea'.

When the waitress came back Catherine said, 'Can you tell me what this is, please?' and pointed to an item on the menu that looked like a series of nightmare Scrabble hands. 'Oh right,' the waitress said, furrowing her brow slightly. 'Well, what that is, is a bit of the calf.'

'What, an escalope?' Catherine suggested. The waitress shook her head. 'No, not an escalope,' she said, 'this bit is from, like, the inside of the calf.' There was the faintest pause and then she burst out laughing, 'The inside of the calf! I guess I made that sound really, really delicious!' We had the salmon.

In the centre of Oudenaarde's Grotemarkt, preparations were under way for the weekend's celebration of the anniversary of the birth of local artist Adriaen Brouwer in 1605. Fittingly, perhaps, the centre of activity was a huge sheet of canvas which looked destined to become a very large beer tent. Like Pieter Bruegel the Elder, Brouwer is very popular with the Flemish not so much for the way he painted as for *what* he painted, which was ordinary Flemings doing things the Flemish like doing. Brouwer's work shows people eating, drinking and smoking. The Flemish smoke a lot. To spend an evening in a small bar in Flanders, particularly one of the aptly named 'brown cafés', is to get some idea of what a kipper must feel like. Brouwer took his work seriously and plainly did a lot of research. He was dead at thirty-three. The Flemish did him the signal honour of naming a pie after him.

Brouwer painted in the area around Oudenaarde, Bruegel

in Pajottenland south of Brussels. The two weren't alone in depicting ordinary Belgian life. There was also David Teniers the Younger, a contemporary of Brouwer's who worked in Antwerp; Emil Claus; Constant Permeke, who painted the Flemish fishermen; Valerius de Saedeleer, who worked around Ronse, and, a little way north of Oudenaarde, a group that gathered in the villages along the river Leie just south of Ghent before and after the Great War, which included Leon and Gustave de Smet.

Belgium, in fact, must be one of the most painted countries in the world. Hardly an inch of it seems to have gone un-depicted, whether in local landscape works, or glimpsed, incongruously, through the windows in biblical scenes. There is nothing like it in Britain. While Paulus and Meunier were painting, however sentimentally, the workforce of Charleroi, we had only Lowry. When the lives of the English pitmen were eventually captured in paint, they did it themselves, in Ashington.

When Leon de Smet was exiled in Wales after the German invasion he became famous for his portraits of English writers, including Thomas Hardy. This seems rather apposite to me: Belgians depicted; the British, by and large, tended to describe. Belgium is captured by pigment on canvas, Britain by ink on paper.

Ignoring the lure of the ruined Abbey of Ename, 'whose foundation and early years of existence are now exposed to the public and together they make an open-air museum with a European radiation', Catherine and I pottered happily around Oudenaarde. The shops were the usual cheerful Flemish mix of the sublime and the ridiculous, the chic and the homespun. In my mind I had begun to form an ideal Belgian town, the main thoroughfare of which would be something like this: a clothes shop with a window display of Prada and Calvin Klein; a shoe shop selling Dirk Bikkembergs and Kurt Geiger, and in between them a health-food store with a huge sign in the window advertising pile ointment. Next to the shoe store is a shop selling expensive gadgets and gimmicky furniture including retro lava-lamps and a see-through inflatable plastic sofa, while next to the clothes shop is a pet shop with the name above the door in English, 'Doggy Do-Do'. There would also have to be several chocolate shops and at least one selling the sort of elaborate lingerie that looks like it would come with an instruction manual and a small tool-kit to help fit it. Belgian lingerie and chocolate shops are frequently next door to one another, and on one occasion I have seen the same shop selling both. I imagine this was a specialist store catering to men who like to dress their partners in fancy silk and lace underwear and then feed them pralines until they explode out of it. Though I don't imagine this often, obviously. Honestly.

In the Tacambaroplein there was a memorial to the Belgian soldiers who died during the Mexican Adventure, one of the more bizarre imperial escapades of the nineteenth century. King Leopold I's daughter Charlotte had married Archduke Maximilian of Austria, and it was he whom an alliance of European powers with France at its head decided to make Emperor of Mexico, largely to safeguard loans they felt the Central American's republican government, led by Benito Juarez, might be incapable or reluctant to repay. The Belgians sent 2,000 troops to bolster Maximilian's regime, protect Charlotte (who changed her name to Carlotta in honour of her new nationality) and aid the French army of Marshal Bazaine. The notion of little Belgium helping the mighty forces of Napoleon III gave much amusement to the French, who had by now hardened to the idea that all things involving their northern neighbour were deeply comical. Things weren't quite so funny for the men of the Belgian Legion, only 754 of whom returned home. Their sacrifice was in vain. Maximilian's regime was unpopular, his armies were defeated and he was captured and shot. Carlotta escaped, but the experience had been so traumatic that she went mad.

Catherine and I walked down to the Schelde, crossed the river, spent forty-five minutes looking round the deserted Lalaing House Museum of Tapestries without ever establishing whether it was actually open, then wandered back along Marlboroughlaan (the Duke won a battle just outside the town during the War of the Spanish Succession) and into the park for an ice cream. It was sunny after several days of rain and the grass in the park was a brilliant green. A breeze was blowing from across the hills of the Flemish Ardennes and the Pays des Collines, bringing with it the scent of drying soil.

There was not much going on in Oudenaarde, yet like many other small Belgian towns, in spite of all the recent upheavals, there was something seductive about it. There were pretty Flemish houses, vivid red geraniums in the window boxes; shops with the kind of things you felt you might just buy – another time; the cafés offered good and inventive food (our salmon had come with a zabayon made from wheat beer, steamed hop shoots and barrel-shaped new potatoes) and nobody you saw seemed to be rushing anywhere.

As we walked along a street near the park an old man in a bargee's cap and dark, baggy jacket came out of his house and mounted a heavy, black-framed bicycle. He cycled forty yards down the street to a corner café and popped inside. A few moments later he re-emerged, a bottle of Flemish brown ale in either pocket, got back on his bike and cycled home again. 'We wish you welcome with all our heart,' the Oudenaarde tourist brochure said. Who wouldn't feel affection for such a place?

Four

Although Catherine and I had spent only one night in Limburg, going back to Borgloon after our experiences in East Flanders felt a bit like returning to the security of the parental home.

Borgloon is a small and pretty market town that always looks well-swept and neatly pressed. On one side of it the land drops away, and from a footpath which runs along the site of the old walls you can see for miles across the gently undulating countryside of orchards and pasture, the occasional capricious turret of a castle popping up from behind a screen of dipping wind-swayed poplars.

A breeze blew gently and constantly in Limburg, shepherding clouds briskly across the sky, and the light was as pure as the air. It was not the intense moody light of the Mediterranean, which makes dullness vivid, or the gilded light of India, as golden as ghee; it was a cool, northern light, clear as spring water, distilled and undistorting. Everything bathed in it was sharply defined, refreshed and shivering slightly.

Borgloon is in the Haspengouw, the centre of Belgium's

fruit-growing region. The narrow lanes around the town wind through mile after mile of rolling cherry, apple and pear orchard. On specially marked routes the local council have planted varieties of every fruit tree that grows in the area, so touring motorists and cyclists can stop and taste them fresh from the bough. The council can afford to be generous. The soil in this part of Limburg is fertile. In early summer practically every dish you order in a café, whether it's scampi tails or steak tartar, comes adorned with clusters of strawberries from the owner's over-productive garden.

One day when we felt our equilibrium sufficiently restored we drove west from Borgloon, around the Sint-Truiden ring-road, where a local car-dealership squatted beneath an elevated sign reading 'Buga St-Truiden', and across into Flemish Brabant.

The borders of western Brabant and eastern Limburg are known as the Haageland, the Hedge Country, though hedges seemed, if anything, slightly less numerous than they had been around Borgloon, or practically anywhere else in Belgium for that matter. The Belgians, though, are keen on these little defining titles. In some ways it mirrored the trend in England to name areas after landmarks or famous local people: Hadrian's Wall Country, Brontë Country, Hardy Country. My particular favourite was Catherine Cookson Country, a distinctly unprepossessing part of South Tyneside. When you drove into it from Gateshead the first thing you saw after the sign announcing your arrival in Catherine Cookson Country was a massive Asda, a drive-in restaurant and a sprawling retail park, none of which seemed quite the stuff of Catherine Cookson novels to me. Although I suppose it is possible that among the late Dame's mighty canon there is a story about a plucky northern lass who is ravished by the manager of a fast-food franchise and returns pregnant, yet proud to live with her seven brothers and sisters in a discount carpet warehouse and eventually gain revenge on her tormentor by founding Kentucky Fried Chicken and putting him out of business.

When naming areas the Belgians tend to steer away from people. Which, given some of the people the Low Countries have produced over the years, is probably just as well. 'Welcome to Heironymus Bosch Country' was hardly likely to act as a siren call for tourists. Instead the Belgians focus on local characteristics. They had the Hedge Country, the Hop Lands, the Country of Hills and, most delightfully of all, the area around Halle, which is dubbed the Land of the Basket Cheese.

Somewhere between Sint-Truiden and Leuven we got lost in one of the usual labyrinthine diversions and ended up driving round and round the outer suburbs of Tienen, a jumbled mix of old and new factories, red-brick terraces, sports grounds and misty-windowed corner cafés. We could have been in a small industrial town anywhere in northern Europe, except that only in Belgium would you see the lurid neon sign of a strip joint so neatly juxtaposed with a showroom for sit-on lawnmowers. Some time around the second or third sighting of the Lokaal VK Tienen the car began to fill with a sickly-sweet caramel odour; by the fourth it felt as if we were inside a toffee-apple. The sources of the smell were the towering brick chimneys of a massive sugar refinery. Tienen styled itself 'The Sugarbeet Capital of Belgium'. As we were popped more or less on a whim from the swirling eddy of the suburbs back into the mainstream of the E40 it was a consolation to know that the diversion had led us into one of the few places on Earth that resolutely lived up to the glamour of its billing.

In Leuven we parked in an underground car-park opposite the university library. The library had done well to survive. For some reason best known to themselves, the Germans had rather taken against it. In 1916 they destroyed the entire archive of 300,000 books, and then in 1940 they came back again and this time did away with close to a million volumes. In the first case at least the destruction seems to have been designed to discourage Belgian civilian resistance, presumably by showing just what kind of barbaric nutcases they were up against. The second time was just force of habit.

On the way to find lunch (Catherine and I are hunter-gatherers) we paused to look at Leuven town hall. It was so elaborate the only possible explanation for it was that its design had been doodled by a student during a particularly long and tedious chemistry lecture. A characteristic Belgian hole in the ground had been placed nearby to act as contrast to this masterpiece of Brabant Gothic architecture. Surprisingly it was the hole that was drawing the bigger crowd. It was an archaeological dig. Clusters of people hovered around the edge, peering downwards in the hope of catching a glimpse of a skeleton or casket of treasure. When none materialised after ten minutes they wandered off. I know, because that's exactly what we did.

In nearby Sint-Pieterskirk there were paintings by the fifteenth-century artists Rogier van der Weyden and Dieric Bouts. Van der Weyden was from Tournai. Apparently there were some of his works in the art gallery in that city, but the attendant with the talons had driven us past them so fast I hadn't really taken them in. Bouts was born in Haarlem in Holland and moved to Leuven some time in the 1450s. Apart from anything else his career is testimony to the patina of sophistication a different spelling and pronunciation can add to a Christian name. It's hard to imagine Bouts having had quite the same success in Britain; I mean, can you think of any famous artists called Derek? *Apart* from that man who presented *Mr and Mrs*?

Nowadays Bouts is considered an important figure, but he

wasn't always so highly regarded. The emotionally flat paintings in Sint-Pieterskirk had bounced around Europe for centuries, and were only returned to Leuven in 1918 as part of German reparations for the ravages of war. The Nazis stole them back in 1940 and they eventually turned up after 1945 in a Silesian salt mine.

Two of Bouts's works in Sint-Pieterskirk immediately catch the eye. The first is a depiction of the martyrdom of St Erasmus. In it two men are removing Erasmus's innards with the aid of a winch. The odd thing is that the saint appears remarkably unconcerned. Indeed his face is suffused with the kind of thoughtful yet cheery look that suggests he has just recalled a rather amusing incident which occurred when he was last on holiday. The torturers meanwhile simply look baffled. Possibly, like me, they are wondering how anyone dreamed up such an idea. All I can imagine is that it came in a sudden moment of inspiration – I can see the chief torturer sitting at home having dinner with his wife one evening, when he leaps to his feet with a cry. 'What is it dear, heartburn?' she inquires kindly, mindful that her husband has just scoffed his blackbird pie a little too quickly.

'No,' the chief torturer replies. 'It's just struck me. What if – just suppose, right – we were to insert a large fish-hook through the heretic's navel, attach it to his intestines and then, using strong rope and a complicated mechanism of some sort of block-and-tackle device, we, we, hahahahaha, yes, I like it, I like it! We turn a winding handle ever so slowly and pull them right out?' His wife smiles indulgently. 'Eee, luv, I sometimes wonder where you get them from!'

Presumably in honour of the part rope and knots had played in his martyrdom, Erasmus was later made patron-saint of sailors.

Bouts's second most arresting work is of the Last Supper. This painting proves beyond any doubt that there was no equivalent of *Points of View* or local newspapers in Renaissance Flanders. If there had been Bouts's *Last Supper* would have produced a deluge of correspondence:

Dear Sir,

I draw your attention to a work by local so-called artist Mr Bouts. This painting is supposed to depict the Last Supper. In fact it is nothing short of a farrago. The costumes are totally wrong and through the back window we can see our new town hall. I hardly need tell other readers that the likelihood of being able to see this building from the Holy City of Jerusalem is doubtful to say the least, especially since it was not built until 1400 or more years *after* Our Lord's ascension! No doubt the artist will have some fancy reason why he has chosen to portray the event in so unhistorical a manner. Well, I say this: isn't it time these modern artists stopped dabbling in silly student 'theories' and concentrated instead on getting their facts straight? The situation is no better abroad. My better half and I recently paid a visit to Florence. Here we saw the latest work by a Mr Michelangelo, a statue of the Boy David. As the mem-sah'b remarked to me somewhat caustically, 'If that's really how big David was, I should hate to have seen Goliath!'

Yours sincerely,

Colonel Franck Verhaegen (retired)

Despite the encroaching bulk of the Stella Artois brewery, a mighty modern conjunction of grey and rust-red cylinders and blocks which looks as if it might be possible to take it apart and re-assemble it as something completely different, like a giant steam-roller, it is the university which dominates Leuven. You can feel the presence of an alternative culture here more strongly than in any Belgian town other than, possibly, Antwerp. There are vegetarian restaurants, second-hand stores, specialists in organic unbleached cotton clothing and furniture made from sustainable European hardwoods. And, of course, there are many, many groups of young people clustered around tables in bars, talking earnestly and pretending to have absolutely no sexual interest in one another whatsoever.

'Ah yes, it is true, I know how to steal any make of European car,' a spotty Teutonic youth in the café where Catherine and I had lunch was saying, in a desperate bid to impress on two American girls the kind of wild and crazy outlaw they were dealing with. 'Oh, yeah, right,' one of the girls said. The other was far too busy prising some dry skin out of her ear to offer any response.

The University of Leuven was founded in 1425. For the next hundred years or so it was at the heart of the Enlightenment in northern Europe. Andreas Vesalius taught anatomy here, and still found time to invent the forceps; Dodoneus produced the first scientific work on botany; Mercator and Ortelius the first atlas. Despite their names all these men were Flemish. In those days scholars liked to adopt a classical nickname to give them a certain air of intellectual authority (Mercator didn't need to, his own Flemish name had a whiff of Latin sophistication about it to start with). Oddly enough the only people who continue this ancient custom in our day are Brazilian footballers.

Perhaps the most important thinker to come to Leuven during this period was Geert Geerts, or Desiderius Erasmus as he preferred to style himself. Erasmus was named in honour of the eviscerated figure in the Bouts painting and came close to suffering a similar fate himself on numerous occasions. He arrived in Leuven after spells in Oxford, Cambridge, Bologna and Rome, and founded the College of Three Languages there in 1517. Erasmus was a key figure in the history of the Low Countries. In fact you could say that he was one of the reasons why the Flemish aren't Dutch and, therefore – partly at least – that he was one of the causes of Belgium.

Erasmus was born in Rotterdam, but he didn't have much time for his fellow Netherlanders. He thought they drank too much gin (Erasmus himself suffered from a dicky stomach, and could imbibe only white wine from Burgundy, an affliction also suffered, if memory serves, by Miss Ellie from *Dallas*). I felt rather smug about this for a while, but then I learned that Erasmus didn't have a very high opinion of the English either. He felt we didn't wash nearly often enough. Given that his experience of England was largely confined to universities, perhaps that wasn't such an unreasonable prejudice to have formed. I'm sure male students of the 1500s weren't much different from their modern-day counterparts. They probably bathed regularly once a year, whether they needed to or not.

The Holbein portrait of Erasmus shows the philosopher at the height of his fame. Erasmus has the face of a strict yet fair schoolmaster. The sort who terrorises you as an adolescent not so much by what he says or does as by the fact that he exudes a complete certainty about right and wrong. He looks like the sort of man to whom you would feel compelled to confess any guilty secret. And if you didn't have a guilty secret you would make one up – 'Erasmus, please forgive me, for I can steal any make of European car. What do you mean, "Nonsense"? It's true, honestly.'

Erasmus was the father of Humanism. The Catholic Church of the day believed that mankind was filthy, sinful and wicked by nature, the disgusting Yahoos of *Gulliver's Travels*. Erasmus, on the other hand, believed in the dignity of human life, despite his time in Oxford. He also believed in tolerance, pacifism, education and equal rights for women.

Nowadays that all seems either remarkably reasonable or totally woolly, depending on your point of view. In the sixteenth century, however, it marked Erasmus out as a dangerous revolutionary. Part of the reason he moved around so much was that in those days if a man of his views stood still for too long he was likely to find his feet surrounded by burning firewood.

A pious Catholic, Erasmus was repelled by the corruption of the Church administration in what was then the Burgundian Empire. Controlling Church affairs in the province was traditionally the responsibility of the ruling Dukes of Burgundy. The Burgundians tended to dole out bishoprics and monasteries to any relative or sycophant who was considered too dim-witted or morally repellent for the army. The results were not edifying. The low opinion the Church had of humanity was borne out by the dissolute behaviour of the clergy. The abbot of the monastery of Saint-Aubert, for example, writes quite merrily of baptising the child of a bishop and the daughter of the cathedral's provost, and Erasmus himself was the son of a Catholic priest.

As the Reformation began to sweep through Europe Erasmus's brand of Humanist Catholicism seemed to many in the Low Countries a good alternative to the extremes presented by the old Church and the new Protestantism. It was particularly popular in what is now Holland, where the national temperament seems always to have been disposed towards liberal thought.

By the mid-1500s the indigenous nobility of the Low Countries were on the verge of revolt. Events were preceded by the accession of Charles, Duke of Burgundy (later Emperor Charles V) to first the Spanish throne in 1517 and then, three years later, to that of the Holy Roman Empire. The power bloc of Burgundy, Spain, Austria, Germany, the Low Countries and the kingdoms of Naples and Sicily was huge, but widely dispersed and hard to protect, especially from the French and Turks.

Charles had been born in Ghent and brought up in Mechelen. He was popular with the Flemish, who regarded him as one of their own. Charles was charming, courageous and, perhaps even more importantly in a Belgian context, very fond of food and drink. It is perhaps in honour of the emperor that in Flanders to this day they use the word 'burgundian' in the way the English use 'gourmand'.

In 1555, exhausted by war and his punishing dietary regime, Charles abdicated, handing the throne of the Holy Roman Empire to his brother Ferdinand, while Spain and the Low Countries went to his son, Philip II. Unlike his father, Philip was not fond of rich living. His passions were God and torturing people. Luckily for him the Counter-Reformation meant he could indulge both at once. Nor did the new monarch share his father's affinity with the Flemish. Far from it; he believed the Low Countries to be rotten to the core with heresy. 'I would prefer to lose all my domains and die a hundred times over,' Philip infamously ranted, 'than rule over heretics.' To prevent this disaster occurring the new king sent the Duke of Alva to stamp out the vaguest flickerings of Protestantism, destroy all privileges in the Low Countries and tax, flog, burn and generally batter the inhabitants into pious submission.

The war which inevitably followed is often portrayed as a religious one, but it was largely political. The leader of the rebels was William of Orange, often known as William the Silent (the traditional view of this is that it indicates he was a man of few words, though I prefer to believe the sobriquet was ironic and he was actually a right old chatterbox). Like Erasmus, William believed in religious tolerance. He himself was a Catholic, but many of his allies and indeed his own father were Protestant.

The rebellion against the Duke of Alva initially centred on Brussels, but in the end only Holland, geographically more cut off from Philip's main power bases, was freed from Spanish rule. So it was that the northern half of the Low Countries developed a political and religious life based on the Humanist ideas promulgated by Erasmus; and the southern half, now renamed the Spanish Netherlands, one based on the Catholic absolutism of Philip.

The mark of this time is still apparent. While Roman Catholics make up the largest religious group in the Netherlands they comprise only 37 per cent of the population. In Belgium the figure is closer to 97 per cent. In Holland government and religion have been kept separate. In Belgium the Church has a massive influence in politics, particularly in Flanders. If you've ever wondered why the Flemish and the Netherlanders don't simply get together and form one big Dutch-speaking country then this is your answer.

They did try it briefly. The United Kingdom of the Netherlands was a product of the Congress of Vienna, which carved up Napoleon's empire after Waterloo. It was ruled over by William of Orange, 'a clever man who did many foolish things', and lasted for just fifteen years in an atmosphere of mutual suspicion and hostility so great that when William attempted to replace French with Dutch as the official language of his newly acquired provinces even the Flemish protested against it. Things finally came to a head in Brussels on 25 August 1831, when a performance of *La Muette de Portici* provoked outpourings of anger and violence (opera has exactly the same effect on me, funnily enough). William at first attempted to suppress what quickly became a revolution across Wallonia and Flanders, but his army had no real stomach for it and eventually withdrew, leaving Belgium independent for the first time in history. The two countries still don't exactly get on.

A few months before I set off for Belgium I was talking to a journalist from the Netherlands. I mentioned that I was coming to Flanders. 'Do you speak Dutch?' the journalist asked. I said I did not, but that I didn't think it would be a problem since most Flemish people seemed to speak English.

'Ah yes,' the Dutchman said with a faint smile, 'though of course they do not speak it properly.'

Like the relationship between the English and the Scots, that between the Dutch and the Flemish is not always an easy one. The Dutch tend to look on the Flemish as backward, parochial and stupid. Like the French, the Dutch make Belgians the butt of many jokes. Example. Amsterdam air-traffic controller to Belgian pilot: 'Please state your position.' Belgian pilot: 'I'm in the cockpit!' The Flemish, as you might guess, consider the Dutch to be arrogant and patronising.

One Sunday evening Catherine and I went to a barbecue organised by the Borgloon branch of the Davidfonds, a Catholic book club. When you cross the provincial border from Brabant, Antwerp or Liège into Limburg you are greeted by huge signs announcing 'The Limburgers Bid You Welcome'. Limburgers are the only Belgians who offer visitors such a cheery greeting. Their sense of regional identity is strong. That Sunday was also the day of Borgloon's annual civic dog walk. In Britain it's the sort of event that might attract half a dozen die-hards and political office-seekers, but here hundreds of ordinary people took part. We came across groups of them all afternoon and evening, the collars and leashes of their dogs decorated with ribbons in the town colours of yellow and red, wandering along a pre-planned route in an unthreatening if slightly eccentric demonstration of local unity. It reminded me of the fact that every year there is a Flemish gathering of cyclists who ride in a circle around Brussels to remind the inhabitants of the capital that though they speak French they are surrounded by Dutch-speakers.

There is something at once bullying and yet strangely comical about the idea. It is hard to imagine anything that is less intimidating than the sight of a man on a bike, except possibly a naked man on a bike. I should think that on the day of the symbolic ride the streets of Brussels resound to the warning cry, 'The Flemish are coming! And they're on bicycles!' and the subsequent crash of people collapsing on the ground laughing.

When I commented on the strong sense of local unity in Limburg to the rotund bearded man sitting next to me at the barbecue he laughed. 'Yes,' he said (he spoke English quite properly), 'Limburgers stick together because the rest of Flanders mocks us for being stupid.'

Belgian Limburg borders on Holland. By the standards of the Low Countries it is a sparsely populated region ('The Green Heart of Europe' the Flemish have characteristically dubbed it). In the Netherlands every square inch of ground seemed to be cultivated or built on. When you parked the car outside a restaurant and went in for a meal you wouldn't have been surprised to come out and find that someone had planted turnips on the bonnet and erected a light industrial unit on the roof. Belgian Limburg is the Great Plains by comparison. As a result wealthy businessmen from across the frontier in Eindhoven and Tilburg who want a bit of breathing space buy houses in the province and commute. It is a popular weekend destination for the Dutch.

Later on at the Davidfonds evening, after an 'Irish' band made up entirely of young Flemish musicians had played a set concluding, somewhat confusingly, with a lusty rendition of 'The Bonny, Bonny Banks Of Loch Lomond', we bought tickets for the barbecue which, in a tradition honoured across the world, was presided over entirely by middle-aged men in elaborate aprons. For 300BF you got three pink tickets. 'So you can go back for more two times,' the wife of the man who told me about the Limburgers' proverbial stupidity said. 'In any other place once would be enough, but in Limburg . . .' She pointed at her husband's billowing waistline. The man chuckled merrily. 'I am a Limburger here,' he said, touching his chest, 'and here,' with a pat on his bulging stomach, which wobbled proudly in response.

Appropriately when I asked the Limburger about the Dutch it was to food that he reached for an explanation. 'The difference between the Flemish and the Dutch,' he said, 'can be seen in cheese. Here in Flanders we make many different kinds of cheese. Hard cheese, soft cheese, goats' cheese, sheep's cheese. We make orange, white and blue cheeses. Cheeses with herbs and with rinds soaked in beer. Hundreds of cheeses. Great cheeses. But nobody outside Belgium has heard of them. The Dutch make one kind of very tasteless cheese and all the world knows about it. That is the difference between us and the Dutch. No matter how well we make something we are too shy to tell anyone about it, but the Dutch? Whatever they do . . .' He shrugged, then picked up his plate and went off to get half a dozen more sausages.

Erasmus, whose teachings would play an even more important part in defining the futures of the two neighbouring nations than the dairy industry, didn't stay in Leuven for long. The chance of being accused of heresy in a city which had, by 1521, become a bulwark of orthodoxy against the encroaching Lutherans was too strong. He departed for the relative safety of Switzerland. Erasmus had been in Flanders just four years, but he had left a considerable mark.

Catherine and I arrived at the GB Maxi supermarket on the outskirts of Leuven via another tortuous diversion. It probably wouldn't have delayed us that much were it not for the fact that we found ourselves stuck behind what appeared to be an entire town's worth of children cycling home from primary school. As we crawled along behind this gaily chattering throng for what seemed like hours I attempted to lighten the situation by pointing out items in the windows of the low box-like houses which lined the road. 'Hey, look, a dozen mother-in-law's tongues! Oh wow, a copse of wrought-iron bonsai trees with little coloured glass leaves! How I wish I could be around these parts to hear the tinkling crash of autumn.'

The Belgians were fond of putting rows of things on their front window-sills. They formed neat little displays between the glass and the net curtains. In smarter areas massive Chinese vases were popular; in more ordinary suburbs they settled for brass artillery shells, often punched with elaborate patterns like brogue shoes. Little bulbous cacti were also widely respected for their decorative powers. In a living-room window in Dienze I saw the two things combined in one alarming whole, a spiky cactus sprouting from a phallic shell-case like some kind of sadistic sex toy.

I'm not sure when or how the tradition of ornamental window displays started in Belgium. I did feel that I knew *why* it started, however: it is clearly a means of sending out a sub-liminal message to burglars. It says: 'If this is the kind of stuff I want people to know I own, imagine the kind of tatty shit I have inside.' It works a treat, too; Belgium has a far lower incidence of break-ins than Britain.

I accompanied Catherine around GB Maxi until we found ourselves queuing at the butcher's counter. The sight of the horsemeat always made me feel queasy. I didn't mind the steaks so much, it was the mince I couldn't take. I don't know why this was. There was certainly no logic to it. It was simply conditioning. After all, what really is the difference between eating pony or eating pork, except that we didn't grow up watching programmes called *Champion the Wonder Pig* or reading about the exploits of *Saddleback Beauty*?

'I think I'll have a wander,' I said to Catherine, wafting a hand towards the offending fat-flecked wormish pile of meat. 'I don't know why it bothers you so much,' she said. 'You don't even like horses.'

'I don't like Noel Edmonds either,' I replied, 'but it doesn't mean I want to see him chopped up on a polystyrene tray with a sprig of parsley stuck in him.' (Though come to think of it . . .)

I walked off down the aisle with the vague notion of doing some important research into the Flemish name for Angel Delight and what noise Rice Krispies makes in Dutch. Instead I found myself standing in front of the crisps, pondering one of the world's great mysteries. The British have a notoriously unadventurous attitude to food. The United Kingdom is perhaps the only nation on Earth in which the phrase 'I've never actually had it, I just don't like the thought of it' is regarded as making complete sense. Yet constricted though our palate may be, there is one area in which we let our gastronomic imaginations run riot; a Club 18–30 holiday of the tastebuds. Yes, Britain has more flavours of potato crisp than anywhere else on the planet. Why?

I didn't get much time to ponder this considerable question as a man came up and started asking something in Flemish (at least I assume he was asking me something. He may just have got a lozenge wedged in his windpipe). He was a tall, thin fellow in a cream mac. He looked like Arnolfini in the Van Eyck painting, only his face, if anything, was slightly more gaunt. In fact if his cheeks had been sunken a millimetre deeper they'd have chafed against each other. 'I'm sorry, I'm English,' I said, an expression I used often and to which I always expected to get the reply, 'I bet you are, mate.'

'Ah,' Mr Arnolfini said. There was a pause. He looked slightly embarrassed. 'You are on vacation, yes?' he said eventually. 'Yes. We are staying near Sint-Truiden.'

'Ah, Sint-Truiden.' Another pause. Mr Arnolfini pursed his lips in concentration and shook his head as if to dislodge some piece of information stuck inside his skull. It obviously didn't work. 'No, sorry,' he said eventually, 'my English has phew!' He slid a finger across his forehead to indicate that at some point his English had nipped out for a packet of fags and not left a forwarding address, shrugged his shoulders self-consciously and turned and stalked away.

I continued my quest for enlightenment along the super-market shelves. It had never struck me so forcibly before how slick and marketing-conscious Britain has become. British baby food came in jars with labels that said things like 'Old Ma Scoggins' Award-Winning Wigan-Style Lancashire Hot Pot. With succulent Pennine-reared, heather-fed lamb chops, garden-fresh new potatoes and crunchy spring carrots'. The Belgian equivalent said simply 'Lamb and Vegetables'. The ingredients were exactly the same.

'Aha-hem!' I turned around. It was Mr Arnolfini. He cleared his throat again, then with great deliberation said, 'The apples in Sint-Truiden have not yet ripened.' Then he smiled, nodded goodbye and disappeared behind the tinned fruit.

The following day we took a trip to Hasselt. The Limburgers may have been mocked by other Belgians but they weren't above a bit of mockery themselves. They called the citizens of Hasselt, the province's biggest and smartest city, *Dikkeneke*, 'The Thick Necks', in honour of the stiff collars once worn by the upper classes. Hasselt is famous for the exclusivity of its shopping streets. In Hasselt the windows full of Christian Lacroix and Ralph Lauren stand in stark contrast to the usual provincial Flemish array, best encapsulated for me by a shop in Sint-Truiden which enlivened the street it stood in with a remarkably rich display of string vests. Not, I should add, that

Sint-Truiden was without other attractions. It has many churches, an abbey devoted to St Trudo (whose sole miracle apparently involved having God strike down a woman who was bothering him with paralysis. There's charitable), a museum of dentistry housed in an Ursuline convent and the design studios of a man named Kamiel Festraets, who built a clock that weighs 4,000 kilograms (unfortunately he never perfected a mantelpiece strong enough to hold it). As if this were not enough, Sint-Truiden is also home to Ijssalon Venise, voted one of the two best ice-cream parlours in Flanders in 1994 and a place so totally devoted to calories that even an espresso comes with a side dish of whipped cream and a little bar of chocolate. Ijssalon Venise is simply fantastic. If you are an ice-cream fan you should hurl this book aside right now and go there immediately. For those of you who have resisted the blandishments of Venise's *Coupe Advocaat* (vanilla, coffee and chocolate ice cream, caramel sauce, advocaat, whipped cream, toasted nuts and chocolate shavings) I shall return to Hasselt. Eventually.

We took rather a roundabout route because our daughter Maisie had gone to sleep the minute we set off, and experience had shown that waking her up after only twenty minutes of her morning nap was not advisable. In fact given the choice I would prefer to spend the day slam-dancing with a particularly large and malevolent rhinoceros. I should say at this point that my daughter accompanied Catherine and I on all of these journeys. If I do not mention her it is not through lack of love or pride, quite the opposite. But I have manfully restrained myself from telling you of her myriad sweet, clever and funny ways or the fact that she says 'teddy' when she means biscuit because she was once given a packet of bear-shaped cookies and has (I take this as a sign of genius) *remembered it ever since.* I have restrained myself because it is a long-held opinion of mine that other people's children are like other people's dreams – they are never as fascinating as your own.

As we crossed the Albert Canal I called on Catherine to stop the car, and when she did I leapt out and scanned the waterway. I did this every time we went anywhere near a canal in Belgium. Which meant we made slow progress around Bruges. What I was looking for was the Cataravan. I had seen an advert for this splendid vessel in the 'Vlaanderen Vakantieland' brochure under the arresting headline WATER DREAMS. The strapline beneath was punchy and to the point: 'Can't take your caravan or motor-home on the water? You can!' The Cataravan was a twin-hulled raft which made every caravan an amphibious vehicle, and all for around £450 a week. 'An original water holiday' the brochure boasted, and who could disagree?

We headed north passed the city of Genk. Genk had once been the centre of the Limburg coal industry, but now the pits had gone and been replaced by a number of massive shopping centres, which I suppose at least gave the redundant miners somewhere warm to go and sit in the winter. We turned west and passed through the flat pine-planted land-scape of the Kempen. Somewhere around Zonhoven Maisie woke up and we were able to turn south to Hasselt at last.

We parked near a monument to the Flemish peasants slaughtered by the French during the Boerenkrijg rebellion in 1798, and made straight for the National Gin Museum.

Gin, or genever as it is called in Flemish, was invented in the Low Countries. In Belgium it was once massively popular. Perhaps a little too much so, in fact. In 1880 the ruling Catholic Party passed a law forbidding its sale in cafés. The law was not rescinded until over a century later. This was good for brain cells, but disastrous for the distilleries. Where once there were hundreds, now only four remain. The largest, Smeets, is in Hasselt. The National Gin Museum is housed in one of the old distilleries that didn't make it. We entered behind a coach-party of pensioners from Aarschot. One of the selling points of the museum is that it has a bar which stocks four hundred gins, and the price of admission includes a sample drink. This was clearly a powerful motivating factor for the old folk, who cantered round the tour of the buildings at such a lick they left a vapour trail.

Arriving at the museum bar after a pleasant potter around the exhibits (I was particularly fond of 'the dwelling house', part of which was devoted to the celebration of Doctor Willems, inventor of the vaccine 'against the dreaded rinderpest'), we found the pensioners already departing, possibly off to find a nearby Museum of Hydrated Magnesium Sulphide and a complementary glass of liver salts. I cashed in our tokens for two genevers, one flavoured with blackcurrant and the other so strong I found I had inhaled most of it before I could get the glass to my lips.

Gin was another bone of contention between the Flemish and the Dutch. The Flemings contend that *genever* should be served cold, the Dutch say *jenever* is best at room temperature. Compared to the Diet of Worms this is a minor disagreement, admittedly, but after a few drinks it is probably enough to start a punch-up. What neither Netherlander nor Belgian disagrees on is that the finest gin comes from Flanders.

After Mechelen, Hasselt is said to be the richest town in Belgium. Opinion in the rest of Limburg is that this has rather gone to the inhabitants' heads. 'The people from Hasselt are *so* superior,' a woman from nearby Tongeren told us later that week. 'You know the German supermarket Aldi? It is famous for selling things cheap. Goods with its own label, you know. Well, there is one in Hasselt. But if you talk to people from Hasselt, none of them ever shop at Aldi. If you see them in Aldi one day and later in the week you meet them and say, "I saw you in Aldi the other day," they say, "No, no, no, it can't have been me. I never go to Aldi. I don't even know where Aldi is." But if you look in their kitchen cupboard you find it is full of things from Aldi! Such snobs, the people of Hasselt.'

Apart from shops, snobbery and gin, Hasselt's other outstanding feature is its Kermesse or fair, held every seven years, the star attraction of which is a giant called the Lounge Man who wobbles up and down the streets all day, towing a barrel from which he dispenses warm pea soup to the assembled throng.

A strange festival, but by no means unusual in Belgium. In fact the Belgium town without an arcane ceremony appears as sad, denuded and unable fully to express itself as a Roger Moore with his eyebrows shaved off. In Verviers, in June, a fancy-dress procession ends with a toy cat being attached to a balloon and chucked from a church spire. At Ecaussines-Lalaing they throw a matrimonial tea-party for bachelors and spinsters. The Brabantine town of Overijse holds a pageant on the theme of 'Grapes in History'. The population of Wingene celebrates the birthday of local boy Pieter Bruegel by donning medieval garb and chomping through 1,200 sausages. In Ostend they have the Dead Rat Ball; in Ypres they march in favour of cats every three years; in Oostduinkerke the annual 'Festival of the Shrimp' brightens a whole weekend in June.

In Aalst there are sober giants, Seigneur Ywein and his wife Loretta accompanied by attendants carrying bouquets of onions. In Eben-Emael hooded figures dressed in red and black caper about the streets hitting people with pigs' bladders before cooking a giant omelette. At Arlon the seventeen-foot-high Helleschsman sings of love. In Treignes they hold the mock trial of a large snowman. There are processions of penitents, the plague, candles, the Holy Blood and the Golden Tree. The fields, the sea and the forests around Saint-Hubert are blessed and in Mons the Procession of the Golden

Chariot ends with St George slaying a fearsome dragon with the less than fearsome name of Doudou.

By far the biggest and wildest of all Belgium's festivals takes place in Binche, an otherwise grim market town in the Borinage, the coal-mining area around Mons. The Great Gilles Carnival is a kind of north European Mardi Gras, complete with ostrich feathers, drumming, revels and a considerable tonnage of oranges which are hurled into the crowd as, according to one guide book, 'a symbol of the riches of the Americas'. Anyone who still thinks the Belgians are dull should bear in mind that it is from the bacchanalian outburst in Binche that the English get the word 'binge'.

Five

Adolescence was not a comfortable time for me. There was all the usual stuff plus the fact that I was very tall. Because I was very tall the only way I could get shirts with sleeves long enough was to buy the biggest chest or collar size available. Unfortunately I was also so thin I made clothes props look like they should cut down on the cakes. Shirts with sleeves that reached the base of my hand flapped around my body like a collapsed tent. I spent much of my teenage years looking as if I was making a lonely and ill-advised bid to re-popularise the poncho.

All that had somehow passed over the years. I was feeling pretty happy with myself. After all, I was thirty-seven and I was almost as thin as I'd always been. Only now contemporaries looked on my thinness not as a badge of weakness and immaturity but as a sign that, well, I hadn't got fat. My limbs seemed to pretty much go where I told them and, due to a silent revolution in the clothing industry, I could now get shirts that fitted me all over. I felt good. I felt together. For once in my life, I felt co-ordinated. Then I met Mrs Stalmans and suddenly I was an emaciated juvenile yeti again.

Mrs Stalmans was frighteningly elegant. She had sleek dark

hair, tanned skin and an immaculate smile. She wore a black tunic that set off a gold necklace which had the chic glint of Chanel about it. She greeted us charmingly. I responded. My voice sounded randomly modulated, a wheezing assortment of squeaks and croaks like a Sumo wrestler sitting on an accordion. I didn't even need to look down. After thirty seconds in Mrs Stalmans' company I instinctively knew that after I bade her farewell I would discover a ketchup stain on the front of my shirt. I hadn't eaten anything with ketchup on it for months, and my shirt was clean on that morning, but I knew this would be no defence. The ketchup stain would be there anyway. It was a mystical symbol. A stigmata of gawkiness.

The Stalmans' house was set among an enclave of large detached residences on the outskirts of Ninove, a suburb of Brussels whose only significance to me was as the finish of the Tour of Flanders and home of Slag lager, a beer that would safely qualify as the worst-named in the world were it not for Leroy in West Flanders and their redoubtable Pompeschitter, and Roman of Oudenaarde, whose Tripel Ename would surely be an instant hit with medical students if ever released in Britain.

The house was a spacious advert for modish late-'60s living. There was an open wooden staircase cascading light from an overhead window, angular black leather and tubular steel furniture, abstract paintings and sketches of nudes on the walls. It was dated yet invitingly stylish, a black-and-white photo spread from *Life* magazine; the kind of place you could picture Joan Didion or Jasper Johns lounging around in, listening to the latest Stephen Sondheim record.

We sat down at a dark wood table in the dining-room. I folded myself awkwardly on to my chair and tried to avoid banging my knees, while simultaneously endeavouring to look vaguely urbane. Through the kitchen door I caught a tantalising glimpse of a half-demolished slab of chocolate mousse the size of a paving stone collapsing decadently and tried not to drool. Mrs Stalmans' teenage son, indecently handsome for his years, arrived home from school and joined us at the table.

Mrs Stalmans began explaining about the flat. A relative of hers in Limburg had told us about it when Catherine had expressed a desire to go to the seaside. 'You must stay at the Stalmans' apartment,' the woman had said, promptly pulling a mobile phone out of her bag and punching in the number. Two minutes later we were booked in for the week commencing the following Sunday.

Mrs Stalmans spoke in lightly accented English. Every once in a while, when her vocabulary failed her, she would utter a word in Flemish and her son would discreetly murmur the English word she was looking for like a theatre prompt. The boy's command of our language was clearly excellent, but he was too self-conscious to offer a sentence of his own directly. I empathised.

'It is just a holiday apartment, you understand,' Mrs Stalmans said, 'for family and friends. There are such terrible . . . *rolgardijn*?'

'Blinds,' the son mumbled.

'Blinds, terrible blinds. You must not look at the blinds, please. Oh dear, the blinds, really. Green. So terrible. We should have changed them years ago, but my mother, you understand, insists on doing all the things. Please do not notice the blinds.' We agreed that we wouldn't.

Mrs Stalmans started to draw a map for us. One of the odd things about being in a foreign country is the impossibility of detecting any kind of social nuance. All the guidelines – clothes, accents, articulacy – that normally point the way are lost to us. We do not know if the person we are talking to empties septic tanks or runs the stock exchange for a living. We wander dippily around in this blissful state and when we return to our hotel in the evening and tell the receptionist how we have spent our day her face turns white, her eyes bulge and she shrieks, 'You went where? But my God it's *sooooo* dangerous over there.' And we swell rather with pride and reply, 'Oh really? It seemed quite pleasant to us.' To our untrained eyes abroad is wonderfully classless, overseas societies homogeneous visions of the perfect future. It is the happy egalitarianism of total ignorance. This rule, however, did not apply to Mrs Stalmans. Mrs Stalmans had that cheerful, unconcerned vagueness which is the international sign of a true aristocrat. 'Restaurants?' she said. 'Ah yes, there is a very nice place around the corner. On Albert 1 Laan. Its name? Oh, now . . . Is it? . . . Maybe . . . No, I don't know. But it has a blue front. At least I think it is blue. Or turquoise. Or possibly it is yellow. But you will see it, of course.' She sketched away with her pen.

'When you come on to the sea front here you will see a café to your right. It is called . . . Oh, something. Ship? Boat?'

'The Barge,' her son muttered.

'The Barge. And a shop which sells clothes. A green sign. Perhaps white. Red writing. It has been there a long time. "Bis", yes, that is it. Or is the writing black? Anyway, our block is here, next to it. A few blocks down at most.' She turned the map towards Catherine and me so we could see it. 'And the restaurant I told you about is here.' She drew a circle with her pen.

Her son nudged her, indicating the mark she had just made. 'That's the sea,' he whispered.

'You will come probably from De Panne,' Mrs Stalmans said after the map had been turned back round and she had relocated the restaurant to the less watery surroundings of Albert 1 Laan, 'along the main road where the tram runs, through Koksijde.'

At the mention of Koksijde I abandoned any pretence of sophistication and became idiotically animated. A few years before, I had been travelling south from Nieuwpoort-an-Zee after a hefty lunch at De Vagant – a café whose name, I later learned, was taken from a medieval brotherhood of wandering priests who earned their meagre subsistence by singing psalms at the houses of the bourgeoisie, a piece of information that has absolutely no relevance to the matter at hand, but which simply leaps up and demands to be shared.

As the tram rattled through Koksijde I had seen from the window something which gladdened my childish heart: a hotel shaped like a boat. I had been so excited by the sight of this splendid brick-and-concrete vessel afloat its calm sea of tarmac that I had written its name and address down in my notebook, just in case.

'The Normandie!' I cried with the jubilant, vindicated tone of a man finding a use for a length of wood he has valiantly saved for a decade or more in the face of all opposition from his wife and family. 'That's on the road from De Panne to Koksijde!' I cackled merrily at the thought of it, imagining deck games, dinner at the captain's table and, perhaps, one stormy night, the bulkheads caving in and the male guests gathering in the ballroom to sing 'Abide With Me' while lifeboats full of women and children were lowered on to the car-park. 'The Normandie!' I added again for emphasis.

Mrs Stalmans looked at me, amused, intrigued maybe, but definitely puzzled. 'The ship hotel!' I said. 'That's on Koninklijke Baan, the tram route through Koksijde!' Mrs Stalmans pursed her lips thoughtfully but without success. I endeavoured to refresh her memory. 'You can't miss it,' I babbled, 'it's about a hundred feet from stem to stern, hull painted black, quarterdecks white, three red funnels protruding from its roof, portholes along each bow. You get up to reception via a gang-plank. I bet the staff sleep down below. In hammocks!'

Mrs Stalmans thought for a moment longer then shook

her head. 'I don't know it,' she said. She turned to her son. 'Do you?' He furrowed his brow, his eyes flickered slightly from side to side as if scanning the distant horizons of his memory for smoke from the funnel of the ship-hotel. Eventually his face brightened slightly. 'Yes,' he said quietly, 'I *think* I might have seen it.' I had the unnerving feeling he was just being polite.

After she had showed us how to use the apartment key and where to find the person we were to leave it with ('A tiny man who speaks only French. He does not like sand to get in his stairway'), Mrs Stalmans showed us out. As we walked to the car I said, 'Wasn't she a nice woman?' Catherine started to agree with me and then stopped, tilting her head slightly to one side. 'What's that on your shirt?' she said, pointing to my chest. 'It looks like ketchup.'

Coming through the front door of Mrs Stalmans' holiday apartment I saw what I initially took to be a massive Rothko-esque canvas, three horizontal bars of colour: pale yellow, steel grey and Swedish blue. It turned out not to be a painting but a floor-to-ceiling window containing nothing but a vision of sand, sea and sky. Catherine and I walked out on to the balcony to admire the view further.

'Dag.' An old man with cropped hair was sitting in a fold-out chair about four feet away on the neighbouring balcony. Even by Belgian standards he was big. His massive frame was upholstered with a thick layer of muscle and solid fat. If Willy the killer whale had ever sprouted arms and legs he would have looked something like the man on the balcony. Though only if you painted him ointment pink and dressed him in a velour leisure top and red nylon shorts first. 'Hello,' I said.

The big man smiled. He had the cheery, bucolic face of a Bruegel peasant. 'Ah, Engels?' he said.

'Yes. Flemish?'

'Ja. Vlaams-Brabant. Alsemberg,' he chuckled merrily at the thought of his home town.

I knew Alsemberg, but I couldn't muster the same enthusiasm for it. It was in the Senne valley, a dormitory town for Brussels. On the weekday lunchtime Catherine and I had been there the place was so deserted we got the unnerving feeling there had been a nuclear alert and we had somehow missed it. As we walked along an empty street of terraced brick houses I imagined that below us in specially constructed bunkers the Belgian elite were counting food supplies and wondering if the underground reservoirs held enough mayonnaise and chocolate sauce to get them through a nuclear winter.

Catherine and I had been looking for something to eat. Eventually we'd found a small supermarket. There was one other customer, a little man who looked like the Lada drawings of Good Soldier Svejk. His wire basket contained a two-litre bottle of 70-proof genever and a punnet of strawberries. From what I'd seen these would be the necessary rations to pass a happy afternoon in Alsemberg. We bought some bread and cheese and walked back to the car-park. When we got there a rather flustered-looking woman dragging two young children behind her approached and asked, in French, 'Is this where we catch the Fun Bus?' Catherine told her she thought it unlikely.

I didn't say any of this to the old man on the balcony, of course. I just smiled. He smiled back. 'Nice,' he said, making a gesture at the general surroundings. We agreed that it was very nice. Encouraged, the old man pointed towards the beach. 'Good,' he said. We agreed that it was indeed good. We shall probably never know what other positive English adjectives he had at his disposal because at this point a dog stepped out on to his balcony. It was the colour and size of a dingo with the ratty, vengeful face of a feral urban youth. At the sight of us it began to bark ferociously. '*Schatzi! Rustig!*' the man yelled. The dog kept barking. 'Sorry. Sorry,' the man said to us above the canine tirade. 'Never mind,' we said, indicating Maisie. 'It's time for her bath anyway.'

Every time Catherine or I went out on the balcony thereafter a truncated version of this scene was played out.

'Dag.'

'Hello.'

'Nice.'

'Oh yes, very nice.'

'Good.'

'It's very good.'

Ruffruffruffruff!

'*Schatzi! Schatzi! Huud je mond!*'

Ruffruffruffruff!

'I apologise.'

'That's all right, I think I can hear the kettle coming to the boil.'

The big man sat out on his balcony from nine in the morning until eight at night when the weather was fine. I suppose he must have gone in at some point for calls of nature and the like, though I'm by no means certain. He may have had a system of tubes. As the week went by I caught occasional glimpses of him through the window. Content and unmoving, identical save for the gradually deepening pink of his exposed flesh. I was glad that his pleasures were simple and that sitting out on his balcony gazing at the sea made him so happy, but after a few days I found myself secretly praying for rain.

The first time I had been to De Panne was the day I saw the Normandie. The euphoria of that golden moment soon dissolved in the dishwater insipidity of the town. It had been a muggy autumn day. The sky was grey. The sea was grey. The immense beach was the colour of an old vest, the tower-blocks of holiday apartments stood rigid, pale and grim as a defeated veterans' football team in a communal cold shower. Along the esplanade pairs of white-faced, sunken-eyed people shuffled aimlessly about dreaming of a painless death.

I had been looking for the station and a train to Veurne, but there was no sign of a railway and no signs to one. I asked half a dozen of the undead doppelgängers for help. They all pointed in different directions, or offered Byzantine instructions which sounded like one of the witches from *Macbeth* reading the shipping forecast: 'Ah, north-north-west of here, through the sand dunes, two points east at the apse of the ruined abbey. If you come to a blasted oak you have gone too far.' I had then wandered aimlessly around for half an hour in an estate of ersatz fishermen's cottages the thatched roofs of which rustled menacingly whenever there was a breeze, becoming increasingly jittery and paranoid – the result, I later suspected, of having drunk nothing but beer and coffee for three days (actually that's a bit of an exaggeration. I had, I'm sure, swallowed some water when brushing my teeth).

Eventually I had found a tourist information centre. 'How do I get out of De Panne?' I asked the middle-aged woman behind the desk. She stared at me through a severe pair of butterfly-wing spectacles. For one terrible moment I thought she was going to say, 'But sir, nobody gets out of De Panne' and cackle maniacally, revealing pointed incisors and a blood-red tongue. What she actually said was even more frightening: 'The next bus to the station is in one hour.'

'Can I get a taxi?'

'Yes, but the bus and train is an integrated system, you understand? If you go now to the station you must wait also one hour.' It is a well-known fact that, after the bus terminal, the train station is the most depressing part of any town, no matter how depressing that town itself may be. While I have no scientific evidence to prove it, my belief is that the thought of Stevenage station is the last thing that goes through a lemming's mind as he hurls himself from cliff-top to foaming sea.

'Can I get a taxi to Veurne?'

The woman looked mildly shocked at the thought of such wantonness. 'Yes,' she said censoriously, 'but it would be very expensive.'

'How expensive?'

'Maybe 1,000 francs, I think.'

Eighteen quid to get out of De Panne? If ever I was going to have a chance to use the phrase 'a mere bagatelle', this was it.

When the taxi arrived it proved to be a rather grand white stretch Mercedes with a fin-shaped roof aerial, tinted windows and enough leg room for a giraffe. I hitched up my knees and sunk back into my tan seat with a luxurious, leathery creak. It was probably all the brown ale.

The Mercedes sped from De Panne, Europop so unctuous and repellent it could only come from a compilation tape entitled *Now That's What I Call Mucus!* oozing from the speakers. When we stopped at some traffic lights in Oosthoek the driver turned to me, mopping sweat from his broad brow. If there is living proof of Jung's theory of the collective consciousness it is to be found among taxi-drivers. The world over, from the Mojave Desert to the Mongolian steppes, they speak with one voice. 'October weather?' the cabbie from De Panne said heartily. 'If this is global *vaarming* it is good by me.' Thankfully we'd arrived at Veurne before he'd got round to telling me that he knew the Krays 'and they were all right, mate'.

I had thought I'd never go back to De Panne. Indeed I cheered myself through many a dark moment with the notion. But now here I was again on a bright June day and it really wasn't that bad at all. Catherine and I had lunch at a café specialising in fish and game. The English edition of the menu helpfully translated one dish as 'Hare in the style of your grandmother'. I ordered cod fillet with shrimps and cream. I like hare but I had no wish to see one wearing zip-up felt boots and a navy-blue beret.

Afterwards we walked along the Zeedijk, past bars and cafés, ice-cream parlours and pancake houses, *friteries* and shops whose windows were plastered with day-glo strips boasting '1,000 items for under 500 francs!'. I took this as a sign of encroaching influence from nearby France. Advertising in Belgium was usually refreshingly blunt. Something pithy and to the point such as 'Loads of cheap crap!' would have satisfied the marketing criteria of most Flemish entrepreneurs.

Across on the beach side of the esplanade some children were queuing up for an attraction which offered the chance to pedal various bizarrely-shaped bicycles round a boarded track, while others whizzed up and down the tarmac concourse on electric go-karts, their guardians trailing behind them on massive five-seater pedal-cars or giant tricycles. Games machines ker-chunked and blooped and the toe-curling sounds of Imagination's 1980s hit 'Body Talk' slithered out from the speakers of a merry-go-round. At the southern end of the Zeedijk a massive statue of Leopold of Saxe-Coburg, first King of the Belgians, surveyed this cheery scene.

De Panne was the place Leopold had first set foot in his new kingdom. A span of concrete arched over the bronze monarch, presumably representing a symbolic gateway into Belgium. From a distance, though, it gave the impression that the ruler had been lowered into his nascent state on some sort of trapeze.

We walked across the large paved square that surrounded the statue. Unlike the Zeedijk it was deserted. Leopold stared strictly and Prussianly at us as we approached. The artist had opted for the classic facial expression bestowed on all sculptures of great men: tight lips, firmly set jaw and nar-rowed eyes. It conveyed a mixture of determination, vision and severe constipation. Nevertheless, the statue caught something of the forty-year-old's famous good looks. As a young prince Leopold had been noted as one of the most handsome men in Europe. He had been dashing and romantic too, stiffly reinforcing Bismarck's later description of the Saxe-Coburg menfolk as 'the stud farm of Europe'. In one particularly exciting spell Leopold had succeeded in bedding Hortense, Empress Josephine's daughter, while almost simultaneously fighting her stepfather, Napoleon, as an officer in a Russian cavalry regiment.

By the time Leopold arrived in Belgium in the summer of 1831 he had all but lost that youthful spark. His life after the defeat of the Little Corporal had been a mix of tragedy, frus-tration and farce (but then again, which life is not?). Leopold's first wife Princess Charlotte, only daughter of George IV, had died shortly after giving birth to the couple's stillborn first child. From being husband of the future Queen of England and father of a monarch, Leopold was relegated to the fringe of court life from where he wrote voluminous, sententious letters to his many nephews and nieces and dreamed of becoming regent to one of them, Princess Victoria, an ideal which was thwarted by the traditional longevity of the Hanoverians. An attempt to become King of Greece – which progressed sufficiently far for Leopold to have organised the manufacture of a cerulian blue marquee, in which he pictured himself in regal repose surrounded by Aegean dancing girls – also came to nothing.

The sensual whimsicality of Leopold's Greek preparations were, it must be said, deeply out of character by this stage. Where once he had been a dangerous roué, now the main threat he posed to an unchaperoned belle was that she would wilt from boredom in his presence and strike her head on something hard. During his years of residence at Claremont House in Surrey, the Prince had so thoroughly immersed himself in the role of diplomat and advisor that he could no longer break free of it. His conversation had become a mind-numbing mix of tact, discretion, pomposity and didacticism. By the time he left Dover for Calais on his way to De Panne, members of the British aristocracy had come to regard being trapped in a room with him as a sneak preview of purgatory.

Leopold's favourite pastime was collecting discarded silver braid and grinding it into powder using a machine called a drizzling-box. During one particularly fruitful year he ground up enough braid to make a soup tureen. Little wonder that even his mistress, the German actress Caroline Bauer, was moved to describe him tenderly as 'wearisome beyond endurance'.

Catherine and I left Leopold to his dullness and wandered off across the dunes. Nearby was a more recent statue. It depicted a local fisherman, pipe in hand, cap set squarely. He was life-sized and staring up the coast with his back towards Leopold. It could be that this was simply coincidence, but I thought not. The German king had hardly gone out of his way to endear himself to the Flemish. He had never learned their language and refused to countenance conversion to Catholicism, which he regarded as corrupt and idolatrous.

For all their reputation for plain-speaking the Flemish know how to get their point across in oblique ways, too. It is the sly, droll subversion of a people whose country was dominated by outsiders for centuries. When the Nazis were making preparations for their invasion of Britain, Operation Sealion, they began assembling a fleet of barges, troop-carriers and boats at Ostend. As the autumn of 1940 approached and the invasion seemed increasingly imminent, the shopkeepers of the port began to take a sudden interest in their window displays. By the time the first proposed date of embarkation,

20 September, arrived, the shop windows of Ostend were chock-a-block with water-wings, bathing costumes and teach-yourself-to-swim books. I suspected that the statue of the indifferent fisherman was another example of this pawky sense of humour.

Leopold had not been the first choice of the Belgian government, formed hastily in the wake of the Brussels uprising – that had been the Duke of Nemours, son of the French monarch, Louis-Philippe – but he proved a good one and he soon delivered the link with France his ministers had been seeking from their original selection by marrying Louis-Philippe's daughter, Louise d'Orléans. The couple quickly produced four children, thus guaranteeing the succession.

Leopold was deeply conscientious and, for all his entrenched beliefs, held at least some modern ideas. It was under his guidance, for example, that, in 1835, Belgium became the first country in mainland Europe to build a railway, beginning a programme of modernisation which over the next fifty or so years would transform the country from a largely rural backwater into the most industrialised nation on the continent and the fourth biggest manufacturing power in the world.

While that was going on Leopold battled away – quite literally during the Ten Days' War with the Dutch, which began practically the second he arrived in his new capital of Brussels – to secure Belgium's future. He married off his children with strategic thoroughness, supported some allies moderately, withdrew from some enemies slightly and ingratiated himself with Queen Victoria at every opportunity. The effort took its toll. When Leopold was visited by the British doctor Henry Thompson in 1863, he remarked sadly, 'You see an old man who has suffered long and severely.' Yet he retained his rigidity of spirit right up until the end. On his death-bed one of his daughters-in-law begged him to convert to the Roman

Catholicism of his subjects and his by-now dead second wife, Louise. 'Will you not do so that you may meet your beloved again in Heaven?' she entreated.

'No,' Leopold replied with incontrovertible finality. He died the next day.

On our first morning at the seaside Catherine and I were sitting having breakfast at about nine o'clock when a frenzied metallic clanging began in the distance. Gradually it grew louder, and was then closely followed by the opening and closing of doors in the other apartments in the block and sandalled feet rapidly descending the stairs with a slapping noise like freshly landed fish. I looked out of the window. A white Citroën van was coming slowly along the promenade. There was a bracket above the driver's door. Suspended from it on a leather thong was a glinting, tubular triangle. The driver was sounding it with a steel rod as he drove along. When he pulled up opposite our flat the front entrances of all the blocks in the vicinity burst open to disgorge gobbets of people clutching saucepans of every size and description. They converged hungrily on the van proffering their receptacles. They were Belgians, they were on holiday, they had come to buy soup.

The soup van arrived at nine each morning. Which was more than could be said for the refuse truck. There were council signs up everywhere informing the visitor that rubbish was collected between 0800 and 1100 hours. They told you how to bag the rubbish and where to place it on the street. The only thing they didn't tell you was the day on which the dustbin wagon would come. I suspect that this was because the council didn't actually know. The Flemish binmen were a maverick breed who refused to be pinned down to anything as conventional as a calendar. So, every morning people in the apartments along the promenade put their rubbish out in neat little green plastic rows and then at 11.30 they brought it in again, as if it were a tender seedling they were acclimatising before planting.

This breakdown of communications between refuse workers and council was really rather a pity. The Flemish seaside villages were proud of their rubbish policy. So much so in fact that page six of the glossy Koksijde, Oostduinkerke and Sint-Idesbald tourist brochure features an attractive colour photo of a huge cylindrical wastebin with a black plastic lid. Unlike the rest of the text the Flemish slogan above it is not translated. I like to think it says, 'And why not bring your old junk too? We've ample room for it!'

I went out to make a phone call. The day was bright with a morning haze drifting over the water. The tide was out and the platinum-blond sand seemed to stretch for miles. It reminded me of an old cartoon of two men in ragged clothes crawling through the Sahara, one saying to the other, 'There's got to be a sea out there somewhere . . .

When I came out of the call-box a small man hailed me. 'Monsieur! Monsieur!' He was tanned with white stubble on his cheeks and a smoothly curved nose. He had the hunched posture of a plover, his legs dangled from his shorts like lengths of knotted hemp and he approached tentatively, placing his sneakered feet with elaborate care as if walking through a field of cattle wearing flip-flops. 'Excuse me, sir,' he said, 'but I am a collector of telephone cards and wondered, perhaps, if you might have any you have finished with?'

I handed him the one I had just used. It carried an advert for *101 Dalmatians*. 'Oh, thank you, sir,' the man said, studying the card. 'Thank you very much. It is most gen—' He broke off. From across the street his finely tuned ear had detected the sound of a receiver being returned to its cradle. He spun on his heels as a large elderly lady in pink bermudas squeezed herself out of a telephone booth with an almost audible pop. 'Madame!' he called. 'Madame!' And he set off towards her as fast as his cautious tread would allow.

That afternoon we drove over to the Paul Delvaux Museum in Sint-Idesbald. The car-park was packed, and as we walked towards the pretty collection of fishermen's cottages which houses the museum large numbers of people were proceeding down the path in front of us. When they got to the door of the museum, however, they veered off to the left. The Delvaux Museum had a rather nice café attached, and that was where they were going. The Belgians like visiting museums and beauty spots, but it is cafés that really attract them, as the figures show. There are 35,000 cafés and bars in Belgium, one for every 285 citizens. This is twice the ratio in Britain. Put a café somewhere, anywhere, and the Belgians will go to it. The opposite holds true too. A Belgian hill without a café athwart its crest is a hill that goes unclimbed. Unlike their Dutch neighbours, the Flemish have never been a great seafaring people, they have not explored or set up trade networks stretching far and wide. If the New World had boasted an unrivalled selection of bars and restaurants, however, you can bet they'd have been there centuries before Leif Ericson.

Catherine and I went into the Paul Delvaux Museum. I have in front of me now the entry ticket. After Magritte and Ensor, Delvaux is Belgium's most famous modern artist. He was born in Antheit in the Meuse valley in 1897 and his early work mimics the social-realist painters from nearby Charleroi. After a visit to a Brussels exhibition of work by Dalí, De Chirico and others in 1930, Delvaux abandoned smokey scenes of urban deprivation in favour of a particularly personal form of surrealism. Delvaux's work is dream-like enough, but compared to Magritte or Dalí, his dreams seem remarkably narrow and unvaried. They are usually about the

1. A quietly confident Paul Delvaux assesses the opposition at the annual Sint-Idesbald El Wisty Look-Alike Competition.

2. A startled Georges Simenon spots a woman he hasn't had sex with.

3. King Leopold II.
Imagine what it was like watching him eat soup.

4. A man in Binche cheerfully oblivious of the fact that
a gigantic tarantula spider is about to drop on his head.

5. Belgium's top Spice Girls tribute band go through their paces.

6. A member of Liège's elite Poop-Scoop Unit prepares for action.

7. A judge in the Brussels gymkhana dressage event becomes suspicious.

8. Ecaussines-Lalaing: the Duchess of Windsor struggles to get to grips with Jean-Paul Gaultier's latest brassiere.

9. In sixteenth-century Flanders synchronised pickpocketing was a popular sport.

10. 'Well, normally you'd allow about half a kilo per person for a starter, but if it's for a main course ...'

11. A pair of Belgian vets marvel at what
sometimes turns up in the stomach of a poodle.

12. Eddy Merckx's cunning was legendary.
Here he makes illicit use of a cleverly disguised sail.

13. A plainly fed-up 'Lange Wapper'
endures yet more taunts about his nickname.

14. An awkward moment in Wallonia: it's '80s revival night and
everyone has turned up as That Bloke From Visage.

15. The Rabot fortress, Gent. Debate still rages about whether the new extension really blends in.

16. Bruges: the traditional craft of untangling fishing lines.

same things: naked women, trams and trains. Sometimes Delvaux puts aside the trams and trains for a brief moment in favour of classical ruins, but the naked women are a fixture. His vast canvases are teeming with them.

I first came across Delvaux's work in Veurne, a few miles inland from Sint-Idesbald. Veurne is an eminently respectable town. It is home to the International Museum of Bread, Rolls, Cakes and Icing (easily recognised by the gigantic white mixer at the gate), and has its own gastronomic delicacy, the Veurnse Slaper. I'd like to tell you what one tastes like but every time I went into a shop to buy one I was overcome with a fit of puerile giggling and had to run out again. My friend Steve and I were in Veurne for a beer festival in nearby Diksmuide. The hotel we checked into was really very sedate-looking, but when we got to our room the first thing we noticed was the painting hanging above the beds. A nocturnal Delvaux cityscape, it depicted two etiolated naked women gazing through a French window at an approaching motorcyclist. From the eager look on their pinched, white faces I could only presume he was a pizza-delivery man. 'Well,' Steve said after we had both given the picture some consideration, 'I'm not bothered about it, myself, but what if we were my parents?' It was indeed a disturbing thought.

Belgian parents evidently took such things in their stride, however. You found Delvaux images everywhere, on the walls of Métro stations, on the lids of biscuit tins and posters advertising beer. In Veurne's little public park there was a bust of the artist. In a move that could surely not have been coincidental Delvaux was peeping through a clump of bushes at a nearby bronze sculpture of a nude girl.

In Britain overt eroticism such as Delvaux's would surely have severely restricted his popularity. In Belgium it seemed to have quite the opposite effect. '[Delvaux's] success,' René

Magritte once commented sourly, 'is due solely to the quantities of naked women he churns out.' Magritte didn't like Delvaux. He thought his work upheld bourgeois values.

Whatever their position in upholding the class structure, the nipple count in the Paul Delvaux Museum must be well into four figures. Naked women line the walls from floor to ceiling. After studying the paintings for a while something becomes clear about Delvaux's nudes: they are mainly the same woman, pale-skinned, straight-nosed, heavy-thighed and with slightly bulging dark eyes. Sometimes she is a brunette, at other times a blonde; occasionally she is adolescent or middle-aged, mainly she is in her mid-twenties, but the face and body remain largely unchanged. If there are two dozen naked women in a Paul Delvaux panel, and there quite often are, the chances are that fifteen of them will be this one.

In a glass case in the centre of one of the rooms of the museum there is a display of Delvaux memorabilia. There are toy trains, letters, sketches, even some of his Christmas decorations. And there are family photographs. Looking at them it quickly becomes obvious that the woman with whom Paul Delvaux was so obsessed was his wife. Perhaps this was what Magritte was getting at. Given the opportunity to fantasise sexually about any person or object of his choosing (His mother! A trombone! His mother's trombone!) Delvaux had picked the woman to whom he was married. It was hardly the stuff of revolution, though personally I found it rather endearing.

Paul Delvaux lived into his eighties and spent much of his later years at his house in Sint-Idesbald, but he died further north, somewhat fittingly you might say, given the nature of his work, in the town of Knokke.

The ticket from the Paul Delvaux Museum is one of those large ones they favour in Europe. It is the size of a postcard.

On the front is a detail from one of Delvaux's paintings. It features, as you might expect, two naked women. Beneath it is the name and address of the museum. On the reverse side of the ticket is an advert: 'De Beauvoorder. Fine Meat Products. Salted and Fresh'. On the front a painting of a pair of nude women; on the back an advert for a butcher. Belgium in miniature.

Six

One evening I went out to call home. My father answered. He asked where exactly we were. 'We're at a place just north of De Panne,' I said. 'When you look south you can see the chimneys at Dunkirk.' There was a slight pause, then my father said, 'That's where your Uncle John was killed.'

John was one of my father's three elder brothers. He was a Flight-Sergeant in the RAF, a Spitfire pilot. Photos show a handsome man with deep-set eyes and thick blond hair, side-parted. Before the war he wears double-breasted pin-stripe suits, turn-ups on the baggy trousers; smokes a pipe. In the Western Desert he has on a life-jacket, khaki shorts, hands thrust into the pockets. He has hairy English legs, a half-grin, squints slightly into the camera and the sun.

John was a journalist on the *Middlesbrough Evening Gazette*, not a career pilot. He read Hemingway, was heavily sarcastic, played for the village cricket team (his girlfriend was the scorer). When people talk of the innocent victims of war they think of women and children. Yet John was surely as guiltless as anyone; his only crime was to have been born at the wrong time in the same century as a malign German lunatic.

My father has his brother's log-books, the pilot's record of his missions and flying hours. Before they took off they filled in the date and the duty; when they returned they wrote in remarks and flight times. John's comments are jokey, slangy and sardonic. But for the final entry, a reconnaissance flight, there is no flippant summary, just an empty space.

This was what Belgium had been for generations of Britons: a place where things ended. It could have been an uncle or a brother; boyfriend, or husband, or father. Volunteer, conscript, or hard-bitten professional. It could have come at De Panne, or Oudenaarde, Waterloo or Quatre Bras, Mons or Ramillies, on the killing-floor of Flanders, in the rubble of Antwerp, or among the autumn leaves of the Ardennes. The English, Scots, Welsh and Irish had come here for centuries and dropped in droves. I sometimes wondered if the British antipathy towards Belgium didn't stem from some subconscious knowledge that whenever the words 'We're going to Belgium' were heard back home, the only people gleefully rubbing their hands in response were unscrupulous undertakers.

My father and I finished our conversation. I hung up the receiver, thought some of these things, and left the telephone box. The door clunked shut behind me and a croaky French voice said, 'Excuse me, sir. I am a collector of telephone cards . . .'

The British weren't the only ones who fell here, of course. Belgium is, as Michelet wrote, 'the meeting-place of wars', where the plains are fertile because 'the blood does not have time to dry'.

One morning Catherine and I drove north, along the coast road that ran between the beach-front developments and the scalloped sand dunes which stretched hundreds of yards inland, concealing little estates of holiday cottages. At Nieuwpoort-Bad there was a huge circular war memorial to the 35,000 Belgian soldiers killed in the Great War and a statue of their commander-in-chief, King Albert. It overlooked the sluices which controlled the entrance to the intricate series of canals and channels of the IJzer valley, used for transport and to drain the land since the days of the Dukes of Burgundy.

Albert I (or Albert, King of the Belgians, as he preferred to style himself) succeeded his father, the ruthless, white-bearded libertine, Leopold II, in 1909. Albert was not a particularly regal figure. He was tall, gangling and wore thick glasses which gave him a permanently astonished appearance. He was self-conscious, awkward in company and absent-minded. One contemporary said he looked 'as if he was thinking of building something'. Which, given his nationality, is a distinct possibility. Albert was a man destined to be shaped by events. His observation after the Great War that Belgium had been 'cornered into heroism' was just as applicable to himself.

His reign began less dramatically. One of the first things Albert did was to synchronise Belgian time with Greenwich Mean Time. Belgium was the first country in Europe to do this. Although the situation did not last long (just twelve months, in fact), for a while at least King Albert and his subjects found themselves nine minutes behind Paris, four minutes behind the rest of France (Paris has always been ahead of the French provinces, though I'm sure the notoriously humble and diffident Parisians rarely mention it) and a full twenty minutes adrift of Holland. Those of us who have trouble remembering where British summertime puts us in relation to the continent, chronometrically speaking, should just thank our lucky stars we didn't have to read a pan-European rail timetable in 1910.

Life for King Albert might have continued on this quirky course had it not been for one thing: Germany wanted to invade France, and Belgium was in the way. Fearing a war on two fronts, German military strategy was based on a swift and decisive blow against France followed by a more leisurely tussle with Russia. The campaign against France would take the form of a right hook that would loop round to the south of Paris. Once Paris fell, the rest of France would capitulate. This was known as 'The Schlieffen Plan', in honour of its devisor, Count Alfred von Schlieffen. By the time it was put into operation the Schlieffen Plan was twenty-three years old, yet somehow it still managed to take Britain and France by surprise.

As the major powers eyed one another cagily, like Wild West gunfighters wondering who was going to surrender the moral high ground by reaching for his weapon first ('It was self-defence, sheriff'), Belgium had determined to remain neutral. This was not as easy as it sounded. For as the French Foreign Minister Claude Cheysson once remarked, 'Pacifism isn't a policy. It is a headache.' And if anyone was guaranteed to give you a migraine it was Kaiser Wilhelm II. On 2 August 1914 the German ambassador delivered a letter to King Albert. It gave him a choice: either he could allow German troops to march through Belgium to invade France or . . . German troops would march through Belgium to invade France.

To his eternal credit Albert rejected the first option, which would have spared his country physically if not morally, and so effectively declared war on Germany. The chances of achieving anything which resembled even a token success were virtually nil, but the Belgians fought bravely while Britain and France vacillated. By this time it was clear that Foch, the French commander, had conceived the same unjustifiably low opinion of Belgian soldiery as Marshal Bazaine had held half a century before in Mexico. (The attitude of France's military elite towards their sometime ally was maintained by General de Gaulle, who dismissed Belgium as 'a country invented by the British to annoy the French'.)

As Belgium's forces retreated westward before the Germans Albert attempted to rally the northern part of the country with the cry, 'Flemings! Remember the Battle of the Golden Spur!' This was unfortunate in some ways because the enemy in that engagement had been Belgium's current ally, the French. Indeed, the rebellion which led up to the battle had included a pogrom against French-speakers in the city of Bruges, provoked by the introduction of a tax on beer, and was led by workmen whose slogan was, 'Walloons are false! Kill them all!'

The Battle of the Golden Spur is the Flemish Agincourt, and followed a similar pattern to that fight. It took place on a muddy field just outside the city of Kortrijk in 1302. The Flemish army was a motley assortment of noblemen and weavers armed with knives tied on the ends of sticks; opposing them was the flower of French chivalry under King Philip the Fair. Things looked bad for the Flemish, but happily for them the French knights employed their traditional tactic in these situations of spending twenty-four hours ridiculing their opponents' grubbiness, insignificance and complete and utter lack of breeding and then galloping headlong across the sludge to get slaughtered.

The French nobility were eventually done away with in the Revolution, though it is really a wonder they lasted that long. Unfortunately their sense of military tactics lived on in the French officer class, who continued to believe that the panache of a headlong rush by Gallic soldiers was irresistible, despite firm evidence presented against that notion in several major conflicts of the nineteenth century, including most notably the Franco-Prussian War, in which the Belgian-baiting Bazaine's own performance was deemed so feeble he was court-martialled. The French attitude in 1914 may have irritated King Albert, but to be criticised as militarily incompetent by such men was surely a form of compliment.

Catherine and I turned right just before the circular stone memorial and the bronze equestrian statue of Albert and came on to one of the little back roads that runs alongside the river. The day was bright and still. The sky, rich blue and dotted with sedentary clouds as pale as the inside of oyster shells, looked as if it had been painted in oils as the backdrop for a theatrical production. We drove along slowly, past lock-keepers' houses, narrow hump-backed bridges, scaring the occasional heron into ponderous flight. In the fields tractors with specially widened wheel-bases to prevent sinking put-tered about on arable land which was flat and fertile and several metres below sea level.

By the time the war had stretched into its third month the only bit of Albert's country still in Belgian hands was the tiny south-western corner demarcated by the IJzer and the low ridges east of Ypres, and the Allies were even struggling to hold on to that. As the Germans launched a series of attacks on Belgian positions along the river and the railway embank-ment beyond, Albert took a fateful decision. On the night of 29 October 1914 Belgian troops slipped into no-man's-land and opened the locks and sluices on the Noordvaart canal. By the following morning the Germans were no longer sepa-rated from their objectives by shell-cratered and boggy ground but by a vast sheet of water which covered the farm-land through which we were now driving. The forces of King Albert and Kaiser Wilhelm would face each other across it for the next three years.

We drove on, passing a little Russian Orthodox church, its roof patterned with red, white and blue shingles. Bearded, long-haired and black-robed monks were out tending the gar-dens; strapping Rasputins among tumbling walls of orange nasturtiums and genuflecting ranks of yellow and scarlet antirrhinums. A mile later and we were in the little town which had once formed the southern end of the Belgian line, Diksmuide.

I had been to Diksmuide before, in the autumn of 1996. That first experience had not been a happy one. Steve and I had gone there for the annual beer festival. I had been looking forward to it for months. I imagined a hall full of hirsute robust men (and hirsute robust women, too – there's no gender bias here) sampling ale from the local brewers such as Dolle and Van Eecke, nibbling sausages and Ghentish mustard and perhaps some of those little cheese squares they give you in Belgian bars along with pots of celery salt and paprika.

The first sign that something was wrong had come as Steve and I walked across the Grotemarkt from the station. A coach passed us. It came from Bradford. 'Oh,' we thought, 'how nice. Some more English fans of Belgian beer.' Seconds later another coach swished past, this time from Sittingbourne. Coaches from Oldham, Hull, Sheffield, Newark and Southampton followed in swift succession.

By the time we got inside the Boterhalle it was packed with whooping English people in party headgear. On a podium in the centre of the cavernous room a Bavarian silver band with the combined weight of a great blue whale were playing 'The Happy Wanderer'. As they oom-pahed and poom-pahed through this merry tune the bandstand began to revolve. Swirling, sweating tuba-players waved; the crowd waved back. 'Foll-dah-ree, foll-dah-ra, foll-dah-ra-hahahaha!' a Yorkshire bloke in a sombrero bellowed lustily, his awesome belly wobbling in a manner that suggested it formed a considerable subsidence hazard for passing pixies.

The stage came to a juddering halt. 'Unt now,' the master of ceremonies intoned, practically bursting his lederhosen with bonhomie, 'let us be on our feet for "Ze Birdie Song".

You all know "Ze Birdie Song", don't you?' Oh yes, indeed we did. A Liverpudlian woman in a day-glo pink fright-wig leapt on to a chair and began pumping her elbows in and out with the fury of a bagpiper attempting a stereo rendition of 'The Sabre Dance'.

The Diksmuide beer festival still had over four hours left to run, and already the horns on the plastic viking helmets were drooping impotently and the queue for the toilets was longer than the one in Bexhill Post Office on pension day. In front of us a shaven-headed youth in a Gillingham football shirt placed his head gingerly down on the table, groaned, then fell asleep.

A knot of local policemen stood in one corner of the hall chatting and joking. They seemed remarkably relaxed considering that usually when the English turn up in Flanders in these numbers, it is a surer sign than even the arrival of Kate Adie that trouble is about to break out.

Fleets of waiters and waitresses passed smilingly back and fourth through the fug of cigarette smoke, aftershave and hair-spray fumes, huge trays laden with lager balanced on their palms, seemingly oblivious to the potential for mayhem in their midst. Even when the band broke into 'Agadoo' the Flemings didn't flinch. I found myself recalling the words of Julius Caesar: 'Of all the people of Gaul the bravest are the Belgians.'

There is another massive drink-up in Weize, East Flanders, and at nearby Poperinge, capital of the Hoppeland and quadrupletted with the other astringent beer-flavouring centres of Hythe, Zatec and Wolnzach, they hold a carnival in celebration of hops – though only every three years, because, let's face it, any more than that and the hops are likely to turn all big-headed and hoity-toity on you and stop returning your calls.

In the Boterhalle the band broke into another recognisable holiday tune. It seemed a pivotal moment. I thought:

well, here I am in Belgium surrounded by drunken English people, listening to a red-faced German band playing 'Y Viva España'. This truly *is* European unity. Then I said to Steve, 'How much longer do you want to stay?' and he replied, 'Oh, not much longer. Let's give it a couple more hours, eh?'

At the exit two minutes later, Steve was still laughing. 'You should have seen your face just now. Bloody hell, if it had sunk any faster you'd have got altitude sickness.'

A kindly Flandrian on the door said, 'Stamp your hand for returning, gentlemen?' 'I am not returning,' I said with what I imagined was splendid Oatesian finality before stepping out into the cool, damp and comforting night.

In the town square twenty or more coaches from England were lined up in rows. The drivers huddled together, smoking and telling war stories about contra-flow systems. Steve and I walked round the corner to a café and ordered a beer made at the Dolle Brewery three kilometres up the road in Esen.

It came in a self-consciously wacky bottle with a snowman on it, but the contents were syrupy, sweet, powerful and delicious. The beer is called 'Stille Nacht' and it is aptly named, because more than two bottles of it would send even a hardened drinker into a coma. As I sipped it I tried to think of something positive to say about events in the Boterhalle, but my mind kept turning back to 'The Birdie Song', the bobbing stetsons and the satin slacks and the only thing that came into my head were the final words of Conrad's Captain Kurtz as he lay in anguish somewhere in the Belgian Congo: 'The horror! The horror!'

On the way back to Diksmuide railway station we passed a *friterie* with a big sign up in the window saying 'Kip aan't Spit'. It looked like sound advice to me.

The following day Steve and I had returned to Diksmuide to watch a vital top-of-the-table clash in the West Flanders League between the local boys and Gullegem, a suburb of

Kortrijk. With the mud and the sporadic outbreaks of violence it looked as if the two teams were re-enacting one of the darker episodes in the area's history. During the Great War Diksmuide had been so pulverised by artillery that when they came to rebuild it after the armistice the only way they could locate the site of the town was by using maps. Perhaps this had given the new Diksmuide an extra durability, like the broken limb that heals stronger. Because, remarkably, the Grotemarkt and the Boterhalle had survived unscathed the onslaught of the night before.

On that trip I had seen for the first time the IJzertoren, which lies on the town's western edge. It is an 84-metre-high tower which forms a cross at the top, marked with the letters AVV-VVK. Fittingly for a Flemish memorial the IJzertoren is made out of brick.

In the flat landscape of West Flanders something this tall stands out for miles around. On the train journey down from Ghent the IJzer tower comes into view a quarter of an hour before you reach the station at Diksmuide.

The guide book I had with me described the IJzertoren as a Belgian war memorial. 'Well,' Steve said when told this as the train trundled passed it, 'it may be appallingly ugly, but as a symbol of the monstrous futility of it all it would be hard to beat.'

Coming back to the IJzertoren with Catherine it quickly became obvious that the guide book had told only half the story. We parked the car and walked through the arched Pax Gate into a garden called 'The European Peace Domain'. Up ahead was the IJzer tower, in front of it a battered stone cross some twenty feet high, also decorated with the letters AVV-VVK, '*Alles voor Vlaanderen – Vlaanderen voor Kristus*' (All for Flanders – Flanders for Christ), and what I at first took to be a carving of a gull, but which turned out to be a fulmar, symbol of Flemish nationalism.

A pair of workmen, muscular, moustachioed and stripped to the waist like figures in a Meunier painting, or a Frankie Goes to Hollywood video, were pounding away with sledge-hammers on the roof of a stone crypt. Noise reverberated around the Peace Domain as we walked up the path to the IJzertoren.

To say the IJzertoren is a war memorial is to understate its role. To say it is Belgian is to miss the point entirely. The brick tower is not about Belgium but Flanders, and it is not simply a monument to the Flemish dead, but also a symbol of radical Flemish nationalism and – and this part is perhaps even more typically Flemish than the building material – a great histori-cal complaint made monolithically solid. The IJzertoren is about oppression.

I knew the Flemish felt aggrieved about years of mistreat-ment. And if you have spent any time among the Flemish you will certainly know about it too.

In a bar in Ghent the day before the Tour of Flanders, Steve and I had met an Austrian cycling fan who lived in the city with his Flemish wife and their teenage kids. The Austrian had been listening to us talking and came over to tell me that he thought I looked like the rider Edwig van Hooydonck. 'You could be his twin,' he laughed. Personally I found this far from flattering (and I'm sure Edwig would have felt exactly the same if he'd been there). That was not the Austrian's main mission, however. He had overheard that we were strapped for cash and appalled by the price of everything (the pound was doing one of its periodic attempts to limbo dance under all European currencies) and wanted to recom-mend a reasonably priced hotel to us. We thanked him for his concern and had a brief chat. When he had finished his beer the Austrian had left, but he'd then come dashing back in again fifteen minutes later. 'Oh good,' he'd wheezed, 'I hoped you would still be here. I just spoke with my wife about your situation and she says that if you need to you may stay at our apartment. But' – he held up a cautionary finger – 'only for a maximum of three days and no more.' He handed us a card with his address and phone number on it and left again.

'What an astoundingly kind and hospitable man,' I said to Steve when the Austrian had disappeared. 'Indeed,' Steve said, 'but I think we'd better go before he comes back and offers to let us sleep with his wife.'

Talking about Belgium the Austrian had said: 'I like the Flemish very much. After all, I am married to a Flemish woman. They are kind, generous, much more friendly than the Austrians. But,' he sighed, 'they cannot speak for more than a minute before they tell you how badly done to they have been.'

Not that the Flemish didn't have reason to complain. It wasn't until the Belgian state was fifty years old that the first speech in Flemish was heard in the parliament building in Brussels. In 1873 an infamous murder trial ended with the wrongful conviction and execution of two Flemings, neither of whom was able to understand the proceedings because they were conducted entirely in French. It was only after this tragic event that Flemish was made available within the Belgian justice system.

Twenty years elapsed, however, before Flemish was recognised as Belgium's second language (although it was and still is the first language of 60 per cent of all Belgians). In the 1920s, when debate raged over whether the University of Ghent should become exclusively Flemish-speaking, a Wallonian MP felt moved to remark that replacing French culture with Flemish culture was like replacing a lighthouse with a candle.

Flemish was routinely ridiculed by the Belgian upper-middle class (even the Flemish-born of whom tended to speak French – the *Franskiljons*, the Flemish nationalists called them) as a backward and barbaric language. Up until the 1950s a Flemish-speaker was as likely to find work as a barrister, army officer or civil servant as an actor with a broad Glaswegian accent was to land the job of a BBC announcer during the days of Lord Reith.

Speaking French was considered intelligent and refined. It was a sign of education and a class indicator; a bit like speaking RP English. You still came across signs of this in older Flemish people, particularly in the larger cities.

In Ghent there is a very traditional confectioner's shop along one of the cobbled streets near the grim Castle Gravensteen, where the trams rumble across a wooden bridge over the Leie. Entering it is like stepping back in time. There are big biscuit tins painted with red-coated soldiers; huge speculoos biscuits cut into the shapes of animals; little digestive sweets flavoured with rosemary and vervain and breath-freshening pastils scented with lavender and wild violet; tubby glass jars, lace doilies and table tops covered in porcelain bowls filled with sugar-coated chocolate mussels, oysters and gulls' eggs.

The tall, slender, elderly lady who presides over the shop has her hair piled high on her head and parted centrally to form two distinct mounds. This coiffeur, combined with her build, her round spectacles, slightly hunched posture and habit of holding her hands up at her chest, gives her the appearance of a benign praying mantis. The elderly lady speaks Flemish, but unlike most Flemish-speakers, no English. Instead, she offers a slightly archaic and courtly French. 'If it pleases, Monsieur and Madame,' the elderly lady says, and her stoop gives the impression of an approaching bow, 'I would politely offer to propose the following suggestion for your consideration as an addition to your so far most excellent selection . . .' It is the language that once signified gentility among the Flemish.

Ghent seems to have been something of a centre for French-speakers in Flanders. In the late nineteenth century the city produced three famous writers: the poet Emile Verhaeren, the dramatist Maurice Maeterlinck (winner of the 1911 Nobel Prize for Literature) and the novelist Georges Rodenbach. All of them chose to write in French. Mind you, in the latter two cases at least, that may have been a blessing in disguise for the Flemish. Maeterlinck and Rodenbach's work is morose in the extreme. The former's most famous play, *Pelléas et Mélisande*, was turned into an opera by Debussy in 1902, causing someone to remark, 'All opera has death in it, but this is just death from start to finish.'

Rodenbach's novel *Bruges La Morte*, meanwhile, is so gloomy you find yourself instinctively trying to brush cobwebs off the pages while you are reading it. *Bruges La Morte* tells the story of Hugh Viane. Viane's wife has died five years before the narrative begins. Since then he has led a solitary existence, his only consolation being a relic of his loved one in the form of her long and golden hair which he cut from her head on the day of her funeral and now keeps on display in the sitting-room of his perpetually darkened home. This macabre toupee is destined to play a part in the . . . Oh, but I'm giving away the plot. *Bruges La Morte* is pretty much the sort of stuff you imagine Edgar Allan Poe might have written if he hadn't discovered drugs, but it was highly thought of in its day and drew praise from other *Weltschmerz*-merchants such as Mallarmé and Huysmans.

More surprisingly, Rodenbach's novel is also credited with making Bruges the popular holiday destination it is today. Though quite how lines such as, 'Bruges was desperately depressing at this time of day. That was the reason Hugh liked it so much' (stop that tittering at the back) could have been worked into a campaign promoting the city is hard to fathom. Maybe the Belgian tourist board of the 1890s targeted people suffering from an excess of high spirits with posters reading 'Come to Bruges. It's a real downer'.

Actually my own experience of Bruges was a bit depressing too, but not in the deliciously dolorous sort of way that might have fascinated Rodenbach. What happened was that I went on a day trip there from Ghent. When I arrived in Bruges I decided to take a ride in one of the little boats that putter up and down the canals, because, well, Bruges is the sort of place where you do that kind of thing. I boarded the small craft and sat near the back. A gang of sixteen-year-olds got on a few minutes later and sat in front of me and began laughing and joking in what to my only half-tuned ear sounded like some Nordic or possibly Slavic language.

When the boat set off, the guide, who was also in command of the outboard motor, asked me my nationality and then began giving his patter exclusively in English. Worried that the teenagers at the front of the boat weren't getting the benefit of his description of the Beguinage, I shouted out to him, 'Excuse me, I'm not sure if these people here,' I indicated the adolescents, 'can actually understand English.'

One of the group, at whom I was now smiling with kindly concern, turned round when I had finished and scowled at me. He was a barbarous-looking youth with spots like florid barnacles. ''Course we fucking can,' he snarled. 'We're from fucking Arbroath, you English poof.' I spent the rest of the forty-five-minute trip fearing they were about to jump me and throw me overboard.

Despite which I failed totally to experience any of the 'blackness of imagination' to which Rodenbach so frequently alludes. Probably the flocks of gaily-coloured tourists and the stalls selling T-shirts ('Welcome to Belgium. Our weather is lovely, our policemen honest, our girls beautiful' one announced with typical self-deprecating sarcasm) had driven it away, or simply replaced it with a horror less moodily languid and decadent.

Rodenbach, Maeterlinck, Fernand Khnopff and other *fin de siècle* Belgian artists are deeply morbid. There are a number of reasons for this, some relating to the presence of Catholic imagery in Belgian homes and schools, others to the feeling of foreboding that the coming end of the century provokes. Mainly, though, it was probably just the weight of Belgian history. It is perhaps no coincidence that one of the most valuable raw materials in this country heavy with death is black marble (Belgium is Europe's only source); the preferred headstone of discerning funeral directors everywhere.

When Catherine and I walked up the steps into the IJzertoren we found it was undergoing some kind of re-fit: there were cables dangling from the roof, cracked shards of plasterboard and bags of cement lying in the corners. As with many public buildings in Belgium it was hard to tell if the IJzertoren was actually open or not, but the woman behind the desk assured us that it was.

There was a slide-and-sound show in one of the tower's side galleries. It told the story of the Flemish soldiers in the Great War. It was quite different from the books I'd read on the subject in English. In these works King Albert was portrayed as wise, steadfast, honest and beloved of his soldiers – Albert the Brave; his wife, Queen Elisabeth, a saintly figure whose very appearance would cheer a wounded man into a quick recovery, was the Saint of the Yser (English-language books always translated Flemish place-names into French, as if deliberately to annoy the locals). In the IJzertoren version Albert was none of these things. Instead he was portrayed as a pragmatic Francophone aristocrat who had promised the Flemish all kinds of linguistic and social reforms in order to get them to fight ('Remember the Battle of the Golden

Spur!'), only to renege once the war was over. Soldiers had been ordered about in French, their gravestones inscribed with the words '*Mort pour la patrie*'. Albert was a traitor to these loyal men. Even the decision to open the sluices was done on the advice of a Fleming, Hendrik Geeraerts.

Later I would learn from a Flemish book-dealer I met in Antwerp that Albert's death in 1934, in what I had always thought of as perhaps the most cruelly ironic of all calamities – a Belgian mountaineering accident – was actually suspected to have been a murder carried out by vengeful Flemish nationalists. Although, as the man admitted with a wry smile, the only people who seemed to suspect this were themselves vengeful Flemish nationalists.

The slide-show in the IJzertoren rumbled on. Images of the front-line, quotations from letters, historical details. We learned that by the time Maeterlinck and Rodenbach had become famous there was a backlash against French-speaking among some younger Flemish artists and intellectuals. They looked not to France for inspiration but back into Flemish history, to the days of Erasmus, Van Eyck and Bruegel. Among them were painters such as Leon de Smet, Constant Permeke and Valerius de Saedelaar. There was a political movement, too, which crystallised during the Great War and in the years following the armistice. The original IJzertoren (blown up in 1946, according to the literature that accompanied the sound-and-vision show, 'by unknown individuals who hated the Flemish (probably soldiers)') became one of its sacred sights, and there was an annual pilgrimage to it by Flemish nationalist groups, a tradition which continues to this day. Though how the monument's professed message of Peace, Freedom and Tolerance squared with the political aims of far-right, openly racist organisations like Vlaams Blok (who believe in the repatriation of foreign workers) was hard to say.

Catherine and I took the lift up the IJzertoren. In the

centre of the cross at the top of the tower there were windows. From nearly three hundred feet up on a sunny day you can see a lot of West Flanders. There was plenty of evidence to bear out Michelet's observation. Farmland stretched for miles around – wheat, rape, the blue-green stubble of newly planted leeks and acre upon acre of pasture speckled with herds of grazing dairy cattle. The area around Diksmuide was famous for its butter. You saw it on sale all over Belgium. Hence the Boterhalle, home not only of the horrendous piss-up I had witnessed, but also the annual Butter Festival, which hosted, according to a brochure I had picked up from the lady at the ticket desk, 'six traditional cheese-throwing events'.

It was a timely reminder of the happier side of Flanders, because there was something unsettling about the IJzertoren. Its mix of religion and patriotism; the talk of blood and fatherland; the imposing, ugly buildings; the posters and postcards downstairs of the annual pilgrimage, the yellow-and-black flags of Flanders in their hundreds, flapping in the breeze; and the pictures of the Pax Gate lit with pale-blue spotlights – all carried echoes of more sinister political rallies. Ones at which Vlaams Blok and their shaven-headed chums might have felt distinctly at home.

Nationalism, however well-intentioned, has always been a beacon for autocrats and their willing subjects. By the 1930s the main Flemish nationalist party, the Vlaams Nationaal Verbond, was leaning heavily towards fascism. There was collaboration by a minority of both French- and Flemish-speakers in Belgium during the Nazi occupation, but only Flanders was rewarded – if that is the term – by being allowed to form its own SS units. They helped run a concentration camp at Breendonk near Antwerp. After centuries of subjugation the Flemish had reason to be angry. But perhaps the people who blew up the original IJzertoren had reason to be angry, too.

When we came out of the tower, still slightly dizzy from the descent in a lift that looked alarmingly as if it was in mid-service, the two Flemish workmen on the roof of the crypt had stopped for a coffee break. 'You like the museum?' the younger of the two shouted down in English as we drew level. 'It's very interesting,' I said diplomatically. The workman who had asked the question translated this to his mate. The other man laughed and yelled something at us in Flemish. The younger man laughed too. 'He says he can't imagine anyone coming here unless they are forced to!' and he shook his head, before turning and pretending to punch his friend in the face.

We headed south from Diksmuide, now driving along what had been the British front-line. When my grandfather had been a boy at Archibald School in Middlesbrough, the war had been raging here, and there'd been a map on every class-room wall marked with little flags to show where units containing relatives of the children were based. After three years of almost motionless stalemate the names of the villages we passed through – Pilckem, Zonnebeke, Hooge – would have been as familiar to them as their two-times-table. My grandfather's eldest brother, Joe, had joined up at sixteen, motivated no doubt by patriotism but surely also by the prospect of excitement and escape from the poverty of indus-trial Teesside.

We parked the car at Sanctuary Wood. There was a memo-rial here, on 'Hill 62', to the Canadians. Like all the Com-monwealth cemeteries it was a picture of neatness. Pale pink roses grew in beds among maple trees and bark chippings. As we walked about we disturbed a great green woodpecker which disappeared over the ridge in bobbing flight. It was the only sign of life apart from the stuttering of a lawn mower in a distant garden and the occasional throaty croop-croop of a lovelorn wood pigeon. Hard to imagine that this area had once been a muddy, roaring, smoking hell, compared to which the blast furnaces of Middlesbrough must have looked as comforting as a home hearth.

It was more atmospheric inside the nearby Sanctuary Wood Museum, a strange, dank place, entered through the café of its owner, a man in his forties with a lugubrious, drooping moustache. A couple of lunchtime drinkers were sitting at the bar hunched over their beers, talking in low voices among stuffed animals, bi-plane propellers, Uhlan helmets and *pickelhaubes*. It didn't seem the sort of place you'd come for a riotous night out.

There had once been scores of these little privately-owned museums along the front. Set up by enterprising locals, they were filled with memorabilia picked up off the battlefields – a small compensation for the destruction of villages and land and the fact that every time a farmer set to with a plough he ran the risk of being blown to eternity by a previously unexploded shell. They had been a decent business. But then the Germans had returned to Belgium and cut off the museums from their main source of visitors. The one at Sanctuary Wood is the last remaining.

There are just two small rooms in the museum, but they are stuffed full of every kind of uniform, weapon and ammunition imaginable. Photos and newspaper cuttings line the walls alongside commemorative plates, recruitment posters and patriotic prints – King Albert firing at a German sniper during a visit to the Belgian front-line, that sort of thing.

Outside, at the back, are some preserved trenches and the blackened stumps of blasted trees now overhung by leafy ash and sycamore. The whole place smells of decay, rust and stagnant water. The exhibits are jumbled, badly labelled or not labelled at all. As an example of the curator's art it is execrable, but as a re-creation of the grim dirtiness of the Great War it is probably as near as anything gets.

The contrast between the Sanctuary Wood Museum and the Salient Museum in the Cloth Hall at Ypres couldn't have been stronger. Here everything was clean, well-organised and crisply displayed. Perhaps even more striking to my mind was the difference in tone between the Salient Museum and another battlefield site we had visited earlier in the trip, Waterloo.

We had travelled there from a hotel near Enghien, up through Wallonian Brabant, the crumpled industrial town of Tubize, where the closure of the local steelworks earlier in the year had brought 80,000 people out on to the streets to protest, and the ghostly avenues of Alsemberg. At Waterloo there were coach parties. Groups of Japanese following leaders armed with pennants on sticks, ponderous American teenagers and chattering Portuguese schoolchildren. The events of 1914–18 were treated with gravity and respect; Waterloo as a kind of fancy-dress parade with guns. The reality was, however, that a soldier in 1815 was far less likely to survive than one a century later. But hey, that was ages ago, right? And just look at those lovely uniforms!

Lenny Bruce once said, 'Tragedy plus time equals comedy.' It was plain that when it came to battles, tragedy plus time equals pageant. Nature renewed itself and so did the human spirit. When the bicentenary eventually comes up there will probably be groups of men who spend weekends in the summer re-enacting Passchendaele at church fêtes for charity.

After Ypres we headed up the cobbled slope of the Kemmelberg and pulled in to the car-park of the Café Belvedere. From the garden to the side of the café you had a commanding view over to the turrets of Ypres's Cloth Hall and the low scarp of the Messines ridge. On top of the ridge you can see the spire of Mesen's village church, the crypt of which was once the billet of Corporal Adolf Hitler.

The Belvedere had been built on the site of a hotel

destroyed by Hitler's compatriots in the Bavarian infantry when they captured the Kemmelberg in April 1918. Before that the hill had been in the hands of the French, and the Belvedere and its attached bell-tower had been a key observation post for senior Allied commanders.

We went into the café for pancakes and coffee. A light rain was falling and it was almost two hours since our lunch; mealwise, at least, we were going native. The Kemmelberg and the surrounding villages are border country, so close to France that even the Flemish families chattering in the Belvedere peppered their speech with *mercis* and *ça va* and the owner talked merrily and unashamedly in French on the telephone. On the opposite slope of the Kemmelberg there was a large memorial to the French dead of 1914–18 set above an ossuary containing the remains of 5,000 unidentified soldiers. From the memorial you were said to be able to see Lille, ancient capital of Flanders. We decided to walk off some of the whipped cream by going to have a look.

We strolled along the road across the flat, wooded crown of Kemmelberg, past a hotel and alarming red notices warning of the possibilities of being shot if you wandered off into the trees during the autumn hunting season. There were half a dozen cars parked on the gravel in front of the French memorial. I walked absent-mindedly past them. When I stopped to read the inscription on the obelisk, Catherine, who had been a bit behind, came up and nudged me. 'There are people in those cars,' she whispered. 'Wow, spooky,' I replied wittily.

'You don't understand,' Catherine hissed, 'there are couples in those cars . . . you know,' she made that slight head-raising gesture which is the subtle English mime for 'rampant animal rutting'. 'Don't look round,' she added, somewhat pointlessly, in my view, since I don't know anybody who wouldn't react by looking round instantaneously when told that scenes of steamy carnality are being played out behind them. The cars were lined up pointing away from the road and into the undergrowth. Some had fogged windows, a few swayed rhythmically.

I turned back to the French monument. 'Crikey!' Catherine said. 'A rainy Wednesday afternoon in West Flanders. Who would have thought it?' But by now I was less sanguine about the scene than she was because I had spotted something else. 'I don't know how to tell you this,' I said quietly, 'but there are some rather seedy old men hiding in the trees. Don't look round!' I added, singularly failing to follow my earlier wisdom. 'God, there are,' Catherine said when she turned back again. 'Do you think they're . . .' she gave the slight head-raising gesture which is the even more subtle English mime for 'voyeurs watching other people engaged in rampant animal rutting in a car and perhaps furtively masturbating beneath their coats at the same time'. I nodded. Which in this case just meant, 'Yes.'

'I think we'd better go,' I said. We turned and strode purposefully towards the road. It was one of the few times in my life when I have found it impossible to resist the urge to whistle a cheerful tune.

'That was strange,' Catherine said when we reached the safety of the Belvedere. People having sex while parked athwart a mass grave being observed by blokes hiding behind bushes. Strange it certainly was. But what made it all the more disturbing was the thought that when they went home that night one of the furtive men from the undergrowth might have cast his mind back over the day and remarked to himself, 'Hey, I thought *I* was a bit odd, but that weird English bloke had brought his family with him.'

Seven

There are some truths of human existence that are incontrovertible. One is that when you are on your own in a hotel room in a strange foreign city, Eurosport will always be showing clay-court tennis. Another has it that when you are alone in Brussels after dark and you have had just enough alcohol to give you that vague feeling of numbness at the nape of your neck, the last thing you should do is go into a railway station.

The railway stations of Brussels at night are no place for anybody who might be susceptible to depression. The first time I arrived in the Belgian capital it was 10.30 p.m. on a Friday. I got off the train from the airport at Brussels Nord. As I walked through the cavernous tunnels to the Métro, thoughts of loved ones left behind filling my head, the strip lights buzzing above and my footfalls echoing across the emptiness to be heard, as far as I could tell, by no fellow human being, a static crackle emerged from the hidden speakers of the tannoy. It was followed shortly afterwards by the melancholy tootling of Acker Bilk's 'Stranger On The Shore'. Harder men than I would have broken.

On that first night in Brussels I had imagined that the choice of music was targeted directly at me, by some sadistic member of Belgian Railways' staff who had spotted the airline tag on my holdall through the security cameras and thought he'd have some psychotic fun. On later visits, however, I came to see that this was actually standard practice. Each evening after sunset the stations of Brussels filled with mournful jazz. 'Midnight In Moscow', 'Harlem Nocturne', practically anything by Jan Gabarek wailed plangently across concourses and down subways. A cynic might suspect the whole thing was sponsored by manufacturers of Prozac. It was nothing of the sort. Rather, the Belgian authorities had cunningly harnessed the psychological power of music in a successful campaign to eradicate late-night violence. Railway termini are a preferred battleground of thugs and drunks all across Europe. Belgian stations are different. Here peace reigns even on the busiest Saturday night. That is not to say Belgium does not have its share of inebriated louts; it does. But when they turn up at the stations belligerent with drink and sexual frustration they find themselves confronted not by riot police but the haunting trumpet of Miles Davis and the theme from *Ascenseur pour l'Échafaud.* Two verses is all it takes. Soon they are staring into the awful abyss of their loveless existences, forget all about fighting and instead go home to write self-pitying poetry or stick their heads in gas ovens.

Forewarned, the next time I arrived in Brussels alone (Catherine and Maisie having made that trip to Munich) with the sun about to disappear over the horizon, I raced across the Gare Centrale and headed straight for my hotel. Once there I flopped down on the bed and did what anybody would do in the same situation, began flicking through the twenty-four or so TV channels on offer in the hope of coming across people having sex.

I was disappointed. All the Flemish channels seemed to be

showing *A Touch of Frost*; the Walloons were watching *Inspector Morse*; the French, chat-shows; the Spanish, variations on *Blind Date*; and the Germans were enjoying comedy based on the European tradition of mime. Thankfully a Dutch station was showing the legendary American soap opera *The Bold and the Beautiful*. In it, a famous surgeon with an improbably deep voice was lying on an isolated mountainside dying from a gangrenous gash sustained in a car wreck. Luckily he had the young wife of an arch-rival with him for comfort. As his life ebbed from him and the snow fell, the surgeon confessed his affection for her. The women wept with joy (love means never having to say, 'Jeez, the stink of that suppurating leg-wound sure is a passion killer') and burrowed under the blanket with him. As they groped one another the surgeon gazed into the woman's tear-filled eyes. 'You are all I dreamed you would be,' he enunciated sonorously. 'So young, so . . . supple.'

The Bold and the Beautiful was rubbish, but it was Dostoy-evsky compared to the shite served up on the Italian channel Rai Uno. I had made a study of Rai Uno over the months I had been in Belgium and as far as I could tell it had only one programme. This involved a short, pot-bellied bald man in a tuxedo jabbering away to an assortment of six-foot-tall, large-breasted blonde women. What the point of it was, I'm not sure. The only workable theory I came up with was that it was some sort of gambling game in which the audience bet on how many capacious cleavages the dumpy bloke could gaze into before he finally dribbled on one of them.

Ten minutes of Rai Uno and I was ready to do something desperate. Go to a Belgian football match, even. Don't get me wrong, Belgian non-league football was fine. In fact it was something of a home away from home; the domain, as is non-league football the world over, of Charles Hawtrey lookalikes, middle-aged men in leather trench-coats who have modelled their hairstyles on that of the lead singer from Chicory Tip, and old white-haired ladies in ten-foot-long knitted scarves who yell, 'Referee, you're about as much use as an ashtray on a motorbike!' at five-minute intervals throughout the match. Unfortunately the paper I had didn't list non-league fixtures. Anderlecht were playing at home, but that was hardly the lure it might once have been . . .

The waitress in the café in Ghent explained how to get to the Ottenstadion, home of KAA Gent. 'The Decascoop cinema is much closer,' she added helpfully when she had finished. I grimaced. The indigenous Belgian film industry had produced some notable features over the years. There was Jaco van Dormael's *Toto the Hero*, for example; the ultra-violent *Man Bites Dog*; the lesbian vampire classic *Daughters of Darkness*, which deserts Transylvania in favour of off-season Ostend ('It's dead around here at this time of year' a hotel porter remarks archly); and, of course, *The Sexual Life of the Belgians, 1956–78*, starring, written and directed by Jan Bucquoy, one-time owner of the Brussels Underpant Museum. Sadly, such fine offerings are few and far between. In Belgium, as in most countries, the bulk of films come from America.

'I could see a Hollywood film in England,' I said. 'You could see a football match in England also,' the waitress said. I have been a Middlesbrough fan for thirty years, with all the imperviousness to logic which that implies. I went to the Ottenstadion.

In England sporting traditionalists like to divide places into football or non-football towns. The categorisation goes way beyond whether the town in question has a league club based in it. It has to do with a burly old-fashioned roughness, an ingrained passion. Grimsby and West Bromwich are football towns, Exeter and Cambridge are not (and not just because they are cities, either). If you were to apply similarly nebulous criteria to nations, then Belgium would definitely be a football country.

The referee in the first World Cup final, M. Langenus, was a Belgian. Belgian club sides once did well in Europe. Anderlecht and Standard Liège are famous names to older fans, and Mechelen won the Cup-Winners' Cup as recently as 1988. The country has produced at least two world-class players since the war. The first was Paul van Himst, who must have featured in every football annual I ever had as a boy, in the section at the back headed 'World Stars', probably next to Sandro Mazzola. Van Himst was a forward with Anderlecht. He had immaculate, side-parted hair and generally looked like he might have driven one of the Minis in *The Italian Job* wearing string-backed gloves. The second world-class Belgian footballer was Eric Gerets, a wing-back whose unhygienic hairiness was surely an over-compensation for having the middle name Maria. Gerets hailed from Genk, played first for Standard Liège, where he was implicated in some nefarious shenanigans involving bribes to rival teams, then in Italy for Milan and finally, and most famously, with PSV Eindhoven in Holland. Gerets is now manager of Club Brugge.

I have had a soft spot for Belgian football ever since staying up until the early hours of the morning to watch the national team overcome the Soviet Union 4–3 in an epic second-round encounter in León during the 1986 World Cup. Belgium owed their victory to a couple of dodgy goals and a mighty performance from Jan Ceulemans. Ceulemans was a hulking blond man whose jarring body movements suggested his limbs had only met one another that morning and were still not sure if they were going to get along. One incident from Ceulemans' magnificently big-hearted display stands out in particular. Late into extra-time in the sweltering Mexican heat, the Club Brugge forward broke from deep inside his own half and galloped away from the Soviet defenders. As he bore down on Dasayev, Big Jan hit an invisible wall of fatigue. Unable to dribble round the goalie or even place a shot, he simply wellied the ball high into the crowd and then collapsed flat on his face. It remains one of my favourite football moments, a perfect vignette of the passionate and pointless heroism of it all.

I went through the turnstiles at the Ottenstadion and stood behind the goal. The stadium, two uncovered terraced 'ends' and two impressive grandstands, was no more than a quarter full. KAA Gent are a bit of an enigma. They are the top team in Belgium's third largest city, and yet have never won the national League Championship. Two domestic cups is all they have to show for a century of endeavour. You are forced to conclude that, despite its size and heavy industry, Ghent is not a football town. The best that can be said for KAA Gent is that they have one of the smartest badges in European football – a bust of a Red Indian in a feathered war bonnet. Though what this proud warrior of the Great Plains has to do with Ghent, Belgium or football in general is anybody's guess.

Gent's opponents were Liègeois. Liègeois were Liège's second most successful club after Standard, but even they had won the Belgian league five times. As it turned out this was to be Liègeois's last crack at adding to that tally. Beset by financial problems they merged with some fellow strugglers at the end of the season. The new club has never had the same support. Partly, I suspect, because many older fans collapsed with asphyxia during the first chant of '*Allez Royal Tilleur Football Club Liègeois*'.

The game kicked off. It was a dull affair. Perhaps the whole thing was best summarised by the silver band who sat up in the left grandstand. Before the game they had entertained the crowd with jolly tunes and old singalong favourites; midway through the first half they broke into the Funeral March. The people around me, numbed, no doubt, by years of mediocrity, absorbed it all without a murmur. Mind you, since many of them were scoffing smoked eels perhaps that's just as well. Things brightened briefly about fifteen minutes from the end when an African player began to warm up on the touchline and the crowd took up the chant of 'Ari Balanga! Ari Balanga!' The object of their affections duly stripped off and trotted on to the pitch. A couple of fancy ball tricks later and Gent were 1–0 up, the silver band playing 'Congratulations'. And that was how it finished. I vowed that next time I'd take the waitress's advice and go to the Decascoop. Or stay in my hotel room watching *Thief Takers* with Dutch subtitles.

The following morning I woke early and went out for a walk past the Musées Royaux des Beaux-Arts and along to the Palais de Justice, once the biggest building in Europe. In light of the Dutroux affair the epic dimensions and resolute sturdiness of this towering hulk seemed bitterly ironic. A more suitable monument to the Belgian justice system might have been a wheely-bin.

I cut back down the slope heading towards Notre Dame de la Chapelle and what I always thought of as the centre of the city. René Magritte described Brussels as 'erotic'. It had plainly shed some of its allure since his day. The whole city had a slightly abandoned air about it. There were some wonderful buildings, some beautiful areas, but the main feeling you had was of neglect. You could come across streets of derelict buildings anywhere in Brussels – just behind the Bourse, for example, or in the posh suburb of Uccle, where the pavements in front of the grand and rather pompous 1930s detached houses were cracked and uneven with proletarian dandelions dancing among them. I suspect this air of abandonment stemmed from the fact that the city didn't really belong to anyone. For all the Flemish claims to it, they knew the city was not occupied by Flemings and, though the bulk of its inhabitants were French-speakers, Brussels was not Wallonian either. The arrival of the EC, with its legions of politicians, lawyers and bureaucrats, added a transient ex-patriate community to the mix. People came in, used the city and then left. Brussels felt like a rented house: the tenants might clean it, even decorate it, but they weren't going to spend any money on doing it up.

Somewhere near the Rue au Buerre I passed a Greek tav-erna with a menu helpfully translated into English. I couldn't help thinking the owner would have done a better trade if he'd kept things in his native tongue. Somehow taramasalata sounds a good deal more appetising than 'spawn mousse'. Whatever its advertising merits I took this menu as a sign. I weaved my way into the Petit Rue des Bouchers, picked a restaurant at random and ate an enormous Belgian lunch. Actually that's a tautology. All meals in Belgium are enor-mous. Later that day I heard what I thought was a ripple of gunfire. It turned out to be a coach-party from Oldham grad-ually exploding in a nearby café.

The portions are big in Belgium and the food is great. The Belgians are not given to self-promotion. Centuries of being taunted and bullied by their neighbours have taken their toll. The average Belgian is so self-effacing as to make Michael Palin look like Muhammad Ali. Canadians seem braggardly by comparison. But one thing Fleming and Walloon alike will tell you proudly is that 'you never eat badly in Belgium'. And this is true. Because if France is the gastronomic heart of Europe then Belgium is the continent's stomach.

'The French love food,' an ample fellow told me once over a medieval plateful of spit-roasted pork, braised chicory and caraway-flecked rye bread in the garden of a café on the river Leie near Ghent, 'but the Belgians love eating.' Through-out Flanders and Wallonia there is plenty of evidence to back up this assertion. It doesn't take many Belgians to block a pavement, and stout middle-aged burghers wander about in the road in small towns confident that no driver would dare run into them for fear of writing off his car.

Buses and trams were going in all directions when I waddled into the Place Montgomery an hour or so later, but the one I wanted, the Number 44 tram to Tervuren, was nowhere to be seen. I stood at the stop and marvelled once again at the revolving destination signs on the fronts of Brussels buses. Although the vast majority of inhabitants of Brussels speak French as their first language, the city was officially declared bilingual by the Belgian government in 1966. This was a conciliatory gesture towards the Flemish activists, one of whose catch-phrases remains 'Brussels is a Flemish city' (though as they insist on saying this in their own tongue most people in Brussels are oblivious of the fact). As a consequence all the street and direction signs in the Belgian capital are in two languages, and so are the signs on public transport. The problem here, however, is clear: which should come first, the Flemish or the French name? The bus company had cunningly avoided any controversy by using revolving signs. That way nobody came first or last and offence was avoided.

The revolving signs were a clear reminder of just what hard work it is living in a country which has three official languages, is divided into a trio of exclusive language zones, has a bilingual capital and several cities with 'protected linguistic minorities'. That the German-speaking enclave of Eupen was isolated way over in the east was, I suppose, a small consolation, especially for the guards on Belgian trains. These poor buggers certainly had their work cut out. Aside from their normal duties they had to keep careful track of exactly which linguistic area they were in during a journey and make their announcements accordingly. On the seventy-mile trip from Brussels to Kortrijk, for example, they had first to declare the destination bilingually as Kortrijk and Courtrai; as the train moved out into Flemish Brabant they simply said Kortrijk; when the train crossed briefly into Hainaut it was just Courtrai; and when it came into East Flanders it was Kortrijk again. What happened if they made a mistake I never discovered, but there are enough language fanatics in Belgium to suggest that at the very least one of those angry letters written in green ink on lined file-paper that invariably begin 'In all my eighty-five years as a . . .' would be winging its way to the head office of the SNCFB (or, as the Flemish – unhindered by the baroque circumlocutions of a romance language – more pithily knew it, the BS).

And still I waited in Place Montgomery (Montgomeryplein). No tram to Tervuren, or even Tervueren, appeared. After half an hour or so a tram coming the other way stopped and the moustachioed driver yelled across to me in English. How he could tell I was an Anglophone I'm not sure, but it made a refreshing change. Being tall and blond I normally get mistaken for a German. Even by Germans. In fact, whenever I am in Germany local citizens who are lost or confused seek me out specially and ask for directions or explanations. Once, walking down a busy shopping street in Cologne, I was stopped every fifteen yards by people searching for hospitals, government offices or simply wanting to know how to operate drinks-vending machines. Somewhere around the sixth time it happened the friend I was with, who was a Czech exiled in Germany, said, 'They recognise you as the *Ubermensch*, Harry. If you stayed here a few more days they would elect you Chancellor.' I suspect he may have been joking, but I still keep it in mind as a future career option.

'What are you waiting here for?' the driver shouted.

'The 44 tram.'

'It does not go from here.'

'But it says 44 on this sign.'

'Yes, but also it says that you must go downstairs to the terminus under the ground to get it.' And so, I presume, it did, in a couple of languages – neither of them, unfortunately, mine.

'I have been past two times already,' the driver said, 'so when I came back again and you were still here I knew something was wrong.' Even more than his accent the kindly seriousness of his tone marked him out as a Fleming. I thanked him profusely. 'If it hadn't been for you,' I said, 'I'd have been standing here all day.' 'Oh no,' he replied solemnly, 'I do not think so.' In the face of all the evidence it was pleasing that he still gave me credit for some initiative.

The 44 tram rattled out along the edge of the Forêt de Soignes (or the Zoniënwoud). The sun was shining, the sky was a rich Alechinsky blue, the new leaves on the beech and birch trees a vivid shade of lime-green and the air was filled with the moist, loamy smell which speaks of spring and the urgent need to change your underclothes. Dr Johnson once said that his idea of bliss was travelling in a fast coach at night in the company of a beautiful woman (though I may possibly have transposed two adjectives in that sentence). Not having much experience in that direction, I can't really judge, but I have a feeling that travelling in a speeding tram through shadow-dappled woodland on a bright day in a city in which you are never more than four hundred yards from a great meal and the kind of beer that can numb your knees in thirty seconds must run it close.

The tram terminated at Tervuren and I walked up towards the domed splendour of the Musée Royal de l'Afrique Centrale (or Koninklijk Museum voor . . . Oh, I'm sorry, I'm bored of this now). The museum was opened in 1910 to house King Leopold II's West African hoard. The Belgian monarch was a collector on a grand scale. When he visited the Paris exhibition of 1900 he brought back a couple of souvenirs. Others might have stuck with an Eiffel Tower tea-towel and a pétanque set; Leopold opted for a Chinese pavilion and a Japanese pagoda. Yet even judged by these epic standards the West African collection is exceptional. The building which houses the museum was specially commissioned for the job. It was the only completed part of a much grander scheme which was also to have included an Oriental Museum, a school for overseas administrators, a concert hall and, this being Belgium, a large restaurant.

When my father was about twelve, he and a friend took the train from Middlesbrough through to Whitby to visit the town's little museum. Like most museums in those days, and indeed up until the 1970s, Whitby Museum housed a motley assortment of pinioned moths, preserved puffer fish, edged weaponry from around the world, eggshells and dead animals. My father and his friend were particularly intrigued by some stuffed birds in an unlabelled case. 'What sort of birds are these?' they asked a hunched and wall-eyed attendant.

The man shuffled over to them. 'Way, now,' he said in a wheezy North Riding accent, 'you know yon cliffs as lie just south of here?' My father and his friend nodded. 'Way,' the man continued, 'there's some little brown birds as sort of circle over them cliffs.' He dropped his voice, leaned down towards them conspiratorially, looked from side to side, then said, 'We calls them . . . shitehawks,' and with that he skulked off.

I have a feeling the Whitby shitehawk-watcher would have felt rather at home in the Royal Museum of Central Africa, Tervuren. The museum has the exterior of a Louis XV château and the dimensions to match. The inside is so old-fashioned it is almost a museum piece in itself. You walk long, pillared corridors that echo to the sound of your footsteps, past marbled walls covered with spears, swords, shields, painted mahogany masks and mysterious objects that could be either wind instruments or penis gourds, or possibly both if the owner got lucky. There is a gigantic pirogue made from an entire hollowed-out tree, an exhibition on the lifestyle of the pygmies, iridescent butterflies, beetles the size of baby booties, rococo birds' nests and an array of stuffed mammals which speaks of carnage on a grand scale.

The brief issued by Leopold to his curator when it came to wildlife seems to have been to go out to the Belgian Congo, kill at least two of everything that moved and bring the carcasses back to Tervuren. It was an assignment for a blood thirsty Noah. The exhibits range in size from mites to elephants, from fleas to water buffalo. An extended family of gorillas stare glassy-eyed from an ersatz jungle, while nearby a static army of ants work on a building project they will never complete.

In many ways this array of slaughtered beasts is a fitting monument to the man who assembled them. For despite stiff opposition from pitiless monarchs across the globe, Leopold II comfortably carries off the title of Supreme Regal Bastard of the Nineteenth Century. This, after all, was the man whom Empress Augusta of Germany found so morally repugnant that after his visits she took the precaution of having the state apartments exorcised by her chaplain; whose single response to the news that his eldest daughter, Louise, had been incarcerated in an Austrian lunatic asylum was to write to the attendant telling her 'to keep a close eye on the mad woman'; and who was so blasé about public opinion that when he was named in a London court as the client of child prostitutes he did not even bother to deny it.

Leopold's gifts in the area of outrageous dastardliness were manifold, and he exhibited them to the full during his thirty-year campaign to grab, hold and ruthlessly exploit the tract of Africa which would later become the Belgian Congo and supply the many natural treasures of the Royal Museum of Central Africa.

As a young prince Leopold had travelled widely. He quickly formed the opinion that overseas possessions were a necessity, if only to swell his own bank account. By 1860 he was on the case, sending a pointed gift to the Belgian Minister of Finance during a trip to Athens. A piece of Grecian marble, it is inscribed with the subtle message 'Belgium needs a colony'.

Whatever his real views, Leopold had inherited some of his father's gift for diplomacy and obfuscation. He saw that simply to march out and cut himself a chunk of Africa or Asia would land him in trouble with Britain and France, who rather regarded such behaviour as their prerogative.

Instead, in 1876 Leopold called together in Brussels a meeting of explorers, philanthropists and churchmen. He was, he told the assembled throng with a disingenuousness that would have brought a flush to the stubbly cheeks of Richard Nixon, deeply concerned about the plight of the African. Arab slavers still roamed the Congo basin. The poor natives, heathens every one, lived in fear, squalor and ignorance. Leopold wanted to put an end to human bondage and bring the benefits of civilisation and the word of God to these sad, benighted folk. Some cynics might suggest he was trying to build an empire. Nothing could be further from his mind, for, 'If Belgium is small, she is happy and contented with her lot. I have no other ambition than to serve her well.'

So moved were the delegates by Leopold's words that instead of shouting 'They all say that, mate!', they agreed to his idea of forming the Association Internationale Africaine (AIA) to carry out his aims, and, since Leopold was the driving force behind the founding of this humanitarian body, they readily elected him its chairman.

Over the following two years Leopold used his stewardship of the AIA to accomplish . . . absolutely nothing. Soon the other members of the association, tired of the inertia, ceased to pay it much attention. After a while they more or less forgot about it all together. At which point Leopold dissolved the AIA and formed a new organisation in its stead, the rather similar sounding AIC (Association Internationale du Congo). The AIC had the same flag as the AIA and many of the same professed aims, indeed most of the world looked on them as one and the same. This was what Leopold wanted. Because while the AIA and the AIC might share many similarities, there was one important difference between them. Unlike the AIA, the AIC was under the complete control of Leopold by dint of the fact that he was its only member.

One of Leopold's first acts as head of the AIC was to commission the explorer, Henry Morton Stanley, to travel to West Africa. Leopold's instructions to Livingstone's rescuer show that while he didn't always choose to use it, the Belgian king had a shrewd grasp of public relations. Stanley was not to build a colony, Leopold told him, certainly not! His job was rather to bring together independent African states into a federation of free Negro republics under the protection and benevolent guidance of the AIC. Stanley carried out his task with his usual thoroughness and determination, mixing diplomacy with brutality, beads with bullets. Soon African chiefs all across the Congo basin had signed away their independence to an organisation with a blue and yellow banner and its headquarters in Brussels. Euro-sceptics may wish to pause a while at this point and have a good old rant.

Having established his Un-colony, Leopold now set about gaining international recognition for it. Other European powers were becoming increasingly suspicious of Leopold's motives, so he turned instead to the United States, whose politicians at that time displayed a more trusting nature. President Chester Alan Arthur, newly inaugurated following the assassination of James Garfield, was a devout Baptist and quickly fell under the spell of Leopold's talk of missionary work and the war against human bondage. He gave the

Belgian monarch his unqualified support and diplomatic recognition to the 'independent states' of this 'neutral' confederacy. (Later American leaders were less sympathetic to Leopold. When someone suggested to Theodore Roosevelt that the ruler of Belgium should be invited to the St Louis Exposition he hammered the table with his fist and bellowed, 'We don't want him! He's a dissolute old rake!').

By 1884 the world's other major powers had fallen into line with the US and recognised the new nation. As reward for the faith Arthur, Bismarck and the rest had placed in him, Leopold delayed for a whole year before doing what he had intended to do all along, declaring himself King of the Congo Independent Free State, sole ruler of 920,000 square miles of Africa.

In one way, at least, Leopold had not lied about his intentions. Since the Belgian government refused to have anything whatsoever to do with the Congo it was not, strictly speaking, a colony; it was simply an extension of the royal estates at Laeken. By a mix of duplicity, sleight of hand and the sort of cunning manipulation of language that would have a modern spin-doctor purring, Leopold had taken personal control of an area eight times the size of his own country. As if this were not enough he quickly extended his territory by sending a military expedition eastward to the Nile.

A rather bizarre episode followed, in which Leopold approached Britain and asked the then Prime Minister Lord Salisbury if he wouldn't mind persuading the Khedive of Egypt to loan him the Sudan for a while. In exchange, Leopold said, he would allow the British to use the Sudanese people to form an army with which to annex China. Salisbury didn't know quite what to make of this plan, but Leopold's cousin, Queen Victoria, was not so perplexed – she concluded sternly that the Belgian king had 'taken leave of his senses'. (Victoria had never much cared for Leopold. When he was younger she had summed him up thus: 'as unfit, idle and unpromising an heir apparent as ever was known'. Her approbation was perhaps heightened by the euphoric relief at finding someone worse than her own son, Edward, a man who shared some of Leopold's vices.)

Though insanity does seem to have been a hazard for the Belgian Royal Family at that time (as well as Leopold's daughter, his sister Charlotte, widow of Emperor Maximilian of Mexico, was also confined for mental health reasons. For a while she occupied a palace in Tervuren, but it burned down in a fire and she was moved to a moated castle at Bouchout. Leopold, true to his nature, never visited her), Leopold's problems were actually more financial than mental. Despite making such dramatic cost-cutting measures as deleting a course from the royal lunch menu, finding and exploiting the wealth of his new kingdom was proving beyond the King's pocket.

To raise the money necessary for his schemes, Leopold eventually persuaded the Belgian government to lend him a vast sum on the understanding that when he died he would bequeath the Congo, or cash equal to that loaned to him, to the Belgian people. That done, he then went out and mortgaged a vast tract of the land he had effectively used as collateral on the government loan to a bank in Antwerp for a further half a million francs. That this was plainly illegal did not bother Leopold in the least. Indeed, when he was unable to meet his repayment on the Antwerp loan, he demanded the Belgian government make it for him, arguing, with logic if little shame, that should they fail to do so the nation would lose a large part of his bequest. The government gave in and handed Leopold the money to pay off his debt. He then asked them for a further 150,000 francs, which he said they might as well give him now to save him from having to bother them again later.

You may think that this little escapade makes Leopold look like a swindler and charlatan. There is an added twist, however, which elevates him far higher up the league table of bunko-artists and conmen than that. Because it later transpired that the loan from the bank in Antwerp did not exist. Leopold had simply made it up in order to chisel more money out of the Belgian treasury.

Finances secured, Leopold now turned back to the Congo. In a series of battles Belgian-led *askaris* broke the power of the Arab and Swahili slave-traders in West Africa. The news was greeted with rejoicing around the world and the Belgian king was hailed as one of the great humanitarians of the age. Leopold celebrated in characteristic fashion by imposing a tax on the inhabitants of the Congo. The Africans had no money, but Leopold generously allowed them to pay the new tax by working for him collecting quotas of rubber and ivory. Since these quotas were fixed falsely high, the Congolese ended up working for the Belgian monarch full-time and without wages. Thus was one type of slavery quickly replaced by another.

Leopold was now in his late fifties. Knowing that he had only the remains of his lifetime to accrue as much wealth from his fiefdom as possible drove him to ever more extreme measures. The quotas were increased. Tribespeople were worked to death. Villages that failed to fulfil the demands of the King were razed, the villagers slaughtered. Baskets full of their severed hands were brought into Leopold's agents as proof that the notorious 'forest guards' had carried out the punishment. It was, in Joseph Conrad's words, 'the vilest scramble for loot that ever disfigured the history of human conscience'.

I wandered along the corridors of the museum gazing at Rwandan dancing costumes and Kakunga initiation masks. There didn't seem to be anyone else around apart from me, though sounds of human life, in the form of Europop, wafted down from some unseen source. The effect of the tribal carvings, jars of preserved reptiles and Patrick Hernandez singing 'Born To Be Alive' was mysteriously creepy. Luckily, before I suffered a Kurtz-type breakdown and went native, I came across a father and his young son lurking amid a collection of dusty moths that had the wing-span of blackbirds, antennae-like fern fronds and brown-and-black marking patterns that looked as if they may have been the inspiration for furniture-fabric designers throughout Belgium.

As man and boy moved off I followed close behind, glad for some semblance of living company. The lad's enjoyment of his visit was greatly enhanced by the opportunity the long galleries and polished stone floors afforded for the ancient boyish art of sliding; the father showed rather too keen an interest in the bottled tape worms for my liking.

Soon we had drifted away from the museum's twelve million insects and into one of the side rooms. Here there was an exhibition devoted to the exploratory and military expeditions in the Congo. There were captured Mahdist flags suspended from the ceiling, Victorian paintings of Congolese soldiers beating off attacks by the ferocious private army of slave-trader Tipoo Tib, and a battered sailing trunk which had belonged to Dr Livingstone. On one wall was a memorial listing the names of the Belgians who had fallen during the early years of the Congo Free State. There was no comparable list of the Congolese who had died during the same period; even in a building the size of the Royal Museum of Central Africa there are constraints on space. In the ten years from 1896 to 1906 King Leopold II made £3 million in clear profit from his enterprises in the Congo. It worked out at slightly less than a pound per African life.

I walked back up to the tram terminus, bought a can of beer from a vending machine, more for the novelty of it than anything else, and caught the 44 back into Brussels. The day was still sunny and I decided to walk from Place Montgomery back into the city centre via what I think can be said without doubt to be a truly unique institution, the Musée Wiertz.

The painter Antoine Wiertz was born in Dinant. He liked to compare himself to Rubens and Michelangelo, though the artist he most resembles is actually William McGonagall. His work is, plain and simply, rubbish. It is big, weird, badly executed and quite often it comes with a message so thumpingly obvious it would have been far simpler and certainly more aesthetically pleasing if Wiertz had just printed it on a T-shirt. An example: a voluptuous nude woman, 'La Belle Rosine', gazes upon a skeleton labelled, wait for it . . . 'La Belle Rosine'! Life, beauty, all must fade. Crikey!

Whatever he lacked in ability Wiertz made up for in ego. He regarded himself as a talent on a galactic scale. Quite how he came by this idea is anybody's guess, but such was the force of his self-belief that he convinced many others of it as well. Among them were members of the Belgian government who, in the 1850s, agreed to build him a studio just off the Rue Vautier in central Brussels at public expense. In return Wiertz magnanimously agreed to bequeath the studio and a selection of his works to the nation. Whether spontaneous street parties greeted this declaration is not recorded.

The studio, now the museum, is vast. It had to be. Wiertz tended towards giganticism. But that was understandable. For as one of his supporters was moved to explain: 'No surface can be found large enough to contain his genius.' This was, let it be remembered, in the days before the introduction of the postage stamp.

Close by the Musée Wiertz is another of Brussels' singular attractions, the Édicule Lambeaux. This pavilion, designed by Victor Horta, houses some sculptures by the Antwerp-born Jef Lambeaux. Entitled *Les Passions Humaines*, these try rather hard to live up to their description as 'reliefs'. Despite the allegedly shocking eroticism of these sculptures it has to be said that none of the men involved in any of the scenes seems in the least bit excited.

In his book *Waterloo to the Peninsula* George Salas says of Brussels, 'I never saw such a place for dogs in all my life. They swarm.' That was in 1867. One hundred and thirty years later you don't come across so many dogs, but the coiled and reeking evidence that they are around in, apparently, vast numbers is everywhere you step. Practically everyone who has visited the Belgian capital feels moved to comment on this phenomenon, yet the Bruxellois themselves seem oddly unconcerned by it. After a while you begin to sense a defiance in their indifference that almost amounts to pride, and you start to wonder if a steaming heap of canine faeces on a paving slab, unattractive though it is, hasn't come to be regarded by the townspeople as something of a status symbol, in much the way a bulging gut and gout was by medieval noblemen.

As I worked my way carefully back to the Petit Ring only one thing bothered me. I just hadn't seen that many dogs in Brussels, ever. The odd *bichon-frise*, a Yorkshire terrier here and there, the occasional giant schnauzer, perhaps, and once, in a bar near the Colonne du Congrès, I had been introduced to a black spaniel-like creature which the owner described as a 'cheese hound' and which promptly answered my question of 'Why?' by attempting to snaffle a square of smouldering Hervé from my plate with an absent-minded sideways dart of his snout. But I had sighted nowhere near the canine numbers or diversity needed to produce such quantity and variety of crap. They must have been hidden away somewhere.

Or maybe there was something more to it than that. Perhaps dogs were being ferried into the centre of Brussels under cover of darkness on special trains. For years the city authorities had attempted to direct the visitor's attention to the many glories of their city, but it was hard to walk around gawping at Art Nouveau architecture when you knew from bitter experience that the slightest loss of concentration would see you executing a triple salchow on a dark-brown skid-pan (the locals suffer no such problems; trained from their earliest years they negotiate the odiferous hazards as if by some bat-like sonar). Maybe, as a result, the dogshit has over the years become so inextricably linked in the minds of men with the city of Brussels that the two things are now as inseparable in the global consciousness as Venice and its canals, New York and its skyscrapers, Milton Keynes and that eerie feeling that you have slipped into a coma. Perhaps as the dog population of Brussels gradually shrank, the city's councillors were faced with the awful possibility of losing their most potent, globally recognised civic symbol. Their attempt to avert a crisis by creating something new in its stead foundered when the Atomium failed to catch on (and how could it? Imagine the Dutch trying to replace the clog with a gigantic chemistry-lab model of a molecule. The whole thing smacked of desperation), and they were forced instead to call on the population of the surrounding countryside for support. The countryside that surrounds French-speaking Brussels is, of course, exclusively Flemish. The negotiations must, therefore, have been long and hard and at times bitter, but eventually both sides were satisfied. Brussels got to borrow some dogs and the Flemings got a capital city with street signs they could understand.

Mort Subite is one of my favourite bars. It has a nicotine-stained ceiling, the price list painted on to wall mirrors, a waitress who resembles the middle-aged Jeanne Moreau and an intense, chain-smoking clientele who look as if they might still believe that you can overthrow capitalism by drinking too much and talking animatedly about gestural abstraction. It is to my knowledge the only bar in the world that has ever inspired a ballet (by Maurice Béjart).

I ordered a glass of faro and sat staring into it sternly, trying to give the impression that I was a man who spent his days deconstructing bourgeois concepts of beauty rather than speculating on the origins of urban dog turds.

Actually at this point I was thinking about Leopold again. The fact was that although I could work myself up into a state of righteous indignation about his behaviour, there was always part of me that refused to join in. I felt a strange, well, *affection* for the ruthless old poltroon. Because as with certain other deeply amoral men there was a seductive swagger about Leopold II. His total indifference to the feelings of others was a liberation most of us will, thankfully, never know, and it produced some notable moments of cruel humour. Once, for instance, when an attempt was made on Leopold's life and the assassin's bullet whizzed past him and struck and mortally wounded a loyal servant, the King simply sniffed and said, 'My, my, whoever would have thought that ineffectual fellow could have provoked someone so severely.' And when the Bishop of Ostend remonstrated with His Majesty about his sordid private life, saying, 'People tell me you keep mistresses,' Leopold simply smiled and said benignly, 'People tell me the same thing about you, Your Grace. But, of course, *I* choose not to believe them.'

Most memorably, perhaps, when asked how he maintained himself during crises, Leopold replied, 'If you can survive the Belgian national anthem you can survive anything.'

This savage wit is, I am aware, no recompense for Leopold's many grisly crimes, but there are other prize bastards who have not even offered that. Notably Adolf Hitler, Josef Stalin, Pol Pot and the bloke whose dog's poop was at that moment spreading evil fumes through Mort Subite via the sole of my right desert boot.

Eight

In the Pays des Collines in northern Hainaut Catherine and I put down the deposit on a holiday flat. The flat was in the attic above a large, square farm. Smells of stewing beef wafted up the stairs; geese honked in the yard. The farmer's wife had the benign, slightly startled features of an elderly guinea pig. A chatty woman, she spoke so quickly as she showed us around you had the constant feeling you'd come into the story half-way through and were a little too late to catch up.

When Catherine pointed out a donkey in a nearby field, the farmer's wife exclaimed, 'Ah, Julie! She is fifteen. Last weekend the man was supposed to come to see her. Then on Friday the man's mother died and the man had to stay at home to comfort his father. Julie was desolated. That night she kicked down her fence and went in with the chickens!'

After a few seconds it dawned on me that 'the man' who had stood Julie up was a male donkey. I had some specialist knowledge here which I felt would benefit the conversation; just before we had come to Belgium I had met up with an old schoolmate of mine who is a farmer.

I hadn't seen Richard for nineteen years. He hadn't

changed that much. His body had thickened, his cheeks had taken on the characteristic sand-blasted look of the northern agriculturalist and his hands had expanded to the size of shovels, but his face still crinkled up when he smiled and took on a self-deprecating look of bewilderment when some aspect of the story he was telling ran against him. His land was near Kirby Moorside and he had a broad North Riding accent, enunciating his words deliberately and speaking so very, very slowly that every phrase sounded like a paragraph. And you

Had to fight

The urge

To finish

Off all

His sentences for him.

He said, 'There are two things they say you never see: a happy farmer and a dead donkey. Well, one of our donkeys died last month. So that's something out of the ordinary in itself. I said to my wife, Annie, I said, "Oh heck. I'll need a big hole to bury that in and I'll need to get on with it or we'll be in bother with the council."

'Annie said, "Before you set on that, why not give Alan a ring and see if he wants it?" We have this friend called Alan, you see, and he's a taxidermist. Well, he isn't a taxidermist by profession, he's a welder, but taxidermy is his hobby. Don't ask me why. So I phoned Alan and asked would he be interested in stuffing my donkey and Alan said he would, because he thinks Leeds Playhouse are after one. So I took it over in the pick-up.'

'Did he do a good job?' I asked.

'Oh, he hasn't done it yet. He's got the donkey in his freezer. Whether it's whole or in bits, I don't know. And to be honest I don't really want to know. But when you go to his house it's absolutely incredible, really. He's stuffed all sorts. Trout, stoats, terriers, ferrets, everything.'

'But a donkey's a bit different, isn't it?' I pointed out. 'I mean, it's a bloody sight bigger than a stoat.'

'Oh, a donkey's not the largest thing Alan's done, not by a long chalk. Because when an animal dies at Flamingoland Zoo Alan always gets the body. Tigers, lions, he's done the lot. Last time I called round to see him he was out in the garage stuffing a giraffe.'

The first part of this story seemed particularly relevant to the situation at hand, so, mustering my French, I said to madame, 'For the donkeys to die it is very not normal, I am certain.'

Madame looked at me as if I was mad. 'No, monsieur,' she said matter-of-factly. 'All animals die, it is the way of things.'

I shrank slightly, an airy-fairy urban liberal crushed by rural common sense. Afterwards Madame never treated me with quite the same respect. I imagine that even now, as you are reading this, she is in conversation with a friend at another farm saying: 'The English! How can we let them have any say in the Common Agricultural Policy? I had one staying with me once. He thought the donkey had the gift of eternal life. No, Hortense, not any specific donkey, all donkeys! You laugh, but these people have a say in how we poor Belgian farmers make our living. It is *incroyable*!'

Of course, I could be greatly over-estimating the impact I had on her life.

In the kitchen of the farm I handed over a BF1,000 note for the deposit. 'Ooh!' the farmer's wife cried excitedly at the sight of it, 'the new note! I have read about it, heard of it, but never yet seen it!' She called out, 'Marie! Auntie! Come and see!'

A rangy woman emerged from a side room clutching a broom. She had a peroxide bouffant, rosy, wind-burned cheeks and a denim shirt. She looked like she might break into 'Stand By Your Man' at any moment. Instead she sauntered over to inspect the new note, a big smile on her ruddy face. 'It has King Albert on it,' the farmer's wife informed her joyously.

Another door opened on the opposite side of the room. This time an old lady trundled into view clutching a manila wage packet aloft like Neville Chamberlain returning from Munich. She had battleship-grey hair and such a pronounced stoop that gravity carried her perpetually forward. The only way she could stand still was to grab a piece of furniture and hang on to it. The farmer's wife waved the 1,000-franc note at her. 'Auntie! The new one. Here it is!' The old lady stared at it, proclaimed astonishment, then glanced up at Catherine and me. 'Netherlanders?' she asked. We told her we were English. She smiled. 'The English,' she said, in English, with a haughty inflection that suggested she received tuition from Dame Edith Evans, 'the English are always welcome here.'

We thanked her. 'Do you know Yorkshire?' the old lady asked. I told her that I am from Yorkshire. 'I have friends there,' she said. 'Mr and Mrs Robinson, perhaps you know them?' I shook my head. 'Mr Robinson,' the old lady said in an attempt to jog my memory, 'works,' she waved the manila envelope skyward, 'up a tower.' Before she could explain further she lost her grip on the table and disappeared out of the door Marie had come in through. I never saw her again. Though a month or so later we passed a woman who looked remarkably like her seventy miles to the north, heading towards Antwerp.

After we had unloaded the car we drove off southwards through pretty pastureland, enclosed between clusters of low hills. The roads between Ronse and Ath are narrow, but this did less to deter the speed of the oncoming traffic than the sight of a pursuing biker gang in the rear-view mirror. Vehicles hurtled towards us, dust spiralling in their wakes, then, seconds before a head-on collision, swerved into the concrete storm guttering, shuddered briefly, terrifyingly, and then zoomed past with so little room to spare that flies reposing on our respective doors were instantly fused together. By the time we had reached the N60 near Leuze we had cheated death by suicide driver on half a dozen occasions, my hands were so sweaty I could no longer grip the dashboard and the outer side of our Peugeot was streaked with *pâté des insectes.*

Belgians have a reputation as the worst drivers in Europe. People say this owes much to history. Driving licences weren't introduced in Belgium until the early 1960s, and all you had to do to get one then was apply for it. There was no practical driving test until a decade later.

A personal view is that the Belgians' swashbuckling driving methods and apparent delusion that the brake pedal is actually a spare clutch, to be used only when the original one wears out, owes less to the past than to Belgian road signs. These are generally placed so discreetly or mysteriously in relation to their purpose that locating them requires more skill, luck and judgement than the average spot-the-ball competition. As a result, you usually do not notice them until you have passed whatever it was they were warning you about or directing you towards. Whatever their other limitations, Belgians are experts at U-turns. They get plenty of practice.

Roundabouts are another source of dangerous confusion. They are rather new to Belgium, and no certain etiquette has as yet evolved about the correct way to deal with them. Some Belgians hold fast to the belief that those on the roundabout should have right of way, while another group maintains that priority should go to those joining it. As a result, roundabouts are best approached in one of two ways: circumspectly, or wearing a blindfold. On the road between Tongeren and Sint-Truiden there is a sign, tucked away discreetly in the middle of a holly-bush, warning you of an approaching roundabout. Underneath it there is a message in Flemish. I am not sure what it says, but I have a feeling it reads: 'Roundabout ahead! Have you any last requests?'

And then there is the notorious *priorité à droite*. This gives right of way to vehicles entering a road from the right no matter what the circumstances or relative status of the two merging roads. Back-alley, lane or cart-track entering an urban throughway – it makes no odds, vehicles can come torpedo-ing in from the right as they see fit. Or at least they can some of the time. Priority to the right does not apply to all roads. This is hardly the help it may first appear, however, because the system of divining which roads it *does* apply to is so arcane that even a language as flexible and richly complex as ours cannot fully explain it. Suffice to say that one of the rules of *priorité à droite* is that, should the person entering from the right hesitate, even momentarily, then their priority is immediately forfeited. This bold and, frankly, insane clause ensures that those who choose to take advantage of their right of way do so with a disregard for personal safety which would draw gasps from a kamikaze pilot. In Tournai we were travelling along a main road when a man shot out in front of us from a side-street with only a couple of yards to spare *on a bicycle*, his only protection the knowledge that the full weight of Belgian justice was on his side. God, how I wish we'd hit him.

Another problem facing the foreign traveller is, predictably, the language divide. Direction signs are in the language of the region, and the name of your destination can alter significantly as you cross linguistic borders. Suddenly Malines turns into Mechelen or Antwerpen Anvers. It helps if you have memorised a few of the more obscure ones before you set off. For while you don't need to be blessed with the gift of tongues to guess that Louvain is Leuven and that Namen and Namur are one and the same, what of Mons and Bergen, Tienen and Tirlemont, Borgworm and Waremme? And how did the Flemish come to call Lille Rijsel, or the

Walloons to know Sint-Truiden as simple, de-sanctified Trond?

A further point about Belgian direction signs is that they tend to stop suddenly as you approach your destination. This is, I think, a nod towards the independent streak of the natives. The Belgians traditionally do not like being told what to do. This intolerance of instruction is a source of national pride. Belgians regard road signs as gentle advice rather than direct orders. 'You take the first right after the bend,' a Belgian will tell you when you ask for the best route out of town. 'Er, but,' you venture, 'I think that's a no-right turn. There's a sign a couple of yards before it, tucked behind a bus shelter.' 'Oh yes,' the Belgian replies cheerfully, 'but if you take any notice of that you will have to go all around the houses.' To a Belgian a 70kph speed limit does not mean 'Do not exceed a speed of 70kph on any account', it means 'Do not exceed a speed of 70kph on any account unless you are in a hurry or driving an open-topped sports car and wish to impress watching girlies'. Whoever designs the system of direction signs makes allowances for this self-reliant streak. As a result a typical sequence of Belgian signs might read: Genk↑; Genk 24; Genk→; Genk 12; ←Genk; Genk 8: Genk You can find your own bloody way from here, surely?

The aim of fostering rugged individualism in the motorist finds its greatest fulfilment in the Belgian diversion. Belgians have an almost mole-like fondness for holes, and to appease the craving the local legislatures employ men in luminous bibs to go around, more or less at random, and dig cavities in the middle of roads. A diversion sign is then cunningly positioned at a strategic point *in full and open view of motorists*. A series of similarly well-placed and easily spotted directions then guide the driver through a tortuous sequence of twists and turns until he is way out into the hinterland, at which point they stop abruptly and the fun begins. What joy awaits!

You drive around for hours looking for a clue as to your whereabouts, but your efforts are hampered by the local habit of placing village or town signs at the entrance to the parish rather than the conurbation itself. Sometimes you can drive in and out of a place three or four times in the space of a few miles without seeing a single dwelling.

On you go, scanning the horizon for church steeples or motorway lights (in this area at least Belgium leads the world. Belgian motorways are the best lit in Europe. The lights are so closely spaced and bright they provide the country with the only motorway system on Earth that is visible from outer space. True!). Head-scarved women out tending crops wave at you as you pass, and wave again with only slightly diminished enthusiasm when you pass them again two minutes later. If you are fortunate enough to be graced with offspring you are in for an added bonus, because at this point, in response to the growing tension in the air, he or she will begin to bawl their lungs out until they are puce in the face and the car windows have all steamed up, and you will attempt to rally his or her spirits by singing snatches from favourite TV programme theme-tunes while simultaneously reading a map, scanning the now oddly flat and featureless landscape for geographical clues and keeping an eye open for maniacs zooming out of expertly camouflaged slip roads. At this point the sound in your car will be something like this: 'Tinky Winky, Dipsy, Laa Laa . . . Hoepertingen? How the hell can this be Hoepertingen? . . . His tinkling bell says he's the happiest little fellow in all . . . Isn't Luik Liège? . . . There's Big Ears and Tubby and Mr Plod . . . Have we been past that life-sized multi-coloured inflatable camel before? . . . And lots of other friends . . . What do you mean, you can't remember? How can you not remember something as bizarre as tha*watch this moron in the Datsun he's not going to stop* . . . It's sixpence an adventure and he'll take you *for Christ's sake*, Hoepertingen again!'

At first this may seem very frustrating and stressful, but after a while you realise it has taught you a valuable lesson. You have learned the Taoist approach to navigation. You simply sit back and abandon yourself to unalterable fate. Belgium has more yards of road per square mile than any other nation in Europe. Eventually they will take you where you want to be. It was in this relaxed manner that we found our way to the village of Tourpes.

Tourpes had an outstanding attraction, Brasserie Dupont. In any other country a brewery might not rate as a tourist destination, but this was Belgium.

Beer occupies the same place in the Belgian national consciousness as roast beef does in Britain. Georges Simenon said, 'The smell of freshly poured beer is the smell of my country,' and right up until the 1950s Belgian children were offered a choice of milk or weak brown ale to accompany their school lunch.

Belgium is the greatest brewing nation on Earth. Other countries produce good beer, but nobody attacks beer-making with the verve and manic inventiveness of the Belgians. Most brewers find a quality formula and stick with it; Belgian brewers are restless tinkerers. In Germany or the Czech Republic they might concoct a fantastic brew and then sit back and watch it roll off the production line for the next five hundred years. In Belgium they've no sooner come up with a finely balanced mix of hops and barley than they're saying to themselves: 'Well, this is pretty damn good, Paul old boy, but I wonder what it would taste like if we added a dash of crushed cinnamon, a hint of coriander and a handful of dandelion leaves to the mash?'

The Belgians never stop experimenting with beer. They use different grains – wheat, spelt, oats, buckwheat – often in combination; huge varieties of hops and malts; drop in fruit in the form of sour cherries, raspberries, apples, strawberries, dried orange peel or even, in one case, figs; perk up the flavours with spices ranging from ginger to aniseed; use rock or candy sugar, or sometimes honey in the mash. To anyone else the sight of may-blossom is simply a happy harbinger of summer, to a Belgian it's the inspiration for a new ale.

As if this were not enough, the Belgians have bulked up their indigenous brewing traditions by filching styles from other nations. Indeed, such is the Belgians' love of beer that they even managed to draw a pint or two of comfort from one of the darkest episodes of their history. Between 1914 and 1918 Belgian and British troops spent plenty of time together on the front line around Diksmuide. From their contact with the Tommies the Belgian soldiers developed a taste for British ales. After the armistice was signed and the British were packed off back to Blighty, the Belgians started making these beers for themselves. Nowadays lots of Belgian breweries produce a Scotch ale, IPA or stout. And the odd thing is that since they still use the old recipes and brew to the original strength (most of our nation's beers are nowhere near as strong as they once were; the result of government worries over the effect drinking was having on industrial output), if you're British and want to drink the sort of beer your great-grandfather might have knocked back on his way to work in the morning, just about the only place you can do so is Belgium.

The result of all this tradition, borrowing and tampering is a range of beers that is, often quite literally, staggering. The average Belgian bar serves around twenty different beers, but in the specialist cafés you will sometimes find a bound list running to that number of pages. Of course it would be untrue to say that the process of mix-and-match works every time. The almost legendary Minty, which comes from the makers of Delirium Tremens, for example, is a bilious green

181

colour and tastes like Special Brew swigged with a mouthful of toothpaste. And those hawthorn flowers really are very, very bitter indeed. But failures are surprisingly few, and when a Belgian brewer really does nail it, as with the sweetly scented Dubbel Domus Honigsbier, or Drie Fontienen's spritzy pink raspberry lambic, you are in the kind of flavour territory that would have Jilly Goolden reaching for her thesaurus.

The man at Brasserie Dupont was dark and his face was so crinkled up with wrinkles and laugh-lines you felt that when he was younger it must have been at least twice as big. He was wearing navy-blue overalls and Nike trainers. His feet were the size of bread rolls. When we'd arrived he had been shifting pallets of beer crates with a fork-lift. He was so tiny he practically needed a step-ladder to get down from it.

We had only called in to buy some beer but when the small man heard we were from England he insisted on showing us round. He was proud of the brewery, justifiably so – even by Belgian standards the beer Dupont produces is exceptional. The small man scurried about the brown-brick brew plant, pointing things out, setting machines in motion, opening and closing doors and hatches and tapping dials. All the while he was chattering away. He had the ability to keep four of five strands of thought running simultaneously. It was as if he had taken his conversational topics for the day, cut them into bite-sized chunks, chucked them into the air, then stuck them back together again at random, William Burroughs-style. He said: 'Fermentation takes place at 25°C. Eric Cantona! What a player! Of all the mobiles I tried, I found Nokia the most reliable. Well, of course, we get twenty-four different channels here. Me, though, I follow the Gunners. Spent grain goes to our farm as cattle feed. BBC, Sky, Canal Plus, Eurosport, we have all of them. In this tank the mash is one hundred per cent organic. But in Belgium Excelsior Mouscron are my team. I believe there is one now, no bigger than the ordinary, with a built-in fax. Amazing! Ian Wright, Wright, Wright! Hahaha! My son is mad on Manchester United. There's a full call-back facility and colour LCD. Total production 6,500 hectolitres a year. Although because I don't speak Dutch a third of them are useless to me. And FC Metz of France.'

By this time we were up in the office paying for the beer, or trying to. The small man was more interested in giving us promotional material than taking our money. 'Here, you must have this. Oh and these, of course,' he kept saying, handing us great wadges of beer mats and brochures. Would we still be here in August? he asked. Resisting the urge to reply that it was a fair bet at the rate he was going, we shook our heads. Pity; we would miss the Parade of Giants in nearby Ath. He showed us a tourist-board flyer with a photo of some huge, brightly painted dummies bumbling round a crowded Grande Place. They looked like the type of thing that used to provoke wheezing, hysterical laughter in Stuart Hall during *Jeux Sans Frontières.*

'Some of these, yes?' The small man passed me half a dozen leaflets for a place near Philippeville that claimed to be 'the only museum in the world devoted exclusively to brewery trucks'.

Later, when we were loading our box of beer and our towering heap of glossy paper into the back of the car, we heard a cry from behind us and the small man came scampering across the road shouting for us not to go. He had something special for us he had almost forgotten. Dupont, he said, were going to start selling their beer in Britain. They had just had a poster printed in English. He would like us to have one.

The poster is now framed on the wall of my office. It is an advert for a *bière blonde* called Moinette, which is so rich and robust in flavour you almost feel it should be served with croutons. Taste is an individual thing, but I'm willing to bet that if experts around the world composed a list of the greatest beers, Moinette would be in or around the top ten of most of them. Not that the brewers at Dupont are prepared to make any such outlandish claims on their own behalf, you understand. The poster features a photo of a bottle of Moinette on a barrel outside the entrance to the brewery. Above it is the modest slogan, 'Moinette. A Really Good Belgian Beer'. Every time I look at it I smile.

When we told the man at Dupont we were heading for Aubechies Archeological Site he said, 'Ah, yes, for the special event.' The woman behind the checkout at Superette Linda in Tourpes said the same thing.

On the way there, at Blicquy, a *jeu de balles* team in red-and-white halved shirts and black jogging pants were beginning to warm up for their afternoon match. They were batting a ball the size of a satsuma about with gloved hands, on what looked something like an elongated and netless tennis court marked out on the village square with pinkish white paint.

Jeu de balles is a game played across Belgium, Holland and northern France. It is said to be derived from pelota. Like macaroons and the dreaded *escavêche*, it was a left-over from the days of Spanish rule. Standing among a respectable crowd of villagers I had watched a game being played a few weeks before at Treignes in the Viroin valley. What had surprised me most was not the sport itself, which had the wilful haphazardness of one of those games invented and played exclusively by public schoolboys, but the fact that there were so many fans brave enough to occupy the pitch-side benches. The ball was made of wood and pinged about the court as if propelled from a musket. Every once in a while a player would mis-time his clout and the hard little pill would whizz over the ducking heads of the audience and ricochet around off the walls of the surrounding buildings. It was little wonder the spectators followed the game with such intense concentration or that so many of the old folk in the crowd seemed to have removed their teeth before coming out.

We made a wide circuit round the *jeu de balles* players and went into a bakery. When the young woman behind the counter heard us discussing what to buy in English, she smiled. 'You have come for the special event at Aubechies,' she said. There seemed no use fighting public opinion any longer. We agreed with her that we had.

As we left the bakery armed with a couple of loaves of bread and enough croissants to give severe indigestion to a Foreign Legion battalion, a mini-bus pulled up in the square and a group of hirsute and tattooed men in tartan suits jumped out, looking for all the world like a Caledonian Grateful Dead tribute band. One of the men shouted across to the *jeu de balles* players for directions. The hairy troop were going to Aubechies too. Only they *were* the special event.

Aubechies is a reconstructed Iron Age settlement. Once you had got through the gift shop and walked up a narrow tree-lined path you found yourself in a hamlet of thatch and timber buildings. There were homes, barns and out-houses, animal pens, authentic dung heaps and the heavy smell of woodsmoke. Celtic re-enactors like the ones we'd seen in Blicquy, with drooping moustaches, pony-tails and blue tribal insignia etched on their biceps and forearms, hammered away at anvils, pumped bellows, chopped timber and scraped animal hides. Coach-loads of rotund Belgian pensioners rumbled up and down between the soot-stained houses and exclaimed with relief when they discovered a large Celtic pavement café doing a busy trade in Iron Age crêpes and coffee.

Beyond the outside tables of the café, wild boar rooted and wallowed in a muddy sty. 'THESE ARE DANGEROUS ANIMALS' a sign above them instructed severely. 'DO NOT ATTEMPT TO TOUCH THEM.' The word 'NOT' was underlined twice. A pair of burly men in houndstooth blazers, black slacks and loafers, the uniform of the bourgeois Belgian weekender, were leaning over the fence directly beneath the sign scratching the ears of a large, bristle-haired sow.

We circled the settlement, popping into a house every once in a while and being regaled with details of Celtic building, bread-making and bee-keeping skills by men and women in muted plaids to whom the Celts represented a bygone Golden Age, when there was still a spirit of community, everyone knew his or her place and you could leave your back door open when you nipped round to your neighbours to borrow a cup of woad. The Belgians were keen on their Iron Age roots. Their hairy Celtic forebears, the Belgae, had ruled a kingdom that stretched from the North Sea over to Switzerland. They were noted throughout Europe for their ferocity in combat, brilliant horsemanship and the high opinion they had of themselves (*Belgae* means 'The Boasters'). It's easy to see how modern Belgians, noted throughout Europe for chocolate, lace and being a bit on the dull side, might be seduced. But could the Belgae really have been happy? Admittedly, inside the houses at Aubechies it was dark enough to gladden the heart of any houseproud Belgian, but I think the lack of fringes and tassels on the furniture must have worn them down eventually.

Some way beyond the Celtic village was a Roman temple. Compared to the village it was relatively free of visitors. The Romans have fallen out of favour these days, while Celticism is big again, and not just in Belgium. I suppose the Celts are simply more romantic and in tune with the spirit of our age. Nowadays people prefer to imagine themselves as mystical, musical hunter-gatherers with a deep understanding of nature rather than order-conscious empire-builders with a deep understanding of sewage systems. I had some sympathy with the Romans here, if only because the English seemed to have taken over their role of dull but disciplined modernists in the minds of many Europeans.

A few weeks earlier I had found myself embroiled in a peculiar argument with the lugubrious heron-like proprietor of a record shop in Oudenaarde, which seemed to me to have been sparked by just such a prejudice. I had gone into the shop because I had seen a tape of a young folk musician, Eliza Carthy, in the window. When I asked about it, the man said, 'It is good. I like Irish music very much.'

'She's English,' I said. The man shook his head. 'I don't think so,' he replied with the peevish finality of Telly Savalas dismissing a Brylcreem salesman. 'I'm sorry,' I said, 'but she is. She's from Yorkshire. She lives in Whitby.'

While resolutely refusing to acknowledge that there could be any substance to my fanciful notion of an indigenous English folk musician, the record-shop man attempted a diplomatic side-step. 'Her music is, I think, Irish,' he said.

I wasn't letting him off the hook so easily, however. 'No,' I said, 'her music is English. Look, I've got nothing against Irish music and I'm sure Eliza Carthy hasn't either, but she makes a point of playing English music because she is herself English,' and with a cry of glee I spotted something on the cassette case that bore out my argument. 'See?' I said, brandishing it at the man. 'It says here, "All the songs are English except for 'Bonaparte's Retreat'." Do you see that?'

The man studied the gatefold for a moment. 'Her name is Irish,' he said eventually.

There was a stall beside the Roman Temple selling drinks with Latin names. 'I wonder what *marcellis* is?' I said to Catherine. 'Sort of an aperitif in the vermouth style,' a clipped English voice coming from behind us said. We turned to find a bearded man dressed in Romano-British garb of tunic and trousers. A shepherd's plaid shawl was fastened to his shoulder with an elaborate bronze brooch. 'Not bad stuff, actually,' the Romano-Briton said. 'Though not a patch on the Celtic beer. Now that's super. Made to an ancient recipe, apparently. Hopped up with all kinds of wonderful stuff.'

'Apple,' I said, 'bay leaves, green peppercorns, lemon balm, cumin, juniper, coriander, ginger and lemon balm.' I had been reading about the Celtic beer, Cervesia, in one of the leaflets we had been given at Dupont. Cervesia might have had the authentic pre-Christian taste, but it had been brewed by a Walloon with a mobile phone and a passion for Tony Adams.

The Romano-Briton sensibly ignored this piece of factual one-upmanship. 'Are you staying for the feasting?' he asked. 'What time does it start?' wondered Catherine, who is always up for a bit of feasting. 'Oh, later on,' the man said, then, dropping his voice to a low whisper that would have sent a shiver down the spine of Peter Cushing, he added, 'after we burn the Wicker Man.'

In the end we didn't stay for the feasting. We went back to the café and had a couple of bottles of Cervesia, after which I tried to persuade Catherine that we should begin a 'The Wicker Man Is Innocent' campaign. We had by this time checked out the bloke in question. He was strapped to a stake near the entrance to the settlement surrounded by bundles of kindling. The Wicker Man was about ten feet tall, but he didn't look that heavy. I reckoned that if Catherine created a diversion by dancing naked on a table, with a bit of luck I could have cut his bonds and carried him away to safety without too much bother. I could picture us hurtling across the rolling plains of Hainaut towards a blood-red sunset, the Wicker Man tied to the roof-rack of the 205, hordes of axe-waving re-enactors and bulging, feast-deprived Belgian OAPs in maddened pursuit.

'Just how strong is that Celtic beer?' Catherine said when I had finished. It was only 6.4 per cent, but I think the juniper might have got to me a bit.

Back at the flat in the Pays des Collines, the farmer himself came up to meet us. He didn't look much like the farmers I am used to. He had long white locks, a neatly clipped beard and a raffish cravat. If they ever produce a French-language version of *Doctor Who* he would be ideal for the title role.

'Enchanted! Marvellous!' the farmer gushed charmingly, clasping our hands. 'My wife, I trust, has explained about the toilet? It is connected to a septic tank. You must not flush anything else down it, you understand. Nothing else. No . . . no . . .' He searched for something likely, but unembarrassing. We waited for what seemed like a long time. Finally the farmer said, 'Nuts.'

The following day we went for a walk. We hiked up a nearby hill, past copses of deciduous trees and ramshackle farms with signs advertising potatoes, goats' cheese and chickens for sale. In the buttercup-speckled meadows there were Belgian Blue cattle – *le Bleu-Blanc* as they were known in Wallonia. Large beasts with bulbous buttocks, the pink flesh showing through their fine white fur gave them a Rubenesque glow.

It was a bright day, but nobody was about. That was one of the differences between Wallonia and Flanders. On any but the most inclement days the Flemish would be out busying themselves. They were fanatical tenders and tidiers. It was something they shared in common with their linguistic cousins the Dutch. When my friend Steve was living in Maastricht, there was supposed to have been a major outbreak of mindless violence one Saturday night in the main square. When he went down there on the Sunday morning he could find no evidence of it. 'I didn't really expect to,' he said. 'In Holland even the hooligans take their debris home with them.'

The same sensibility existed in Flanders. Hedges were clipped, borders were weeded, front-door steps were polished. If you drove out early in the morning it was not uncommon to see Flemish women sweeping the road in front of their houses. They stopped at the dashed white line. In Viane we saw a woman with her right leg in plaster half-way up a twenty-foot ladder scrubbing the metal shutters on her bedroom windows. And once from a train window I am sure I saw a farming family out in the fields near Kortemark dusting the leaves of some scruffy leeks.

In Wallonia people were a bit more relaxed. It wasn't that they weren't house-proud, it was just that you got the impression the French-speakers might have regarded a broken limb as a reasonable excuse for grubby shutters.

Catherine and I strolled on a bit and then stopped at a fork in the road. There was a spring nearby. A laminated sign was nailed to a post next to the spring, declaring the water drinkable and giving a great list of data about its chemical and mineral content. As we studied it and wondered who would have gone to all the bother of placing it there, a four-wheel-drive flashed past, tooting. It was *Monsieur* from the farm.

When the farmer had first made his remark about not flushing nuts down the lavatory I had assumed that in his embarrassment he had simply chosen the wrong word. The more I replayed the scene, however, the less likely that seemed. *Monsieur* hadn't simply blurted out the word 'nuts', he had considered it very carefully first. He had weighed the situation up.

We in Britain have countless pieces of obscure received wisdom about foreigners. You must never blow your nose in front of the Japanese; Turks like fat women; burping after a meal is good manners among the Arabs. Some of these may be true, some untrue and some a mix of fact and fiction, but since we have these views of other countries it seems reasonable to assume that other countries have similarly arcane notions about us.

As a schoolboy I had gone to stay with a family in Norway. The Norwegians lived on a farm overlooking a lake. They had a barn in which they smoked the fish the father caught through a hole in the ice. On my first morning I went down to breakfast. The family – mother, father, grandmother and four children – were gathered around the kitchen table. They greeted me warmly. We started chatting. When I asked for the teapot, however, the gathering fell silent. I poured a cup of tea and reached for the milk jug. As the first drop of milk hit the steaming tea the family burst into laughter. A round of applause followed. When they had recovered sufficiently from their merriment, the father wheezed, 'We had heard it said that the English did this, but we did not believe it!' and the assembly cracked up again. They lived high in the mountains and the Scandinavian winters are long.

Was it possible that among Belgians some similar half-believed truths about the English existed? Was the prevailing assessment of Anglo-Saxons that we are a well-organised, unmusical people with the besetting vice of blocking U-bends with our discarded filberts? Was the Walloon equivalent of 'He's got a kangaroo loose in his attic' the phrase 'He's as nutty as an English toilet'? Do Flemish schoolkids call conkers 'London drain-stuffers'? If this is indeed a Belgian opinion of the British, you may think it a wild and erroneous one. Perhaps you would be right. But it would certainly explain what happens to all those bowls of brazils, hazels and walnuts you see on people's sideboards at Christmas, wouldn't it? Because, let's be honest, nobody actually eats them.

Nine

The train from Tongeren to Liège rumbled through the farming land of the Haspengouw, past rolling wheat fields and teams of toiling Sikhs crouching amid the rows of strawberry plants. Near Glons we crossed yet another linguistic border and the Haspengouw became the Hesbaye. At Liers there was a café with the name of the owners stretched across the windows like the sun-strip on a Ford Cortina; at Milmort the station yard was dominated by a permanent obstacle course of jumps and rope swings and rows of tyres built for . . . who? Local children? Waiting passengers? Railway porters? After Milmort tall water-towers and bulky relay stations began to appear, then the first of the conical slag-heaps with their spiny covering of tiny pine trees. Soon the train was running parallel to the river Meuse and we were into the industrial dereliction of Liège itself, with its redundant blast furnaces and unattended coal quays. Even the air had a gritty texture. The hop town of Poperinge was twinned with Hythe in Kent. Liège looked like it had a suicide pact with Consett.

The first and only time I'd been to Liège before was on a Sunday morning in mid-April. The station had been deserted, the only sign of human life a crackling recording of popular piano classics coming over the platform tannoy. Steve and I had come to see the start of Wallonia's biggest bicycle race, Liège–Bastogne–Liège, organised by the singularly titled Royal Cyclist's Pesant Club Liègois.

Outside the station several locals, including the man in the tourist office, a couple of tram-drivers and a road-sweeper, told us to go to the Opera House, but the race wasn't there. We stood around for a while until a Gewiss team car flashed past. We attempted to follow it and failed. Another team car and half a dozen riders, this time from the Mercatone Uno squad, whizzed past at the top of the street we'd just left. They were heading east. We marched off in pursuit. A combined bunch of cyclists from Lotto and Mapei-GB suddenly appeared round a corner and headed towards us going south. And so it went on. After four or five more futile attempts to chase speeding cyclists Steve and I realised we were no longer alone. We had been joined by a couple of Germans, a Dutch father and his two sons, a quartet of Italians and a rather forlorn Australian, all looking for the start line and plainly fooled by what must have appeared to them our decisive manoeuvring. Together our multi-national force continued to stride determinedly but hopelessly about like a troop from some medieval pageant society re-creating the Peasants' Crusade. Eventually the others disappeared, possibly raped and murdered by unscrupulous Venetians, and Steve and I gave up on the race altogether and went to get some breakfast instead.

We found a bakery, bought armfuls of provender and took our supplies to a little public garden on the Rue Fabry. The sun was shining, the day was warm, Liège was silent except for the distant peal of church bells and a throstle warbling his love song amid the blushing bower of a nearby cherry tree. We sat down on a bench and opened our bags of goodies.

Smells of fresh pastry, vanilla and cocoa filled the air. No sooner had we finished subconsciously congratulating ourselves on the quality of our existence than a white Citroën appeared and stopped ten yards away. The passenger door swung open and a Groenendael shepherd dog jumped out and squatted down without so much as a preparatory sniff. Thirty seconds later and several kilos lighter, the shaggy black dog jumped back in the car which promptly drove off.

Steve and I looked at one another. Before we could utter even the most perfunctory *ugh*, however, a Fiat pulled over on the opposite side of the road and exactly the same scene was played out, this time featuring a white standard poodle in the starring role. The action was repeated again and again, with Dobermanns, wire fox terriers, Alsatians and once with a Borzoi which sprang agilely from a Renault Clio with French number-plates. Soon the garden, pristine when we arrived save for a light beading of dew, was dotted all around with little doggy slag-heaps. If you think this sounds totally disgusting, then just imagine how much more disgusting it would have been if you were eating a warm *pain au chocolat*, as I was at the time.

On that visit to Liège I'd alighted at the Gare de Guillemins. For deeply unsentimental reasons this time I got off at the Palais station, right in the heart of the city. The day was hot (too hot for Catherine and Maisie, who had rejected the decaying industrial heart of Wallonia in favour of a swimming-pool in the Limburg countryside and unlimited access to ice cream) and I walked along to the Palais des Prince Evêques, the Palace of the Prince Bishops. In what may well have been a two-fingered socialist gesture to their former rulers, the Liègois had chosen to decorate the massive open area in front of the imposing seventeenth-century palace with a collection of bus and tram stops and a large car-park. The last of the Prince Bishops was expelled from Liège by French

194

revolutionaries. If they ever do make a return I think they'll probably look for a residence with a better view from the front windows, though they're unlikely to find one that is quite so convenient for Marks & Spencer.

The Prince Bishops had held both religious and secular power in Liège from around AD 900 until the arrival of the spirit of equality, liberty and fraternity in 1794. During that time they had maintained Liège's independence from the Burgundians, the Spanish and the Austrians, instilling in the locals along the way the strong sense of their unique regional identity which persists to this day.

The upheavals in Paris brought out the radical side of the Liègois. The city was the first outside France to declare itself in support of the Revolution, and ever since then Liège has been seen as a bastion of liberal, left-wing and at times simply bloody-minded militancy. It was the citizens of Liège, for example, who, under the leadership of the inspirational 'Peg-Leg Charlier' Rogier marched west to support Brussels after the 1830 rebellion against the Dutch. An independent Belgium was the consequence. It was Liège too that was the centre of unrest over working conditions that sparked riots in 1886 in which two dozen protesters were shot by the Belgian army, and at the forefront of the general strike in 1893 that resulted in the adoption of universal male suffrage. Between 1945 and 1950 it was the socialists and communists of Liège who were central in the campaign that brought about the abdication of King Leopold III and almost split Belgium in half in the process. In 1961 a series of violent clashes between demonstrators and police around the city presaged reforms that led to greater autonomy for both Wallonia and Flanders.

The Liègois were as proud of their defiance as they were of their legendary *joie de vivre*. However, one man's free-spirited stander-up for human rights is another man's bone-idle troublemaker, and perceptions of the citizens of Liège in

195

other parts of Belgium, particularly the Flemish-speaking parts, were not always entirely positive. Feckless and awkward were two frequently applied adjectives. On top of which usually came allegations of shady dealing among the local socialist politicians. Comparisons between countries are usually misleading and often pointless, but in this case it's probably not too far-fetched to say that the Liègois is the Belgian Scouser.

Inside the Museum of Wallonian Life it was dead. I was the only visitor, perhaps because I was the one person persistent enough to find the door in among all the scaffolding and builders' mess. This was a perennial problem in Belgium. Practically everywhere seemed to be in the middle of an overhaul. In Tournai the entire Grande Place had been dug up; in Veurne the streets leading into the market-place had been reduced to gullies of sand and mud; and in Ghent the Graslei was a heap of cobbles. It was as if Belgium was desperately dolling itself up in preparation for a visit from some wealthy in-laws who just might be thinking of leaving it something in their will. (The situation is exacerbated by a system which guarantees federal parity when it comes to public works. If 100 miles of road is re-surfaced in Flanders, then 100 miles of road must also be re-surfaced in Wallonia, whether it needs doing or not.)

After some confusion over whether the Museum of Wallonian Life closed for lunch – a sign on the front door said it did, but the hours had been scribbled out with a biro – I forced my way in. Behind the ticket counter was a pair of legs and a length of dark skirt. I gathered together some tatters of French and then coughed politely. The body and head that belonged to the bunting sticks dropped into view from behind a row of high shelving that formed a partition wall separating the gift shop and ticket booth from the entrance hall. The head, which had curly dark hair and a slightly stern countenance, murmured an apology while the legs stepped down off the hidden chair. 'Good day,' I said after what I considered a decent interval. 'It is possible for me I entering? But perhaps I think you are to be hours of lunch for closing?' That at least is what I imagined I said. In reality it may have been total gibberish.

The woman, who clearly had huge reservoirs of sang-froid, smiled pleasantly at my words and assented. To what exactly I wasn't altogether sure, so I bought a ticket and went in.

The Musée de la Vie Wallonie is housed inside an old Minorite monastery, and every once in a while as I strolled around it I caught a glimpse of the cloisters and sunlit courtyard through one of the narrow windows. Museum staff were sitting out eating sandwiches and enjoying the warmth. I was glad to see them because the museum itself was a bit sinister. In part this was because a large chunk of the exhibition was taken up with Wallonian folklore, and much of Wallonian folklore involved phantasmagoria. Far from regarding this as something unhealthy that was best not mentioned, the Walloons appeared rather proud of it all. Indeed, the whole of Belgium seems to rejoice in this darker aspect of its past: there are witches' festivals in Nieuwpoort and Beselare; in Ellezelles there is a community mural on the gable end of a house devoted to local witchcraft; while practically every product you buy from the Ardennes seems to feature pixies, gnomes or broomsticks somewhere on the label.

The necromancy was one factor. Mainly, though, the creepy atmosphere in the museum was down to the extensive collection of marionettes. Puppet theatre is popular in Brussels and perhaps even more so in Liège. Hundreds of dolls from the Imperial Royal Old Theatre and the museum's own puppet troupe were lined up in ranks along one wall in one of the more shadowy parts of the second floor. Sooty or Scott Tracy they were not.

About three feet tall and dressed in an array of costumes

that ranged from medieval armour to business suits, they had floridly painted faces and psychotic, staring eyes. Many smiled, mockingly it seemed to me, revealing stained yellow teeth. Something about the marionettes' gleeful menace put me in mind of the notorious 1960s children's TV programme, *The Singing Ringing Tree*, which was imported by the BBC from somewhere in *Mitteleuropa* apparently with the express intention of giving my entire generation nightmares for the rest of our lives.

Although I couldn't see him, I guessed that somewhere in this ghastly legion was the figure of Tchantchès, hero of Liège puppet drama and the unofficial patron saint of the city. As well as being rebellious, good-hearted and irrepressible, Tchantchès (Walloon for Francis) is said to enjoy getting drunk and head-butting people. He is, apparently, the archetypal Liègois. Which is hardly a comfort to the visitor.

I walked past the puppets slowly, fixing them with a steely glare because I had a suspicion they could scent fear, but then a gust of wind from an open window set their wooden limbs clacking together and I bolted into a side room devoted to capital punishment. I never thought I'd be relieved to see a guillotine.

Using a route that didn't involve going back past the puppets – I'm sure I heard them sniggering – I made my way to the exit. In one of the network of bustling streets just off the admirably named Rue Saucy, I bought some chips and a jumbo sausage that must have used up practically the whole elephant. My shaken morale was bolstered by the sight of a gents' outfitters with a large sign in the window announcing 'Upstairs! 500 pants!'

With its coal and steel and notoriously corrupt ruling socialist party, Liège has a pleasantly familiar feel to anyone who, like me, has spent most of their life on the fringes of County Durham. The similarity between the two communities was further reinforced in the impressive Museum of Wallonian Art. The gallery is designed rather like a helter-skelter. You take a lift to the top and gradually descend through a chronologically arranged collection of paintings that takes you from Henri Blés to Paul Delvaux in a slightly dizzying spiral.

Somewhere around 1920, I stumbled into a huddle of elderly cleaning women sitting under a big, misty-green Albert Raty canvas of the Ardennes. All of them were smoking and one had a bare foot resting on a red plastic mop bucket. She was plainly relating the finer points of a recent operation on an in-growing toenail to an appreciative audience. You didn't need to speak French to know what she was saying. 'It was that Dr Delcour. He said to me, he said, "Mrs Closson," he said, "in my forty years in medicine I have never, I *have never* seen pus like it! Green it was!" He's very good, Dr Delcour. Very good. Mind you, I wouldn't let that Dr Marnix fella touch me. Our Clothilde's Frank went under him for his gall-bladder and now he's up and down at night like a bride's nightie. He was lucky, mind. Round our way they call that Marnix "The Widow Maker". Is he, Astrid? Your Claude? When? Well, I expect it'll go all right, honey. I mean, he can't kill 'em all, can he, or he'd get struck off.' For the only time on the entire trip I was momentarily overwhelmed with homesickness.

I walked along Rue Léopold, birthplace of Liège's most famous son, Georges Simenon, across the Pont des Arches and on to the Outremeuse, legendary stamping-ground of the dreaded Tchantchès. A densely populated island formed by a fork in the river, this was once the district of the tanners and weavers. It is sometimes referred to as the Free Republic of Outremeuse, and holds a place in the mythology of Liège similar to that which – and here comes the third in the series of those comparisons between countries I said were misleading and pointless a few pages back (I'm nothing if not

199

inconsistent) – the East End does in London, much of it born of a similar mix of sentimentality and the binding ties of hardship, though at least the inhabitants of the Outremeuse have never suffered the indignity of being impersonated by Dick van Dyke.

I wandered along the narrow streets, past the small museum devoted to the composer André-Modeste Grétry. Born in the Outremeuse in 1741, Grétry is usually described as 'the father of comic opera'. Having once sat through a village amateur dramatic society production of *The Merry Widow*, a personal view is that it's a shame he didn't take precautions.

Georges Simenon may have been born in central Liège, but he spent most of his childhood living in the crowded streets of the Outremeuse. His family – insurance salesman father Désiré, with his waxed moustache and Tintin quiff; snobbish mother Henriette and obtuse younger brother Christian – moved house fairly regularly but never to anywhere more than a few hundred yards from the Rue Puits-en-Sock where Simenon's paternal grandfather had owned a hat shop.

Considering he was a man of letters, numbers feature an awful lot in most summaries of Simenon's career. He was born in 1903, and in a fifty-one-year period stretching from 1921 to 1972 wrote 193 novels in his own name, including 76 devoted to his most famous creation, Inspector Maigret, and at least two hundred others under, probably, eighteen pseudonyms. On top of this he also knocked out twenty-five volumes of autobiography, three volumes of collected journalism, four collections of short stories and more than a thousand short stories which were never collected. His books have been translated into eighty-seven languages and enjoyed total global sales in excess of 500 million. His novels have been committed to celluloid on 55 occasions while 279 have been dramatised for television.

Simenon wrote for six hours a day, during which time he rattled off ten thousand words, smoked six pipes and drank two bottles of good claret. He confined himself to a written vocabulary of two thousand words. Most of his books were completed in eleven days (thirteen if you count the two days he spent thinking about them before starting to write). He was nicknamed 'The Steamship Novelist' by literary critics and rarely wrote less than half a dozen books per year. In his most productive phase, during the late 1920s, this figure rose to a peak of forty-four.

Simenon left Liège for Paris when he was nineteen. He spent a couple of years living on a sailing boat, moved house thirty-three times, lived in five different countries and visited over a hundred more. He married twice and had four children. At the height of his fame he occupied a thirty-room mansion on the shores of Lake Geneva, where he employed eleven servants. He died in Lausanne in 1989, aged eighty-six.

In the blizzard of figures that blows around the life of Simenon, the one which sticks most often in people's minds is ten thousand. This is the number of women with whom he claimed to have had sex. He made this announcement during an interview with Federico Fellini in 1977, apparently prompted by the Italian film director's remark that he always made love wearing a brassiere.

Simenon did not name this figure off the top of his head; he said he had calculated it mathematically. The figures of the case are this: Simenon lost his virginity at the age of thirteen and made his calculation when he was seventy-three; ten thousand women in sixty years works out at roughly 166 per annum, or slightly over three a week. Later on, his second wife, Denyse, ridiculed her husband's suggestion, saying Simenon was prone to exaggeration on these matters and that the actual total was probably no more than 1,200. Which really cut him down to size.

Whichever figure comes nearest the truth, it is certainly entirely appropriate that Simenon once lived at a house in Arizona named 'Stud Barn', and that the administrator of the Centre d'Études Georges Simenon at the University of Liège should at one time have been a Madame Swings.

With all the impressive statistics, it is easy to forget the quality of much of Simenon's work, which is very high indeed. Although he had begun life as a writer of pulp fiction and continued to knock out Maigret books (which the novelist himself deemed 'semi-literary') for largely commercial reasons up until 1972, his literary reputation rests on a series of more serious novels, his *romans durs*, perhaps the best known of which nowadays is *The Engagement of M. Hire*, filmed simply as *M. Hire* in 1989. These works drew enormous praise from the likes of Colette, François Mauriac and T. S. Eliot, and led André Gide to describe Simenon as 'the greatest French novelist of the century'. As well as an indication of the high regard in which Simenon was held by the literary elite, Gide's remark also serves to illustrate why there appear to be so few famous Belgians: if the Belgian is a Flemish-speaker everyone believes them to be Dutch, if they are Francophone people think of them as French. Maurice Maeterlinck, for example, is routinely described in English-language surveys of European writers as a 'Belgian-born French dramatist', despite the fact that he didn't actually move to France until he was thirty-six. Nor was it such a surprise to hear the actor Gene Wilder telling Sue Lawley of his love of all things French on *Desert Island Discs* and then going on to pick a record by Jacques Brel to remind him of Paris. Simenon suffers similarly routine and unjustified relocation.

I don't think he would have altogether approved, for although Simenon's best-known character, Maigret, is from the Loire, the author himself was truly Belgian: Flemish on his mother's side, Walloon on his father's. Simenon was well aware of the importance of place and background in forming a writer. He once said, 'All of the feelings and impressions we retain in later life have been collected by our seventeenth or, at latest, eighteenth year.' Simenon spent those first eighteen years in Belgium. Though the bulk of his work is set in France it is, as Patrick Marnham observes in his excellent biography, *The Man Who Wasn't Maigret*, a France observed from the outside, a foreigner's view of the country. The world may have come to regard Simenon as French, but the author himself never did.

The jumbled streets of the Outremeuse, with their red-brick terraces and single-room corner bars and cafés, could be anywhere in Belgium or northern France. They have one distinctive feature, however: the *potales*, little niches in the walls containing figurines of the Madonna. At certain times of the year these tiny sculptures of the Virgin are honoured with gifts and flowers. In the Museum of Wallonian Life there had been photos of things called 'nail oaks', special trees to which the sick would attach items of clothing in the hope of a cure. This old pagan tradition seemed to live on in the Outremeuse in a form more acceptable to the Church. At one time I might have taken a traditional British view of this and categorised it rather sniffily as the colourful yet backward behaviour of a superstitious people. That was before I saw Northumbrians laying bouquets down before a poster of the late Princess of Wales in the window of our local department store.

On the way back to the station I stopped in at a bar that stocked 1,000 Belgian beers. Predictably, the one I was after, Fantôme, was temporarily out of stock. Fantôme is made at a tiny brewery in Luxembourg province. It is flavoured with wild herbs. Every beer writer who has ever sampled it has raved. I had been trying to get hold of it for years without success, and was beginning to lose hope. I suppose at least

Fantôme lived up to its name: only a few people had ever seen it and you suspected many of them were pissed at the time.

When I got back to Tongeren I had an hour to kill before my bus, so I walked up to the main square and sat under a red-and-white umbrella outside a café drinking draught kriek and marvelling at the bronze statue of Ambiorix. Ambiorix was the king of the Eburons, a tribe of Gauls who attacked and massacred the Roman legions just outside the town in 54 BC. Whoever had made the statue had attempted to capture the savage nobility of the man, but had unfortunately ended up instead with a vague *Carry On* campness. The sculpted Ambiorix has a drooping Gaulish moustache, is wearing what can only be described as bondage sandals, and has the fingertips of his left hand pressed to his chest in a gesture that must surely presage a battle cry of 'Ooooh, get her in the fancy mauve toga'.

It was about six o'clock and Tongeren was slipping slowly into another quiet mid-week evening. Opposite the tourist information office half a dozen teenage boys were complying with the little-known Belgian by-law which makes it statutory for every Flemish town above a certain size to have a group of youths who take turns to aimlessly ride a moped up and down its main shopping area for a minimum of two hours per day. Last-minute shoppers and businessmen finishing work strolled past. Compared to the Liègois the citizens of Tongeren looked prosperous, conservative and highly respectable. It was hard to believe the two places were no more than twenty miles apart.

That evening Catherine and I had dinner with a Flemish friend. I told her about another incident that had occurred the first time I had been in Liège. When Steve and I had gone back to the station we had got on a train to take us down to Trois Ponts, to see some of the bike race we'd so comprehensively missed. As we sat waiting for the engine to judder into life, a troop of twenty or so boy scouts invaded the carriage. They were dressed in full regalia, and all wore broad-brimmed Baden-Powell hats that gave them the appearance of a herd of mobile, khaki mushrooms. The scouts were equipped for a major expedition. They were laden down with tents, entrenching tools, supplies and wind-breaks. The boy standing next to us had ruddy cheeks and ears like the handles on a loving cup. A frying-pan and a ladle dangled from his belt. Along the aisle one of his comrades leaned on an arm-rest, a bow-saw suspended from a strap around his shoulder. It was so big it trailed along the ground when he walked with a nerve-jangling shriek. I imagined the scouts were heading down into the deep Ardennes for a woodland camp. I was wrong. Ten minutes out of the city the train stopped in the non-descript red-brick suburb of Angleur, and the troop disembarked. I watched them disappearing off down the platform. The scout who had stood next to us strode purposefully along, the ladle and frying-pan clanging dolefully.

When I had finished my story our Flemish friend smiled, dutifully, politely. 'Perhaps you had to be there,' I said.

Later I began to suspect that our friend's reaction, or lack of it, had more to do with the fact that the incident had occurred in Wallonia. When you talk about Wallonia to the Flemish you can see their eyes glaze over. Mention a town ten miles away but across the linguistic border and they shake their heads, 'No, I don't know it.' Even big Wallonian cities are a mystery to Flemings who live half an hour's drive from them. 'I don't know,' our friend said when I made mention of some mysterious thing I had come across in Liège. 'I have never been to Liège. I have no reason to go there.'

Part of this attitude was undoubtedly down to the sheer smallness of Belgium. Inhabitants of Hasselt might not go to Liège, but they probably didn't make the hour's drive to

Antwerp very often either. The smaller a place is, the less it seems to encourage travel in its inhabitants. The Flemish in particular are notoriously parochial. It used to be said that a Fleming loved only what he could see from the local clock-tower – though in places as flat as the Waasland this might not be quite as small an area as you may imagine.

The narrowing of horizons is tied in too with opportunity. People in Montana will drive three hundred miles to see a concert, in Northumberland they will drive sixty miles, in London they can hardly bring themselves to cross the river.

The visitor to Belgium can, using the excellent rail net-work, quite happily spend a Saturday evening having an aperitif in Mechelen, dinner in Antwerp, a nightcap in Ghent and still be back in his or her Brussels hotel room in time to watch *Match of the Day*. But would you do the same thing if you were Belgian? Probably not. The range of choice (restaurants, cafés, cities, towns, villages) would be bewildering. Better to confine yourself to your local area and avoid the headache. And that is what the Belgians do. Georges Simenon used to tell the story of how his father had once gone on a day-trip with a friend from Liège to the town of Limbourg, ten miles or so to the south. All the time his father was away on his jaunt, Madame Simenon made Georges and Christien pray to God for his safe return. 'It was as if he had left for the Moon,' the well-travelled Simenon noted drily.

That was some of it, at least. Another part of the prejudice was the language divide. The Flemings still smarted over the years of Francophone hegemony and the snooty bullying which often went with it. Arguing against the need for a uni-versity in which Flemish was spoken, an MP named Amelot illustrated the point admirably: 'Science is only for the few, instruction the right only of the elite,' he observed. Plainly those who spoke Flemish fitted into neither category.

The difference between the two factions goes way beyond

language, however. Politics plays a big part too. Belgium's heavy industry was originally located mainly in Wallonia. Though there were the coalfields around the Limburg city of Genk, there was no equivalent in Flanders of the Pays Noir or the Borinage. The coal and steel workers of these areas were, as everywhere else in Europe, predominantly socialist. In a deeply Catholic country such as Belgium this had an added significance. The socialists were Catholics but they believed that the Church and the state were separate entities. As a result, the influence of Catholicism was less obvious in Wallonia.

In the village of Olloy in the Viroin valley, for example, Catherine and I came across a large brick-and-stone church. It was derelict. The stained-glass windows were smashed, the door was padlocked and a goat with a body like a sack of spanners was cropping grass among the gravestones. It was impossible to imagine such a thing in the more conservative and traditional Flanders (as indeed it was the urchins in their tin-roofed cottage). Here the Church played, and continues to play, an important part in government.

Once Catholic doctrine ceased to determine the agenda of the major Walloon parties, the political divergence between French- and Flemish-speakers grew wider and wider. The situation was exacerbated by the unenlightened attitude taken by the Catholic Party, which governed Belgium from 1884 until 1914. Social reform was low on their agenda. In 1910 an extensive sociological survey carried out by Seebohm Rowntree reached the conclusion that 'there is little doubt that the proportion of Belgian workmen who are adequately fed is much smaller than in Britain'. This should, I think, be taken as a black mark against Belgium rather than a ringing endorsement of our own country.

Combined with the campaigns of Flemish nationalists, this produced a result which was singularly Belgian. On the one hand the French language was denounced by Flemish leftists as the tongue of the oppressive middle-class elite; on the other it was roundly criticised by Flemish conservatives as the speech of Godless Bolshevism. Inevitably, trouble between north and south flared periodically, but things reached their nadir during the post-war abdication crisis.

When Leopold III had succeeded his father, Albert I, in 1934, he had been a popular figure. Aristocratically hand-some, Leopold had further endeared himself to his subjects by marrying the beautiful Princess Astrid of Sweden. 'The Snow Princess', as Astrid was known, was a glamorous royal figure, a creature of the society pages and gossip columns. In many ways Queen Astrid prefigured Grace Kelly and Diana Spencer. Like those women Astrid too would die in a car crash. In her case the blame for the accident would always be whispered to be the wild if distinctly Belgian driving habits of her husband. That was in 1935. From then on Leopold's for-tunes changed dramatically.

Always an autocrat, Leopold began to quarrel publicly with his government during the build-up to the Second World War. When Germany invaded in 1940, Belgian resistance col-lapsed dramatically along with that of the other Allies. As it became obvious that the situation was beyond repair, senior Belgian politicians decamped to France and then London to set up what was to become the Belgian Government in Exile. Despite the entreaties of Prime Minister Hubert Pierlot and Foreign Minister Paul Spaak, as well as King George VI, Leopold refused to join them. He was Commander-in-Chief of the Belgian armed forces, he told Pierlot, and felt that to desert his men would be cowardly and immoral.

Unfortunately Leopold was not simply an army officer, he was also the Head of State. And he would remain so through-out the Nazi occupation – years spent, in the main, under a rather relaxed house arrest in the royal palace at Laeken. Just as there would be now, many colourful theories were advanced for Leopold's actions, perhaps the liveliest of which was that he had actually died in the accident alongside Astrid and been replaced by a Nazi imposter named Oldendorff.

What Leopold's motivation was is hard to fathom. Was it an act of principle, or was he hedging his bets? Was he hoping that when Britain finally fell, the Nazis would allow him to rule again, perhaps with the total power Belgium's constitution had previously denied him? Or was his sole concern that someone of authority should remain in Belgium to represent the people in dealings with their conquerors? No one can be sure, but the certainty is that Leopold's decision to remarry in 1941 was a public-relations disaster. A situation hardly helped by the fact that the ceremony was carried out secretly and the news only made public three months later because Leopold's new wife, Liliane Baels, was pregnant.

In the years that followed the Allied victory Leopold's actions during the war would be the dominant issue in Belgian politics. It was a time of upheaval, with governments elected and dismissed with alarming rapidity, none able to resolve the question of whether Leopold should be allowed to rule again or not.

The King waited it out in Switzerland. Finally, in 1950, a referendum was held. After much debate it was agreed that a 55 per cent vote in Leopold's favour would see the monarch's return. Less than that and either a successor would be appointed or a republic declared.

The result was just about the worst possible for all concerned. Leopold got 57.68 per cent of the vote. While the King took this as a mandate, not everyone was convinced. Particularly since the split in the country was so marked. In Flanders, where the Church's backing for Leopold had proved crucial, the pro vote was 72 per cent, but in Wallonia it was only 42 per cent and in Brussels 47 per cent.

Leopold, belligerent as ever, ignored all entreaties and prepared to return to Laeken. As his arrival in Belgium became imminent Wallonia rebelled. Miners went on strike across the Pays Noir and the Borinage, and 80,000 workers marched on the capital and fought with police and royalists outside the gates of the palace. Oblivious, or simply not bothered, Leopold returned anyway. Four days later half a million Walloons walked out of their workplaces. Four days after that, in Liège, police fired on demonstrators, killing three people. The response was more or less immediate: 100,000 workers gathered in the industrial centres to begin a march on Brussels. Belgium was on the verge of civil war.

At last Leopold caved in. On 1 August 1950 he abdicated in favour of his son Baudouin. The crisis was averted. Wallonian militancy had overturned the results of the referendum. Rightly or wrongly, Flanders had not got what it had voted for.

I had expected the Flemish might be angry with the Walloons – for the years of linguistic harassment, the arguments with the Church and the political upheavals that at times ignored democracy. What I had not anticipated was the more or less total indifference to them. To the Flemings Wallonia seemed almost not to exist at all. It is as if in their minds all that stands between Flanders and northern France is a void. Like some disgraced member of the Politburo in an old Soviet photo, Wallonia has been air-brushed off the Flemish map of Europe.

Baudouin proved an ideal successor to his father. After the turmoil he brought peace through dullness. The one trouble-spot of his reign came in 1990, when the Belgian parliament voted to legalise abortion. Baudouin and his wife Fabiola (surely the only member of any European royal family ever to have been named after a self-adhesive, wipe-clean vinyl paper) were devout Roman Catholics. The King's conscience would not allow him to sign the new law. To avoid any confrontation he simply abdicated. For one day Belgium was a republic. The law was passed and then Baudouin was invited to re-claim his throne, which he did. In many ways it was a classic piece of Belgian politics – pragmatic almost to the point of surrealism. It was a throwback to the time in 1893 when the Catholic Party had introduced universal male suffrage, but at the same time given the propertied class extra votes, thus extending the franchise to all men without actually altering the balance of power in the slightest.

The next day I was back on the train from Tongeren to Liège. At Guillemins station I changed trains, getting the westbound express for Aachen. Soon we were chugging out through the industrial suburbs, endless brick and tarmac brightened occasionally by congregations of teenagers, the girls in orange mini-dresses and platform trainers, the boys with splashy pastel shirts buttoned up at the throat: a Meunier painting dressed by Top Shop.

At Battice the train stopped and a large, dark-suited middle-aged man with a head shaped like a half-filled bag of flour got on and sat down opposite me. He glanced at the book I was holding. 'British?' he inquired happily. I nodded and smiled. How is it that no matter where you are on the planet, if you are sitting on a train or bus reading a book about the Second World War the stranger sitting next to you will always turn out to be a German? It's uncanny.

It transpired that the German in this case wasn't actually German as such. I was heading for Eupen, the biggest settlement in the German-speaking part of Belgium, and that was where the man with the bulging jowls was from. The two German-language districts, Eupen and Sankt-Vith (along with French-speaking Malmédy, known collectively as the Cantons de l'Est – though not, presumably, by two-thirds of the natives), have a population of 70,000, the oldest part of which is probably still bewildered as to exactly what nationality they are. Up until the end of the Great War Eupen, Sankt-Vith and Malmédy were part of Germany. In 1919 they were ceded to Belgium under the Treaty of Versailles. In 1940 Hitler claimed them back again. In 1945 they were liberated by the Allies and handed over to Belgium once more.

In Cantons de l'Est terms this was not so unusual. In the previous century, for example, the districts had been part of the Prince-Bishopric of Liège, the Napoleonic department of Ourthe and Prussia; in the space of twenty years the citizens had found themselves governed from Rome, Paris and Berlin and suffered the indignity of having the name of Eupen changed to Neau. Sometimes in Belgium you got the impression that enthusiasm for European federalism was motivated as much by a quest for stability as anything else. Europe seems unlikely to change hands half a dozen times every two hundred years.

Not that the German–Belgian seemed remotely concerned by such matters. He was immensely jolly and had a mighty, robust voice. He reminded me of a time when I was a teenager and had been staying with some friends in Münster. We had gone to a midnight screening of *The Rocky Horror Picture Show*. The youth of the Nordrhein had clearly taken reports of the kind of behaviour that was expected at this event to heart, and responded with Teutonic diligence. Fishnet, stilettos and eye-liner were much in evidence, rice was thrown, dance routines were performed, but most impressively of all, the man behind us reacted to any line or phrase that tickled his fancy by laughing sonorously and then repeating it in rumbling and heavily accented English, 'Ah-row ho ho ho! Voorbitten frooots!' 'Ach-ha ha-ha! Live meents nossing to dare zort! Ha!' He was far better value than Meatloaf.

'I have not spoken English much since school,' the Belgo-German said, 'but here many things on TV and also the movies are subtitled, so if we do not speak English we still hear it often. I have been also to London once.' He lapsed into silence for a moment, then a smile spread across his face, gradually, like treacle spilling from a jar. 'You may explain to me the mystery of pies,' he said. He pronounced pies to rhyme with mice.

'Pardon?'

'The English pice, it is an . . . enigma!'

'Sorry?'

'My first day in London I am buying one of your pice. Here the pice is always apple or berries, you see? So I bite into your pice imagining fruit and . . . it is meat!' He chuckled at the memory of his shocked tastebuds. 'So the next time I buy an English pice I am thinking it will be meat and . . . it is fruit!' He was guffawing so heartily now I began to worry that the strain on his waistcoat might end with the buttons ricocheting about the carriage like bazooka rounds. 'It is,' he said, when he had finally wrestled control of his faculties from the tickly fingers of Mr Mirth, 'a great mystery.'

I agreed that it was, and that England is a very strange place, a place where not only are pies filled with anything that takes the maker's fancy, but where mincemeat can on occasion comprise raisins and lemon peel. I told him that once when my Czech friend had come to stay my mother had said to him, 'I thought it was a bit cold in that back bedroom so I put a bottle in your bed for you.' And my friend had gone upstairs anticipating a nightcap of scotch, or vodka, but had found instead a clammy rubber object filled with hot water.

When I thought I had paved the way sufficiently I asked the man if he felt he was German or Belgian. He smiled broadly. 'German, Flemish, Walloon, British, we are all Europeans now,' he said. It is the only time I have ever heard anyone boom diplomatically. It was a reminder, too, of the other reason so many Belgians were keen on European unity – it was a way to resolve the regional autonomy conflict to pretty much everyone's satisfaction with a minimum of fuss. Simply remove the importance of national government and, hey presto, everyone was happy!

The Belgians had been at the forefront of the formation of the EC. Indeed, it was one of Leopold III's chief tormentors, the sometime Belgian Prime Minister Paul Spaak, who had formulated the original report on which the 1957 Treaty of Rome was based. The Belgians also came up with a rather good name for the new confederation of states, Finebel. According to the Italian writer Luigi Barzini, they liked this because *bel* sounded like the French for beautiful and *fine* is the best type of cognac. Sadly it was never adopted.

'Yes,' the Belgo-German chuckled after a pause, 'we are all part of the Family of Europe.'

I managed to restrain myself from suggesting that if Europe is a family then the Germans are those cousins with the irritating habit of turning up unexpectedly and taking over everything. It would have been deeply unfair on this avuncular and positive man if I had, of course, but I was still smarting from an incident that had occurred at our hotel a couple of nights before. Catherine and I had finished our dinner and taken our coffee through to the lounge, where we had sat at a big round table. After a few minutes a forty-ish German couple had come into the sitting-room. The man, who was big, wildly bearded and generally looked like he had just got dressed after a busy afternoon in the Teutonburgerwald battering Roman legionaries, stomped across the room, glared at us, then spun on his heels and clattered back out again. His wife, who was tall and willowy and wore clothes and a facial expression that suggested she was deeply concerned about the ozone layer, eyed us. 'My husband,' she said in flat, precise English tinged neither with anger nor regret, 'had expected to use that table for his maps in order that we might plan tomorrow's expedition.' Her explanation delivered, she too turned and disappeared out of the door.

'Well!' Catherine said.

'Well!' I agreed. And up until now that had been the most waspish response either of us had managed to come up with.

Later, as I walked up Eupen's distinctly Teutonic-looking main street, I began to feel a bit nervous. It was to do with the German language. Most Flemings understood English, and I had enough vocabulary to make a fool of myself in French, but my German was very limited. I had studied German for a year when I was thirteen and for some reason only two things had stuck in my mind: the handy phrase 'The bear is brown', and that there was something about the gender of certain nouns which at the time I had found mightily hilarious, though I couldn't quite remember what (was it that 'girl' was neuter?). Apart from that I only had the German phrases which every Briton knows by heart: Good morning, Good evening, Please, Thank you and Hands up, pig-dog, quickly, quickly! This didn't seem likely to get me anywhere in Eupen, except, possibly, the local casualty unit.

I walked up to the market-place, dominated by a large cloth merchant's house which now housed the *Grenzecho*, Belgium's German-language newspaper. I had intended to visit the Municipal Museum of Eupen, but my extensive researches had somehow failed to reveal the fact that it is shut on Fridays. Much of Eupen seemed to be in sympathy. Defeated, I walked straight back to the station, stopping off to buy some bread, sliced salami and a bottle of Klosterbier from the local Eupener Bierbrauerei on the way.

The train for Liège was about to depart when the door of the carriage opened and a nun got in. She sat down in the group of seats across the aisle from mine. We bobbed a greeting to one another. When the train set off I got out my bread and salami and my beer. For some reason I was under the impression there were wall-mounted bottle-openers in Belgian railway carriages, but on closer inspection these turned out to be those metal cigarette-stubbing plates you used to see on the backs of seats on British buses. Frustrated, I made a fruitless search of my pockets for some object with which to jimmy the top off my beer.

'Monsieur?' It was the nun. She had got up from her seat and was standing in the aisle beside me. She pointed at the bottle, then to herself and held out a hand. At first I thought she was attempting to confiscate my drink. I envisaged some kind of scuffle followed by arrest and a case that would test the relative strength of Belgian national values even more profoundly than the 1950 referendum. Which way would the magistrates lean, to the man protecting his beer, or the Catholic Church? It would be a *cause célèbre*.

Before I could get any further down this avenue of thought the nun said, 'I will open for you, yes?' I handed her the bottle. The nun raised it up towards her face and for one glorious moment I thought she was going to prise the cap off with her teeth. Instead she turned and disappeared down the train. Three minutes later she came back with the opened bottle and handed it to me with a nod and a smile.

Ten

It was a warm Saturday morning and Catherine and I were sitting outside Pain Quotidien in Namur sipping little bowls of coffee and eating finger-thick brown rolls studded with fat raisins and slivers of walnut. Choral music was wafting and echoing between the four-storey houses of the street. Those new to Belgium would have been forgiven for thinking it emanated from the baroque Church of Saint-Loup opposite. In fact it came from a loudspeaker outside a nearby shop selling upmarket house plants and tall scented candles.

Every so often the musical interlude was given fresh impetus by a man on a bicycle who looped round and round the block. He was dressed in a faded pink cycling jersey and a little decorator's cap, and he was singing one of those downbeat Francophone *chansons* the meaning of which you feel you instinctively grasp. 'Now the summer of our love is ended,' the man warbled as he pedalled past, 'the swallows gone, the nights grown colder / We talk but our words have no meaning / And the flowers in your hat have wilted / Nananana-naaah nananana-naaaah . . .'

Though I had developed a liking for the smaller towns of

Flanders such as Oudenaarde and Veurne, and an abiding fondness for the province of Limburg and the city of Ghent, all in all I would say that Namur was my favourite place in Belgium. Set at the confluence of the rivers Sambre and Meuse, ringed by the thickly forested hills of the Ardennes, and overlooked by a nineteenth-century citadel, the capital of Wallonia is a pleasant place of balconied houses, waterside gardens, second-hand book and antique-dealers and shady, cobbled squares. It is not a place, admittedly, where very much appears to be happening, but it reminded me of something a friend once said about Italy. He had travelled round that country extensively over a number of years and also worked there on occasion. I asked him where he would live in Italy if he had the choice. He thought for a moment and then said, 'I suppose this will surprise you, because to tell the truth it does me rather, but if I think about it I'd probably say Bologna.'

When I asked him why, he said, 'Nothing I can really put my finger on. It's just that I imagine if you lived there you would have a good life.' And this is pretty much what I felt about Namur.

I sipped at my coffee and yawned. We had been in Belgium a couple of months now and our days had slipped into a very gentle rhythm. Meals were the governing factor. We planned our trips around restaurants, *patisseries* and cafés. I felt in doing so we were being true to our host nation. In Belgium the gap between meals is measured not in time but in distance. Catherine and I had gradually made it shorter and shorter. In Namur we were looking to crack the 200-metre barrier.

We had picked our place well. Namur is noted as the gastronomic capital of Belgium. In a country that takes its food very seriously indeed this is no mean title. Like the French city of Lyon, Namur is ideally placed to have assimilated a rich vocabulary of culinary self-expression. Its two major rivers provide trout, perch and pike, their many fast-flowing tributaries, crayfish; the rocky, wooded landscape is home to the favourite delicacy of snails (*caracole* in the local dialect – the symbol of Namur), sometimes served in a mighty *pot au feu*, but equally available, smothered in herb butter, from any of the mobile *friteries* dotted around the city's car-parks. Lamb comes from the rolling hills of southern Hainaut; beef, cream and butter from the rich pastures of Herve and the Voeren; goats' cheese from the flower-speckled meadows of the Viroin valley. In early summer there are strawberries from nearby Wepion, the most coveted in Belgium, and asparagus from the fields around Tienen to the north. In autumn there is game, including wild boar, from the Ardennes and fruit from the orchards of the Hesbaye.

Given the quality of available ingredients it is hardly surprising that the shopping streets of Namur are lined with bars, cafés, restaurants, *chocolatiers*, *confiseurs* and *traiteurs*, the air scented with the smell of apple *beignets* frying on the stalls of street vendors.

I yawned again, popped the last bit of nutty roll into my mouth and glanced across at the Church. The Church of Saint-Loup held a special place in the hearts of Belgians. The French poet Charles Baudelaire had come to the country in 1864 to escape the scandal which had engulfed him after the publication of *Les Fleurs du Mal* (Belgium's constitution, one of the most liberal in nineteenth-century Europe, guaranteed freedom of speech. The country became a favoured haunt of exiled French writers including Victor Hugo, Verlaine and Rimbaud).

In Brussels Baudelaire conceived a passionate hatred of Belgium and the Belgians. In his early months in the capital he wrote to his friend, Ancelle, that in Belgium celibacy was not a virtue since 'the sight of the Belgian female repels any

idea of pleasure'. Such outbursts failed to satiate Baudelaire's anger with the country and its 'gaping' inhabitants,
however. He decided to write a book, *Pauvre Belgique!*,
denouncing a nation in which 'the flowers have no per-
fume'. In 1867 the Frenchman came to Namur on a research
trip. While wandering around in the Church of Saint-Loup
he collapsed, unconscious. Though he was revived, he never
spoke or wrote anything ever again. A year later, back in
France at last, Baudelaire died. It might be tempting to see
this as divine intervention. Medical science, though, said
syphilis.

On the way to lunch we took a slight diversion to the Musée
Félicien Rops. Namur has produced three famous artists:
Félicien Rops, Henri Blès and, most recently, Henri Michaux,
who died in 1984. Despite being born in Namur and having a
Walloon name, Michaux had been educated in Flemish. A
fact which may explain his later experimentation with
mescalin and deep obsession with the notion that human
existence is a series of absurd and random gestures. Michaux's work is moderately disturbing and certainly not the kind
of thing you should plan to spend time with if you are nursing
a hangover. It did, however, send the Nazis into a foaming
rage of denunciation, surely a massive plus-point for any work
of art.

Rops is the only one of this trio of Namurois artists to get a
gallery all to himself. I can't help thinking this is a perverse
decision. Which, given the content of much of Rops' art, is
rather fitting.

Félicien Rops' work falls broadly into three areas: choco-
late-box landscapes (including some rather sweet pictures of
the Flemish coast with bathing huts and strolling couples);
drawings 'specially commissioned for private collectors'
(which sophisticates such as yourselves will instantly recognise as art-world slang for pornography); and scathing sati-

rical etchings the thrust of which seems to be that women are corrupting and sex is evil.

Before I looked at the dates on the pictures I had concocted a rather neat biography of Rops based on his work. I imagined him as a struggling provincial artist forced to take on work from dubious old roués ('Yes, master Rops, very neatly done. But next time you draw me a young girl getting into a rowing boat, forget about the clothes. Except, of course, for the lifebelt and the high-heel boots *snicker-snicker*'), then a member of *Les Vingts* in Paris after the Franco-Prussian War, becoming gradually disillusioned as he watches a life of debauchery taking its toll on friends such as Guy de Maupassant ('Their perfumed loins are the charnel-house of our talents, I tell you, my dear Mallarmé'), and then returning to the valley of the Meuse to rediscover the joys of nature and a simple life ('What care I for the gilded Pandoras of Montmartre when I can gaze upon the goats in the meadow?'). All of which proved to be bollocks, since Rops produced all three types of work continually throughout his life with no excuse whatsoever save presumably economic necessity. Which is a far better reason than any that I came up with.

Catherine, Maisie and I walked up rows of coloured paintings of the Meuse valley and past an etching of a scantily clad and plainly post-coital woman woozily drooling atop a cage full of children, wondering if this was really the sort of thing we ought to have brought a baby to look at (you may think I'm being a bit prudish here. If so, please bear in mind that we are talking about an artist whose work was described as 'obscene' by the De Goncourt brothers, two men who lived far less sheltered lives than myself).

Studying the exhibits (purely in the interests of research, obviously) it was hard to imagine that Rops had once contributed cartoons to *Punch*. As we proceeded down a line of drawings showing women in various states of undress doing all kinds of weird stuff (why is the portly lady in the black stockings and the carnival mask taking a pig for a walk? What exactly is the toothless crone doing with the figure of Death? Oh, I see. *That's* why she's kneeling down in front of him) I imagined the captions in that august Victorian organ: 'Buxom young Belgian lady (about to engage in the act of carnal union with a statue of Zeus): "Now that's what I call a Doric column!"'

The museum shop had a disappointingly tame selection of postcards. I had to settle for a cartoon showing two women bathing in a river. An elderly man is watching them from some nearby bushes, his furled umbrella rising from his hand at an angle of forty-five degrees in what is perhaps the least subtle phallic symbol this side of the Cerne Abbas giant.

Whatever its merits, Rops' work was highly influential in its day. The linking of eroticism and death was picked up by Belgian writers like Rodenbach and Maeterlinck and given a more melancholic twist; the macabre humour was echoed, less bawdily, in the work of James Ensor. Rops' friend Charles Baudelaire said the Walloon artist had a genius as large as the Great Pyramid of Cheops. Having been round the museum devoted to his work I can advance only three possible explanations for this: either Baudelaire had only seen pictures of the Valley of Kings and had not quite grasped the scale of things, or he was exceptionally loyal, or he was a complete and utter numbskull.

Catherine and I pottered along to the Place Saint-Aubain. The large square, dominated by the domed cathedral, was hosting *les échasseurs*. These are teams of local men whose somewhat unlikely hobby is to deck themselves out in Renaissance furbelows, climb aboard a pair of stilts and have fights with one another. Stilt-fighting takes its place among a triumvirate of unlikely Wallonian sports which also includes *jeu de balle* and attempting to decapitate a hanging goose by throwing sickles at it.

While it may look like the kind of thing invented for the local heats of *It's a Knockout* in 1974, stilt-fighting actually dates back more than five hundred years. Stilts were used in Namur from the tenth century because of the frequent flooding of the Sambre and Meuse. Over the years a rivalry had developed between the stiltmen (*échasseurs*) of the old town, the Melans, and the men of the new town on the left bank of the Sambre, the Avresses. By the 1400s fights on stilts had become so common, unruly and violent that they threatened to disrupt Namur's trade and clog up its hospitals. To ease the situation formal jousts were organised and held outside the town hall in the Place d'Armes. Apart from a brief interruption when the *échasseurs* were outlawed by French Revolutionaries, who regarded it rather pompously as 'unfitting to the gravity of the age', it has continued to this day. The Melans wear yellow and black; the Avresses red and white. These two groups are by no means Namur's most unusual body of men. That title must surely go to the Quarante Molons. This ancient club, which is also known as the Society of Liars, makes public appearances in the form of a *mirliton* orchestra. If you can picture forty Arthur Askey lookalikes dressed in pierrot costumes and playing kazoos you have pretty much got the Quarante Molons.

Les échasseurs take their sport more seriously than the Liars do their music. They kick, hack and shoulder-charge one another with a ferocity rarely seen since the retirement of Ron 'Chopper' Harris. Fifteen minutes of watching such brutal exercise and we had worked up sufficient appetite to pop into nearby Brasserie Henry for lunch.

We ate baby lobster and *crêpe suzette*. Fleets of aproned waiters whizzed about the among the potted palms; service doors whumped and thunked. Bedazzled, I went to the lavatory and ended up tipping a posh old dowager five francs, having mistaken her for the rather grand attendant. She seemed put out, but cannily held on to the cash.

Back in the restaurant Catherine pointed out an elderly man who had ordered two main courses and was now feeding one of them, a little plate of tripe sausages, to his toffee-coloured cocker spaniel. It was a sweet scene. Or rather it would have been if the dog hadn't periodically broken off from his feasting to lick his testicles, returning moments later to his meal, his appetite apparently refreshed.

The woman behind the ticket counter in the Musée des Arts Anciens du Namurois took an instant shine to our daughter. 'What a little rascal!' she cooed. 'Her face is full of mischief!'

She had three children of her own, she said, and now she was a grandmother, five times over! Could you believe it! They grew up so fast it seemed like they had hardly learned to walk and the next thing you knew they were leaving home. 'This one is very special,' she said, chucking Maisie's chin. 'She is gregarious and loves everyone! You must cherish each moment with her because her childhood will be gone, *purph!*' Having been up six times the night before I suspect this thought provoked rather the opposite response in me than that which was intended.

We bought our tickets and walked up some stairs to look around the museum's collection of paintings. There were a few by Henri Blès, of whose work I was rather fond. Blès was born in the Meuse valley around 1480, but at some point had moved to Antwerp. He painted biblical scenes and it was clear from them that he pined for the craggy, wooded countryside of home. In fact his interest in the scenery far outstrips his interest in the parables he is illustrating. In Blès' painting of the Good Samaritan, the incident involving the wounded traveller and his kindly saviour occupies one tiny corner of the canvas, the rest of which is taken up by a grossly exaggerated version of the Mosan landscape, complete with towering rocks, wild forests, glimmering, distant cities and some improbably thin camels which look as if they have been made from pipe-cleaners by local schoolchildren.

There were other good paintings tucked away among the reliquaries further on. I was particularly taken with a couple of them: *Christ the Gardener*, in which the Lord was depicted smiling cheerily while digging with a wooden spade in an allotment surrounded by a neat picket fence, and a picture of a slightly balding and nervous-looking Jesus on board a boat with some strapping rockabilly-quiffed fishermen. In Belgium you got used to seeing pictures of Christ looking lean, muscular, bloody and tragic. It seemed to me that the kindness and humanity of Jesus often got overlooked in the headlong rush towards the final torment.

When we came back downstairs the woman at the ticket counter said, 'Do you want to see anything again? You can leave your daughter with me. She will sit here on my knee and will be able to watch you on the closed-circuit TV.' We thanked the woman and said she really didn't need to, but she was insistent, adding, 'If the little one is upset I will call you over the tannoy.' It was one of those awkward situations. Did we entrust our child to a total stranger, or let a person who had made a warm and friendly gesture infer that we suspected she might be the kind of barmy sicko who would steal a baby? It was a choice between offering 100 per cent protection to my daughter, or suffering temporary embarrassment. As a true Englishman this was, of course, no choice at all. I handed Maisie over to the woman, waving aside Catherine's protests.

We didn't actually go far, just back round the corner to the Blès paintings. We gave it a decent interval, about a minute and a half, and then returned to the entrance lobby. The chair behind the ticket desk was empty.

There are moments in your life when it feels as if your blood has suddenly drained through the soles of your feet and is now lying around you in an ice-cold pool that reaches to your waist. This was one of them. It lasted about two seconds. Then a voice called out, 'Madame! Monsieur! We are here in the sunshine!'

Through French windows off to the left we could see the woman and Maisie sitting out on a lawn, surrounded by beds of marguerites and African marigolds. 'Look,' the woman said merrily, holding Maisie aloft, 'she has picked you some daisies!'

In need of a restorative we made our way to a narrow side-street and La Maison des Desserts. Here fabulous cakes, ornamented with glistening baubles of fruit and filigrees of icing and spun sugar, decorated the curved-glass cabinets like tiaras in the window of a Bond Street jeweller's . The owner, a robust-looking woman in a tweed suit, sat by the cash register wrapping home-made chocolates by hand. We ate black-currant mousses, each imprisoned in a bijou stockade of sugar-coated puff-pastry matchsticks, and felt much better.

Namur's citadel was part of a chain of forts which had been built along the Meuse and Sambre in the 1860s to protect Belgium from invasion by France or Germany. They were the brainchild of a Walloon military engineer named Henri Brialmont. The forts were costly to build, expensive to main-tain and had to be constantly updated to keep pace with changes in technology. When invasion finally did come in 1914, the forts of the Sambre and Meuse held Germany at bay for only a few weeks. It was not long, but it was enough to thwart the Germans' master strategy, the Schlieffen Plan, save France and thus condemn Europe to four years of attritional stalemate.

We drove up the winding road to Namur's citadel. There

was a cable-car, but I had been on it once before, in 1996, and I had no interest in repeating the experience. When I think of cable-cars I think of those things in the Alps, railway carriages on wires, and *Where Eagles Dare*. The cable-car in Namur was not like that. There were thirty or so little twin-seater fibre-glass eggs that went up and down the cliff-side in rotation, bobbing all the way like Chinese lanterns. You couldn't imagine Richard Burton grappling with a German stormtrooper on the roof of one of the Namur cable-cars. A couple of squirrels engaged in polite conversation on top of one would have presented a grave hazard. The whole thing looked more like a fairground ride – an impression confirmed by the man presiding over things, a rangy, snaggle-toothed rogue with prison tattoos on his knuckles and the oiled and tufted scalp of a Canvey Island cormorant.

'I desire solely upward to go,' I had said to the man on that first visit, handing him a 100-franc note. 'All tickets are returns,' he'd growled, shoving the money into his pocket. I thought better of asking for it back.

The cable-car jolted forward and began to climb up the craggy hillside. The views out across the Meuse to Jambes were spectacular, but I found it hard to concentrate on them. In the early stages of the ascent I had decided to change seats so I was facing upward. As I did so the car lurched and I attempted to steady myself against the outer-side window only to discover slightly too late that there wasn't actually any glass in it. Though there was no danger whatsoever of me falling out, the very fact that for a split-second both my arms had been suspended over a 200-foot drop made me feel headily vertiginous. I realise this sounds totally pathetic. My only excuse is that it was at a time of great emotional upheaval for me. Catherine was pregnant and as my arms had plunged through the non-existent glass a scene from the unborn child's life had flashed before me. In it she was a young adult, deep in conversation with someone special in her life. She was saying, 'I never knew my father. He died before I was born. In Belgium. In a cable-car accident.' And the other person responded not with kindness or concern but with a bray of derisive laughter: 'A cable-car accident? In Belgium? That's impossible. Everyone knows Belgium's flat as a fart.'

The whole thing was so affecting that when I had got to the top unharmed I could barely manage a brace of pancakes with caramelised apples and whipped cream at the café.

This time the ascent was a good deal less harrowing, but when we got to the citadel we found the whole area had been taken over by a motocross event. Bikes hurtled up and down the steep earth slopes, weaving between the trees, filling the air with snarling squeals and petrol fumes. Maisie burst into tears instantly, so we turned round and went back down again.

You could tell that the bar in Namur was something special because there was a pair of English real-ale buffs outside, one taking the other's photo standing in the doorway. The man with the camera, who I will call Malcolm because that was what he looked like, was wearing a beige anorak. The garment had all the style and finesse those two words imply. As we went past he was saying to the other man (a Colin if ever I saw one) in a nasal estuarine drone, 'You know, I never knew Bernard Shaw was an Irishman.' You can only imagine the shock he will get later in life when he finds out John Wayne was an American.

The owner of the bar, a chunky man with a moustache and the kind of voice that was unlikely to win him any awards from the Noise Abatement Society, greeted me like a long-lost friend. 'You've got a good memory,' I said. 'I've only been here twice before and the last time was over a year ago.'

'Yes,' the bar-owner said, turning to Catherine, 'but the bastard got totally pissed and threw up all over the floor.' His grasp of our native vernacular was very impressive. He'd clearly benefited from a TEFL class. Only in his case the initials had stood for Teaching English as a Foul Language.

The bar-owner loved beer and his list, chalked up on a blackboard, was one of the best in Wallonia. He loved music too, though I felt his taste in this area was a little less discerning. When it's knocking on midnight in a strange city and the table in front of you is filled with empty bottles, the last thing you really need to hear is Grace Slick and Jefferson Airplane doing 'White Rabbit'.

We ordered a bottle of Rochefort 10. The bar-owner's son brought it to the table and poured it for us with some ceremony. Of all Belgium's beers perhaps the most famous are those, like Rochefort, which are made by Trappist monks.

There are five Trappist breweries in Belgium and one across the border in Holland at Koeningshoeven. Despite the fact that they are run by monks, a couple of them are very big commercial operations indeed. The Abbaye Notre Dame de Scourmont, better known to the world as Chimay, for example, produces 103,000 hectolitres of beer per year (if, like me, you struggle to picture things in anything other than the most basic domestic terms, then you might prefer to think of that as roughly 15 million pints), as well as cheeses, pâtés, sausages and a range of children's clothing which, perhaps surprisingly, does not involve even moderate use of sackcloth. Fleets of trucks bearing the logos of Chimay and the equally large Westmalle rumble up and down the motorways of Belgium, Holland and northern France, while Rochefort and Orval are readily available across the rest of Europe, too. Only the Abbey of Sint-Sixtus near the French border in West Flanders remains relatively untainted by commercialism. The three different beers, usually called Westvleteren after the nearest village, come in unlabelled bottles distinguishable only by the colour of the caps: red for Special, blue for Extra and yellow for Abt.

Steve and I had hired bicycles from nearby Poperinge one bright April day in 1995 and, armed with a map of the officially designated 'Hoppeland Route' from the local tourist office, cycled out to the abbey. The route took us along segmented concrete roads through the Flemish hop fields, identifiable in early spring only by the networks of sturdy twenty-foot-high support poles and wires up which the vines grow. We passed shuttered country inns with signs outside boasting of skittle alleys, deserted village breweries, stands of poplar trees and low, rendered farm buildings, the older of them still with dark thatched roofs. When the Northumberland Division had arrived at the Ypres Salient in 1914, these little houses reminded the soldiers of the one-storey dwellings of Tynedale. It was a small comfort, I suppose.

A few miles outside the sweetly named village of Lovie we had come upon one of the neat British cemeteries which speckle the landscape in this part of West Flanders. There were Northumberland Fusiliers buried beneath the clipped grass and, perhaps even more affectingly, a row of graves of soldiers from the West Indian Regiment. The Northumbrians had found something in the Flandrian landscape that reminded them of home, but what must the interned Trinidadians, Jamaicans and Bajans have made of it? Probably the only thing they recognised was the night-time sky.

The countryside between Poperinge and Ypres is usually described as flat. What appears flat when you are in a car, however, often seems to verge on mountainous when you're on a bicycle. By the time we arrived at Sint-Sixtus I had worked up quite a thirst. We parked our bicycles next to the Café In de Vrede opposite the abbey. As we were locking them a white-robed monk appeared. He had a rubicund face, a bald head and a full and snowy beard. If you were ever to sit down and try to imagine what a monk might look like the chances are you would come up with someone pretty much like this. Steve and I stopped chatting the instant we saw the monk and nodded politely and very quietly to him, because if there is one thing everyone knows about Trappists it is that they have taken a vow of strict and total silence.

'Dag!' the monk said cheerily, 'or perhaps I say, "Good day"! You are English, I think from hearing you. Well, that is no problem to me because I talk English quite good also.'

Steve and I were stunned by this outburst. In fact we would probably have been less taken aback if the monk had started break-dancing. We shouldn't have been, though. The perception of the silent Trappist owes more to history than it does to present-day reality.

The brewing monks of Sint-Sixtus owe their existence to Armand-Jean le Bouthillier de Rance, a mid-seventeenth-century abbot at the Abbey of La Trappe in Normandy and founder of the Order of Reformed Cistercians of Strict Observance, the Trappists. For over three centuries the Trappists did indeed work and live together in total silence. Nor did they eat meat, or in some cases even cheese or fish. This was partly the justification for brewing beer: the brothers needed the iron and vitamins (a slightly more spurious course of reasoning had it that beer was permissible since 'it is only liquid bread'. Which is true up to a point, though I've yet to see anyone staggering about trying to punch a policeman as the result of too much toast). In the late 1960s the reforms of the second Vatican Council lead to a relaxation of monastic policy and now, while the monks try to maintain an atmosphere of peace and tranquillity within the monastery, they are free to speak if they wish. I suspect that this is not always the bonus it may at first appear. There were probably no more than a dozen monks at a small abbey like Sint-Sixtus (there are only twenty at the much bigger Chimay), and, given that they share the same life of religious devotion, conversation must be somewhat limited.

I based my theory on the monk outside the Café In de Vrede. He spoke like a man who had a load to get off his chest. The words and phrases came out as rapidly as bullets from a Bren gun. 'You have cycled from Poperinge, I see. I notice the station tags on your bicycles, hired from Belgian Railways. Poperinge is the centre of the Hoppeland, as you may know. There is a museum of the hop there, I believe. Though I have never been to it. You are here specially to sample our famous Trappist beers? They are well-known throughout the world, I think.'

The monk spoke with a slight sing-song inflection. At first I thought he might be Scandinavian. Then he said, 'But you have many fine beers in England also, I hear. Particularly from the brewer's town of Burton-on-Trent. And of course the ale of Kent, your own hop country, is renowned too,' and I knew he was Flemish.

'You make three beers here?' we said when the monk finally ran out of breath.

'Four,' he said with a smile, 'but the Dubbel we keep only to drink for ourselves. And I must say that this is the best of all the beer we make. You know why that is?'

Steve and I shook our heads, though both of us suspected a religious homily was approaching. We needn't have worried. The Belgians take brewing far too seriously to allow God to get mixed up with it, even in a monastery. 'It is because,' the monk said, 'it is fermented without additional sugars. All the alcohol in it is natural from the grain.' The monk grinned benignly at the thought, then, perhaps sensing he might be talking the Order out of a couple of sales he added, 'The other beers are good too, though. Although myself I do not like the Abt. To me it is too sweet. Far, far too sweet. It is a woman's drink!' The Westvleteren Abt was nearly 12 per cent alcohol by volume. The monk had obviously known some pretty rugged women in his time.

'But you will not be drinking the Abt,' the monk said, indicating our bicycles, 'otherwise, I think you take a long way home.' He imitated Steve and I swerving about drunkenly. 'Better you stick only with the Special! So where in England are you coming from?'

I reluctantly offered an answer. At first I had found talking to the monk an appealing novelty. By this stage, though, I had begun to wonder if we would ever get shot of him. I was so dry my tongue was sticking to the roof of my mouth, and the only thing standing between me and a cellar-cold bottle of beer was this chatterbox in a hooded frock. 'Ah, Newcastle. The coal mines are there, I think. "Taking coals to Newcastle" is an expression I have heard. But not now I think in the wake of Maggie Thatcher! In Belgium the coal is further east from here . . .'

'Do the monks run the café, too?' Steve asked. I'm not sure if he knew what the consequences of this enquiry might be, but it proved a master-stroke.

'No, no, no,' the monk said censoriously. 'The brothers running a café!' He shook his head at the total madness of the suggestion, though quite why such a moral chasm should have existed between making beer and serving it I'm not sure. 'No, that would never do,' the monk said with finality and, apparently affronted, he stomped off in the direction of a newly arrived car with French number-plates. As we went into the bar we could hear him saying, 'Dag! Ou peut-être je dit, "Bonjour" . . .'

Sunday in Namur. Catherine and I got up early. In the street outside the hotel a council workman was using a vast vacuum-cleaner called a 'Glutton' to suck up dead pigeons off the road. A woman out walking a chihuahua picked it up and scurried away from him. We drove out of the city past a wig shop which advertised a 10 per cent discount for students and the flea-market on the river bank at Jambes. In Tongeren there was a rather ritzy flea-market, where you heard German and American accents and the air was full of the smell of cigar smoke, new leather, sandalwood soap and money. The flea-market in Jambes was of a slightly more downmarket kind. A row of trestle tables, some blankets on the floor and an array of goods that demonstrated beyond doubt the immense quantity of Viewmasters that must once have been sold in Europe.

We travelled south along the Meuse. There were stalls along the roadsides with cardboard signs beside them advertising 'strawberries' and then 'Wepion strawberries' and then 'Genuine Wepion strawberries'. 'Genuine' was underlined twice, suggesting that somewhere in Belgium there was a roaring trade in counterfeit Wepion fruits.

The road wound along between the river and the jagged cliffs of the Meuse gorge. What small clusters of houses there were seemed to project out across the water or be stuck to the rock face like fridge magnets. South of Anhee the valley parted slightly and Dinant and Bouvignes – home to the Museum of Lighting 'from Ancient times to the present day' and a restaurant which was billed in the English-language version of a local guide as a 'Gastronomic Hatting-place' – appeared up ahead.

Dinant is a beauty spot. Though only in the sense that it is a dark if unmalignant blemish. The popular picture-postcard image of Dinant shows the onion-domed Collegiate Church, the slow moving river to its front and at the rear a sheer sheet of limestone topped by the high walls of the citadel. It looks spectacular. It is misleading. Although wider here than at some other points, the Meuse gorge is still deep, and the result gloomy. Dinant's river-front is dominated by tourist bars and shops selling tacky souvenirs. Cars cruise slowly up and down in the gloaming, the drivers desperately looking for somewhere to park before they get sucked into the one-way system and washed up on to the N97 dual carriageway which swishes traffic along on a bridge high above the river. If you imagine a run-down seaside town at dusk, then that is Dinant. All day.

We went and sat on the terrace of a café which had the picture-postcard view across the Meuse. I had a glass of lager, not because I particularly wanted one but because its name, Coq Hardi, had a certain puerile appeal, and a Croque Hawaiian. Isn't it amazing how a tinned pineapple ring can transform a simple toasted cheese sandwich, slab of gammon or plate of sausages into a Polynesian feast? Just one bite and you can feel the South Sea breeze on your cheek and smell the coconut oil in the hair of the dancing girls. To add to the illusion the café had curved bamboo furniture. It was upholstered with the kind of silky black and gold fabric you normally see on the large-breasted alien maidens in *Star Trek* to whom Captain Kirk says, 'On our planet we call this kissing.' Along the wall opposite the bar were black-and-white photos of Dinant's most famous son, Adolphe Sax.

Sax, the inventor of the saxophone, was born in Dinant in 1815. He had an eventful childhood. In quick succession he tumbled down some stairs, swallowed a needle, collided with a red-hot stove, drank vitriol, breathed in poisonous metal fumes, took arsenic, fell in the Meuse and had a brick dropped on his head by a clumsy builder. As a consequence the locals nicknamed him 'The Little Ghost of Dinant'. Though I should imagine his mother was paler, especially since she also had nine other children to worry about.

Sax was the son of an instrument-maker. He took to his father's profession with a manic boldness. By the age of twenty-nine he had already perfected the instrument which would make him famous. It would be nice to think that when the idea of the saxophone dawned on the young Adolphe he had, whispering away somewhere in his subconscious, the sound of a melodious Stan Getz, breathy Ben Webster, or sweet Lester Young. It would be nice, but it would also be totally wrong. Adolphe Sax invented the saxophone not because he hoped it might one day be considered cool by men in pork-pie hats and wraparound sunglasses, but purely and simply to prove that using the laws of harmonics it was possible to produce a reed instrument which was louder than anything with a traditional metal mouthpiece. To us this may seem a rather pointless scientific exercise, but in the era of the military band decibels were all, and Sax's invention had more volume than any hand-held instrument in history, with the possible exception of the Israelite trumpets at Jericho. If he had named it the cacophone it would have been completely apt.

Not that everyone was immediately convinced. Rivals in the market for lucrative military-instrument contracts claimed that playing the saxophone was 'beyond human power'. In Germany, meanwhile, the inventor of the interestingly-named batyphone brought a lawsuit against Sax 'proving' that his invention not only did not but *could* not exist.

The instrument-maker from Dinant's chance to disprove all allegations against him came in 1845. On the Champs de Mars in Paris the French army organised a competition to determine which was the superior, Sax's saxophone or its chief competitor, M. Carafo's carafon. In a series of tests the saxophone blew its rival away. Encouraged, Sax went off and produced a whole clan of his instrument, ranging from the baby soprano up to the double bass saxophone, a brass beast so massive it could only be played when standing on a barstool.

In 1852 Sax staged a demonstration of sonic power in which a dozen Saxtubas produced more noise than an orchestra of 1,500 traditional instruments. The event was attended by army officers from across Europe. Asked afterwards if they were impressed with what they had just heard the military men replied, yes, but they thought it might turn to rain later.

This was the high point for Adolphe Sax. His instrument was taken up by armies in Europe and America and moved gradually from there into civilian marching bands and on into dance orchestras. Classical musicians, however, continued to turn their noses up at what they considered a vulgar and tuneless instrument. The saxophone never found its way into the symphony orchestra during its inventor's lifetime.

Undeterred by such niceties, or the continual bombardment of lawsuits from embittered competitors which three times drove him to bankruptcy, Sax turned his fascination with loud noises to another area. Frustrated by the allied armies' failure to break the Russian defence of Sebastopol, Sax dreamed up the ultimate siege weapon. The Saxocannon was a mortar which would fire a shell eleven yards wide and weighing 550 tons. It would, according to its designer's gleefully maniacal description, 'tear apart, smash entire walls, ruin fortifications, explode mines, blow up powderhouses – in a word exert an irresistible action of devastation'. Frustratingly for Sax he could find no one willing to build the Saxocannon for him. This was probably just as well. If Charlie Parker had ever got his hands on one, God knows what would have happened.

Adolphe Sax died in 1894. During his lifetime he had patented forty musical instruments and his workshop had manufactured over twenty thousand of his inventions. Although he himself would never know it, along the way this dumpy, obsessive man from a small town in a proverbially un-hip country had changed the course of popular music and culture for ever. Somewhere in this I couldn't help feeling there was a message of hope for all humanity.

We drove up out of Dinant and doubled back towards Huy. Up above the crepuscular cleft carved by the river the country was hilly and pretty. The road dipped and curved between thickets of hawthorn, cherry and elm and stands of ash and maple, there were pale pink rock roses and the pungent early summer smell of wild garlic. Then the Meuse appeared again and spoiled it all.

Though it was hard to imagine looking at the thrumming power lines, haulage depots and other industrial sights which seemed to have spilled up the river from Liège, Huy, like Dinant, had once been a popular tourist destination. People came from across Belgium to take a cable-car up to the cliff-top fort and marvel at the so-called 'Four Wonders of Huy'. These are: the château, the Gothic rose window in the Church of Notre-Dame, the thirteenth-century bridge over the Meuse and the fountain in the square opposite the town hall. After twenty minutes of ambling around Huy I was pre-pared to add a fifth wonder to the list: what the bloody hell am I doing here?

Unfazed by what we had so far encountered, we drove on to the Château d'Aigremont. This brick-and-stone castle is perched on a rocky outcrop overlooking the Meuse. The views from the windows are picturesque, though only if the picture in question was by a latter-day Pierre Paulus. Chemical storage silos, pylons and pipelines lined the river's banks. Dispersed among them were dozens of squat brick and metal sheds. With coils and antennae poking from them at every corner, they looked like they might have been bought in a job-lot from the cellars of Ming the Merciless. Amid the grimness, the roaring powerboat towing a red swim-suited water-skier along the turgid Meuse provided the most incongruous flash of glamour I'd seen since Jennifer Beals removed her welding mask in *Flashdance*.

In the courtyard of the Château d'Aigremont tables and chairs were arranged beneath some striped awning. Charcoal smoke filled the air. From somewhere off in the walled gardens came the thwack and bang of a clay-pigeon shoot. Every once in a while men in husky jackets, tweed caps and moleskin breeches would come wandering into the courtyard with over-and-under shotguns cradled in their arms.

At the door of the château the owner was selling entrance tickets. 'We rent out rooms and the gardens to local businesses and organisations,' she said. 'We have some sponsorship also. We are trying gradually to restore things.' She seemed cheerful enough, though it was a formidable task – reclaiming the formal walled gardens in particular. It was the sort of place where a week of hard work would make less impact than a rabbit on the front wing of a Range Rover. There was a forlorn, slightly haunted feel about the place. '*Le Grand Meaulnes*,' Catherine whispered as we wandered around the empty upstairs rooms. 'Well, what do you expect?' I hissed. 'We've been to three different places today and they've all been crap.'

The only consolation was that Château d'Aigremont wasn't as sad as Château Beloeil. Beloeil was in Hainaut, ten miles or so west of Mons. It was supposed to be one of the most wonderful houses in northern Europe. Guide books raved about it, the gardens in particular: 'One of the most beautiful gardens in the world,' gushed the historian René Pechère. Every Belgian we met swooned at the mention of it: 'Oh yes, Beloeil. It is enchanting, breathtaking!' (When I say *every* Belgian I mean, naturally, every French-speaking Belgian. When you mentioned Beloeil to the Flemish they shook their heads: no, they had never heard of it.)

Château Beloeil was owned by the Princes de Ligne, the most famous of whom was Charles-Joseph, known in the eighteenth century as 'The Prince Charming of Europe'. Charles-Joseph is famous for remarking, 'Every man has two fatherlands: his own country and France.' Though what happened if your own country *was* France he didn't say. Like Charles-Joseph the other Princes de Ligne are usually portrayed as an urbane and intelligent lot. I see no reason to doubt this. They did, however, show an almost supernatural ability to pick the wrong side when it came to combat. When war broke out, those who found themselves opposing the Ligne family were fortunate indeed. Part of the problem was that the Lignes leant towards Austria. In martial matters this was always a mistake, for as a sarcastic American observed after the battle of Solferino, 'The Austrian army exists purely to provide victories for others.'

When Charles-Joseph de Ligne did desert the Habsburgs, however, the results were no better. Napoleon might have looked like a winner; he wasn't and 150 years of family tradition was upheld. So complete is the Ligne family's mastery of picking losers, in fact, that one suspects that if the modern Prince ever came across a boxing match between Mike Tyson and Tinky Winky Teletubby his immediate reaction would be to slap his family fortune on the big blue fella with the handbag.

And perhaps that's what had happened. Because something had clearly gone wrong at Beloeil. The house itself was fine, if a little dull, but the garden? Stunning. Stunning indeed, because any amateur gardener who saw it would collapse from the oxygen overload of sucking in so much air so fast. Thistles wagged their punkish purple heads mockingly from the rose beds; the six miles of hedges, once immaculately coiffeured, had sprouted New Age dreadlocks; the lawns were tussocky; the glass remaining in the orangeries barely sufficient to fill a monocle.

One of the things I'd really been looking forward to on my visit to Beloeil was Minibel, a 1:25 scale model village of all Belgium's greatest landmarks (well, let's be honest, what sort of red-blooded male really travels all that way on a Sunday just to see some seventeenth-century castle filled with rare tapestries, a Canaletto, a pink coral writing desk and three hundred acres of grounds laid out according to the principles of Dezalliers d'Argenville?). This fascinating exhibit was not sign-posted, so I went off in search of it on my own. I found it by crossing a rickety bridge above a stream and clambering over a padlocked gate. It was in a walled section of the grounds, among flower beds colonised by chickweed and dandelions and what might once have been rockeries, but now seemed more like piles of rubble.

Like its surroundings Minibel was not in a good state. Antwerp docks were drained, the armies of the Battle of Waterloo were barely visible through the long grass, and there was an ash sapling sprouting through the roof of Leuven town hall. As I walked among the wreckage of Le Grand Hornu in the haunting stillness of the deserted garden I felt strangely like Charlton Heston must have done when he discovered the ruin of the Statue of Liberty in the final scene of *Planet of the Apes.* Minibel looked like it had been hit by a mini neutron bomb.

Picking my way past the bell-tower of Bruges, bindweed choking its doorways, I cheered myself with the thought that three thousand years hence, archaeologists might uncover the ruins of Minibel and use a reconstruction of its diminutive Antwerp Station to prove that the people back then were a good deal smaller than they are today.

Across the stream, among the straight rows of trees, I

trudged back up the path to the turreted Beloeil. In a country being torn apart by the political fall-out of the Dutroux case, the collapsed and forlorn enterprise which had once been Minibel seemed an apposite metaphor. Too apposite, in fact. It looked like it had been put there specifically for my benefit. Suspecting a trap, I decided to leave it alone.

There was nothing so eerie as Minibel back at Château d'Aigremont. But there was the smell of cooking meat. After absorbing the byzantine complexities of the ticketing system we went to get some food from the barbecue. The middle-aged man in the blue-and-white pinny who was in command of the pork chops asked where we were from. When we told him, his face brightened. 'I am in England often,' he said. 'Are you familiar with New Malden?'

We confessed that sadly we weren't. 'A super place with many facilities,' the man said, beaming at the thought of them. 'Our Rotary Club in Seraing is twinned with New Malden,' he added by way of explanation. It was odd how often you met people on the continent whose main, and sometimes only, contact with Britain came through London satellite towns. In Italy, Spain, Norway and Crete, names such as Harpenden, Watford, Orpington and Hayes conjured up a magic undreamed of in their native land.

After lunch we decided to complete our day by driving around trying to find a petrol station that was open. Eventually, on the edge of Liège, we located a garage with an automatic pump. I had noticed these before. Because most Belgian garages are shut on Sundays the idea is that the automatic pump will provide a means of obtaining fuel for those like us who were insufficiently disciplined to plan ahead. You put a 500- or 1,000-franc note in through a slot and the machine opens the pump until you have put that amount of petrol or diesel into your car. That at least is the theory. What happened in Liège was that I fed 1,000 francs into the slot and got nothing in return except a blank look from the machine, which seemed to say, 'Hey, did you really expect this to work? Where d'you think you are, Japan?'

Epilogue

On our last morning in Namur we went for a stroll. A millinery was on the corner of one of the city's cobbled squares. The hats were displayed in the window on wire stands. If you wanted to try them on you had to ring a bell and the milliner would come down from his workroom upstairs and let you in. The milliner was a young man with a thin, oval face and dark skin. He wore a striped Breton T-shirt, baggy khaki pants and blue espadrilles. His hats were made of straw but they weren't straw hats in the conventional sense. They came in two basic designs. The first was round with a domed crown and in-curling brim, the sort of hat favoured by jazz singer Anita O'Day; the second was more elaborate, a series of circular, gradually decreasing tiers like a wedding cake. Each hat was decorated differently, with thin strips of silk ribbon or coloured paper woven into the straw. They were wonderful, if not particularly practical. One of those things you feel you really ought to own, though you know in the back of your mind that it will only sit on top of a wardrobe gathering dust and providing a sanctuary for nervous spiders.

The interior of the hat shop was triangular and so small

that there was not enough space in it for three people. I stood out on the step. As Catherine tried on hats and endeavoured to think of possible future weddings at which she might wear one, we chatted to the milliner. 'You work in Brussels?' he asked.

'No, we're here on holiday,' we said.

'In Namur?'

'Not just in Namur. We've travelled all round Belgium. It's been a long holiday.'

The milliner looked perplexed. He repeated the notion to himself softly, slowly, 'A . . . long . . . holiday . . . in . . . Belgium,' and thought about it for a while, his eyebrows as neatly woven together as his hats. But it was no good. The concept was just too alien and difficult. It was as if we had tried to explain the theory of special relativity to a three-year-old. Eventually he gave up on it and instantly and visibly brightened. 'In the mornings,' he said, 'the sun rises above the church and fills my workshop with light. It is a beautiful time to work.'

We studied the hats for a while longer. 'We'll think about it and come back soon,' we said, and I think we meant it.

Shortly before lunch we packed the car and trekked across Limburg to Antwerp.

We spent two days among the designer shops, but our hearts weren't really in it. We were at the end of the trip and high fashion had reached a stage where the difference between a garment that would wow the audience at a Paris show and the sort of thing Emily Bishop from *Coronation Street* might have worn to a church social in 1982 was so wafer-thin as to be undiscernable to the naked eye. And besides which, there was something about Antwerp – its chain stores, its vague air of nocturnal menace and the teenage Goths swigging Special Brew around the phone boxes – that was all too familiar. It was a staging-post on the way home.

The ferry from IJmuiden in Holland to Newcastle was busy. The food was lousy. After Maisie was put to bed Catherine and I sat on the floor by her cot in the narrow cabin talking about the meals we'd had in Belgium. The veal with mustard sauce in Olloy-Saint-Viroin, the baked ham and pickled pears in Beersel, the mirabelle plum sorbet in Tournai. Our stomachs rumbled; our spirits sank.

When Catherine turned her light out, I lay on my bunk in the dark listening to the thrum of the ship's engines and trying to remember all the beers I had drunk during the trip. Witkap Stimulo, Stropken, Bink Donker, La Marlagne Blanche, Saison de Silly, Rodenbach Alexander, Poperinge's Hommelbier, Cuvée d'Aristée, Gordon's Highland Scotch . . . Somewhere around the century mark I fell into a deep and rather dizzy sleep.

THE FAR CORNER

Harry Pearson

Covering the game at all levels from St James's Park to
Langley Park, from Roker to Willington, *The Far Corner* is
Harry Pearson's brilliant account of the North-East's
experience of the 1993–94 football season.

A book in which Wilf Mannion rubs shoulders with The
Sunderland Skinhead; recollections of Len Shackleton
blight the lives of village shoppers; and the appointment of
Kevin Keegan as manager of Newcastle is celebrated by a
man in a leather stetson crooning 'For The Good Times'
to the accompaniment of a midi organ, *The Far Corner* is a
tale of heroism and human frailty, passion and the perils of
eating an egg mayonnaise stottie without staining
your trousers.

'Forget Nick Hornby's *Fever Pitch*, this is the football book
of the new age, a mix of heroism, humour and Norman
Hunter, but mainly humour'
Sunday Times, Sports Book of the Year

'Savagely funny and frequently moving . . . Some of the
humour is as full-blooded as a tackle by Bryan Robson,
and if at times the author wanders off at a tangent, like
Chris Waddle on a bad day, then that is the capricious
nature of football'
Daily Telegraph

RACING PIGS AND GIANT MARROWS

Harry Pearson

'After the tale of the supernaturally dense Archway Baby, and a wild digression on the staying power of cinder toffee, I could take no more. I fell from my chair to my hands and knees hooting helplessly, so buckled with laughter that my lower back was in pain'
Pete Davies in the *Independent*

Following his acclaimed book about football in the north-east, *The Far Corner*, Harry Pearson vowed that his next project would not involve hanging around outdoors on days so cold that itinerant dogs had to be detached from lamp-posts by firemen. It would be about the summer: specifically, about a summer of shows and fairs in the north of England.

Encompassing such diverse entertainments as fell-running, tupperware-boxing and rabbit-fancying (literally), and containing many more jokes about goats than is legal on the Isle of Man, *Racing Pigs and Giant Marrows* is without doubt the only book in existence to explain the design faults of earwigs and expose English farmers' fondness for transvestism. Warm, wise, and very funny, it confirms increasing suspicions that Harry Pearson is really quite good.

'Pearson is as tall as he is funny and, believe me, he is very tall'
The Face

'Just as much of a hoot [as *The Far Corner*]. The title explains his remit, but can't do justice to his one-liners and digressions'
Manchester Evening News

Now you can order superb titles directly from Abacus

☐	Racing Pigs and Giant Marrows	Harry Pearson	£6.99
☐	The Far Corner	Harry Pearson	£7.99

Please allow for postage and packing: **Free UK delivery.**
Europe; add 25% of retail price; Rest of World; 45% of retail price.

To order any of the above or any other Abacus titles, please call our credit card orderline or fill in this coupon and send/fax it to:

**Abacus, P.O. Box 121, Kettering, Northants NN14 4ZQ
Tel: 01832 737527   Fax: 01832 733076
Email: aspenhouse@FSBDial.co.uk**

☐ I enclose a UK bank cheque made payable to Abacus for £ ....
☐ Please charge £.............. to my Access, Visa, Delta, Switch Card No.

☐☐☐☐☐☐☐☐☐☐☐☐☐☐☐☐☐☐☐

Expiry Date ☐☐☐☐   Switch Issue No.   ☐☐

NAME (Block letters please) ....

ADDRESS ....

....

....

Postcode ....Telephone ....

Signature ....

Please allow 28 days for delivery within the UK. Offer subject to price and availability.

Please do not send any further mailings from companies carefully selected by Abacus ☐